# Modern
# Christian
# Revivals

# Modern Christian Revivals

EDITED BY EDITH L. BLUMHOFER
AND RANDALL BALMER

UNIVERSITY OF ILLINOIS PRESS
Urbana and Chicago

©1993 by the Board of Trustees of the University of Illinois
Manufactured in the United States of America
1 2 3 4 5 C P 5 4 3 2 1

*This book is printed on acid-free paper.*

Library of Congress Cataloging-in-Publication Data

Modern Christian Revivals / edited by Edith L. Blumhofer and Randall
Balmer
    p.    cm.
    Includes bibliographical references and index.
    ISBN 0-252-01990-3. — ISBN 0-252-06295-7 (pbk.)
    1. Revivals—History. I. Blumhofer, Edith Waldvogel.
II. Balmer, Randall Herbert.
BV37700.M63   1993
269'.24'0903—dc20                     93-31407
                                        CIP

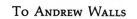

To Andrew Walls

# Contents

# Acknowledgments

This book had its origin in a conference, "Modern Christian Revivals: A Comparative Perspective," sponsored by the Institute for the Study of American Evangelicals and held at Wheaton College, 30 March–1 April 1989. All but one of the chapters began as conference papers, and we are grateful to the authors for their cooperation in the process of revising and editing. The conference was a stimulating time, and we thank all of the participants and registrants for their comments in discussions, formal responses, and informal interaction. The conference proceedings influenced the perspectives that the authors and editors brought to the task of preparing this material for publication. A generous grant from The Pew Charitable Trusts made possible the conference from which this book emerged.

Most of the book manuscript's final editing and production took place at the Institute for the Study of American Evangelicals. The Institute's capable research assistants, Candace Wegner and Kristal Otto, mastered word processing tasks and prepared the final copy. Other staff members gave assistance at various stages of the project. Our special thanks to Kristin Helmer, Mary Noll, Katherine Tinlin-Vaughn, Kurt Berends, and Larry Eskridge. This text has benefited from the careful attention of Louie Simon, editor at the University of Illinois Press.

This book is dedicated to a historian who has dedicated his life to expanding our understanding of the cultural and spiritual significance of Christian revivals around the world.

# Introduction

## ✦

### EDITH L. BLUMHOFER AND
### RANDALL BALMER

The term *revival* has had various connotations throughout modern history. To cite two notorious examples on the American scene, the redoubtable Jonathan Edwards believed that revival was "a surprising work of God," while Charles Grandison Finney declared emphatically that revival was "a work of man." Edwards dedicated his considerable intellectual talents to understanding the gracious visitation of God upon his congregation at Northampton, Massachusetts, while Finney, believing that revivals came about through human agency rather than divine, produced the first in a series of manuals aimed at supplying a formula for the replication of revivals throughout antebellum America.

Such broadly divergent understandings of revival render the task of definition a difficult one.[1] Most Christian revivals have as their object some sort of conversion or experience of grace in the individual. Very often that experience is instantaneous and datable, after the manner of such spectacular conversions as those of Saints Paul and Augustine. Others are less spectacular, and some people prefer to see their spiritual lives as pilgrimages. Modern revivalism, particularly the strain that emphasizes pilgrimage over instantaneous conversion, owes a great deal to pietism, with its emphasis on personal probity and attention to the disciplines of spirituality.

Evangelicalism more generally, with its emphasis on the individual's direct relationship with God, has nurtured revivals throughout the modern period. Whereas Roman Catholicism and the high church traditions teach that God's grace is communicated continually and repeatedly through the sacraments, evangelical spirituality and soteriology is considerably more ephemeral. For most evangelicals the process of establishing, sustaining, or renewing a direct relationship with God is not so simple as being baptized, partaking of the Eucharist, or going to confession. Instead, they have to conjure the requisite sentiments—sorrow for sin, humility before the Almighty, fear of perdition—in order to atone for their spiritual indifference and amend their lives. Revivalism, especially revival preaching, abets this process. Evangelical revivalists, moreover, historically have understood the importance of popular communications and group behavior to touch both the intellect and the affections, and, as these essays indicate, they have been remarkably adaptable to historical and social circumstances. Indeed, the relative absence of ecclesiastical hierarchies or liturgical rubrics among evangelicals has provided them greater latitude to tailor their message to particular audiences.

The essential characteristic of revival (and one implied in the term itself) is that it assumes some sort of decline, whether real or imagined, out of which the faithful are called to new heights of spiritual ardor and commitment. Finney, once again, was quite explicit. "A 'Revival of Religion,'" he wrote, "presupposes a declension."[2] Revivals, then, often build upon a sense of loss and the need to recover a former plateau of spirituality. There is an evocation of a golden, halcyon past that serves as an implicit rebuke to the spiritual languor of those who stand in need of revival.

Various revivals exhibit other characteristics as well. While individual, private regenerations are not unheard of, most revivals are communal events. A skilled and charismatic evangelist can whip a revival gathering into a frenzy, full of passion and excitation. The sheer force of group behavior in such an environment has a powerful influence upon the behavior of individuals. That is not to deny the workings of the Holy Spirit, but merely to suggest that such workings are beyond the ken of human understanding and presumably manifest themselves in particular circumstances.

The essays that follow, first delivered in 1989 at a conference entitled "Modern Christian Revivalism: A Comparative Perspective" at Wheaton College, provide a hint of the various forms that revivals have taken in the modern period as well as the influences that have animated them. In the opening essay, Randall Balmer charts the rise and spread of pietism on both sides of the Atlantic. The eighteenth-century revival of religion known to historians as the Great Awakening, Balmer argues, was not so much the death rasp of Puritanism as it was the confluence of New England Puritanism and the various strains of Continental pietism already flourishing in the Middle Colonies. Balmer goes on to show the continuing influence of pietistic impulses on the evangelical and revival tradition in America.

David Bebbington asserts that the Evangelical Revival in eighteenth-century England was not so antithetical to the Enlightenment as historians have often supposed, an argument that will seem eminently plausible to students of the Princeton theology in the nineteenth century or fundamentalist theology in the twentieth. "Educated evangelicals," Bebbington insists, "were part of an Enlightenment cultural milieu." Indeed, they appropriated the Enlightenment's use of empiricism to understand their own spiritual experiences, and their millennial notions mimicked the optimistic temper of the Enlightenment. In addition, Bebbington contends that evangelicalism shared with the Enlightenment an emphasis on popular education, the duties of morality, latitudinarianism, and a common literary idiom. "The revival," he asserts, "did not turn its adherents into ignorant bigots."

In his essay on Puritan New England, Gerald F. Moran cites the importance of clerical professionalization and transatlantic correspondence as instrumental to the success of revivals in the eighteenth century. Although the scope of the revival itself caught many of the clergy by surprise, they eventually rebounded by "combining old pastoral practices, which they used to guide the revival and counsel their stricken parishioners, with fresh attitudes toward the proper role of the people in the church and the propriety of the pure church." Moran also argues that the revival known to historians as the "Great Awakening" was built upon the foundation of local, discrete revivals in New England dating back to the seventeenth century. He concludes that the Awakening attested to "the capacity of the Puritan system for self-renewal."

In his essay on the Old South, John B. Boles outlines the characteristics of religion during the Great Revival of the antebellum South and the long shadow that evangelical revivals have cast over southern culture, including such aspects as political rhetoric, family life, and even child-rearing. Southern evangelicalism, he argues, was marked by the lay control of the churches, by vernacular preaching, and by an interior faith. Antebellum revivals were social occasions punctuated by ritualized conversions and "rededications." The picture that emerges here is that southern religion was decidedly energetic and enthusiastic rather than contemplative. The Great Revival signaled the triumph of evangelical denominations in the South, particularly the Methodists, Baptists, and Presbyterians. Boles points out what he calls the evangelical churches' "principled compromise" with slavery, which he insists "was not simply a selling out to the forces of black exploitation for the sake of courting planter popularity." Rather, the early antislavery ministers recognized that their freedom to preach in many areas of the South would be circumscribed by their abolitionist stance. In a provocative thesis, Boles also argues that the gradual Christianization of slaves made the entire institution of slavery a good bit more benign and humane by the nineteenth century than it had been previously. Beneath the roofs of many evangelical churches in the antebellum South, blacks even attained a kind of equality with whites, if only for a few hours a week.

In the early decades of the nineteenth century, Richard Carwardine argues, "the United States was not alone in experiencing a 'reformation' in popular religion." In the juxtaposition of the Second Great Awakening in both Britain and the United States, Carwardine finds several common elements. Both cultures were trying to adjust to a new economic order: the industrialization in Britain and the emerging market economy in America. The evangelical theology on both sides of the Atlantic moved dramatically in the direction of Arminianism—witness the transatlantic appeal and influence of Charles Grandison Finney and Methodism. "In both societies," Carwardine writes, "revivals were often the catalysts of progressive humanitarian and moral reform, drawing on and reinforcing established strains of millennial and perfectionist thought," although Britain endured nothing akin to the Civil War, "America's Holy War."

Frederick Hale uses a study of revivals in Norway to suggest the inadequacy of stereotypes of religious life in state-church-dominated cultures and the narrowness of the use of the term in the American setting. The word *revival* as used by American scholars is problematic when introduced into the Norwegian setting, raising as many questions as it answers. Hale focuses on personal spirituality rather than on revival in the churches in order to show how various phenomena usually associated with revival have contributed to the spiritual vitality of Norwegians in ways that conventional religious practices apparently did not.

Annual Keswick Conventions, held in England's Lake District since 1875, have had enormous influence on American evangelicalism. David Bundy examines the origins of the "higher Christian life" spirituality associated with Keswick, carefully documenting the interplay of streams of piety rooted in continental European and British Protestantism with American holiness teaching.

American pentecostalism emerged as a discrete movement at the turn of the century. Its early adherents understood revival somewhat differently than did most American Protestants, many of whom were praying for revival. Pentecostals believed that the last days would be marked by an intense revival that would issue in Christ's physical return. They regarded pentecostalism as that revival, so they announced the presence of long-awaited renewal and thought of themselves as the sign that revival had come. Edith Blumhofer explores the early pentecostal understanding of revival, which differs markedly from later pentecostal expectations that tended to be more typically evangelical.

Early twentieth-century revivals in China, both under missionary auspices and under national leadership, are the focus of Daniel Bays's chapter. "Within a few years after 1900," he writes, "revivals reminiscent in tone and size of those of Finney and Moody were occurring in China. A major reason for this was the dramatically altered climate of receptivity to Christianity in China." He raises the question of whether or not revivalism is a handy and effective means for indigenous Christian leaders to break free of domination by foreign missionaries and concludes: "The tentative answer in the Chinese case is that, in the first part of the twentieth century, it was. This may also indicate the long-term historical significance of the phenomenon of revivalism in a global Christian context."

The rapid growth of evangelical and pentecostal movements across Latin America in recent years is common knowledge. Several important studies by social scientists have begun to address both the dimensions of the change and its social implications. Everett A. Wilson examines the social orientation of Latin American evangelicals. Despite allegations that these movements support oppressive regimes and oppose revolutionary politics and social progressivism, Wilson argues that "Latin American evangelicals are committed to taking control of their own destinies and are themselves effective agents of social change."

In an overview of revivalism in the past generation, David Edwin Harrell, Jr., offers a close look at several major players. "From Billy Graham to Pat Robertson," he notes, "we have witnessed the southernization of American revivalism and the Americanization of southern religion."

Finally, in a highly personal account appropriate to the emotional and personal nature of revivals, George A. Rawlyk, who delivered the keynote address to open the conference, reflects on the theoretical models that have informed his own work on Canadian revivalism. In addition, Rawlyk offers his thoughts on the professional perils he has faced within the Canadian academic community for challenging what he calls "the compelling power of secular bias" in the mainstream of Canadian historiography. Rawlyk cites the example and the support of religious historians in the United States—Nathan Hatch, Mark Noll, and especially George Marsden, among others— as critical in his own development as a historian of evangelicalism in Canada. "If neo-Marxists can write neo-Marxist history," Rawlyk asks, "why should not evangelical Christian historians—like Marsden—write from an evangelical Christian perspective?" In an intriguing coda to his address, Rawlyk makes clear that, despite his avowed religious sympathies, he is unwilling to remain uncritical of North American evangelicalism. Drawing on the work of Douglas Frank, Rawlyk adopts a Marxian critique of evangelicalism, which, he believes, has so capitulated to consumerism—"the insidious antithesis of essential Christianity"—that it has lost its prophetic voice.

## NOTES

1. The editors thank Russell E. Richey for the benefit of his reflections on the nature and definition of revival.

2. Charles Grandison Finney, *Lectures on Revivals of Religion*, ed. William G. McLoughlin (Cambridge: Harvard University Press, 1960), 9.

# Modern
# Christian
# Revivals

# 1

# Eschewing the "Routine of Religion": Eighteenth-Century Pietism and the Revival Tradition in America

✦

RANDALL BALMER

THERE ARE OBSTACLES aplenty to appreciating pietism and the role it has played in shaping religion in America. First, there is the question of definition. The *Oxford English Dictionary* (1971 edition) defines *pietism* as a movement begun by Philipp Jakob Spener at Frankfurt am Main "for the revival and advancement of piety in the Lutheran church" and characterized by a "devotion to religious feeling, or to strictness of religious practice." Such a definition rightly points out the interiority of pietist faith, but it ignores the earlier development of Reformed pietism (or "precisianism") in the Netherlands.[1] It also slights the institutional dimensions of pietism and fails to suggest the ecumenical bias of the movement, a bias that only compounds the difficulties of definition because pietism transcended confessional boundaries and took different forms within different traditions.

Indeed, pietism covers the spectrum from conservative, orthodox, liturgical members of state-church traditions to separatist groups who reviled the "four dumb idols" of the state churches—baptismal font, altar, pulpit, and (in Lutheran lands) confessional—to radical prophetic groups alienated from both social and institutional church life. What they held in common was an emphasis on spiritual discipline and affective religion rather than mere intellectual assent, and a bias against ecclesiastical hierarchies and religious pretensions. Pietism, moreover, can also be viewed in the context of a larger revival of religious fervor and revolt against formality, ceremonialism, scholasticism, and moral laxity that (when defined broadly) encompassed quietism among Roman Catholics in France, Spain, and Italy, Wesleyanism in England, and even Hasidism in eastern Europe.

Another obstacle facing the student of pietism in the colonies is the dearth of pietistic literary records, at least relative to the Puritans of New England. In some instances the records are adequate, as in the case of Heinrich Melchior Mühlenberg's *Journals* or the sermons of Theodorus Jacobus Frelinghuysen.[2] Most of the extant literature, moreover, from Johann Conrad Beissel's mystical writings to Bernardus Freeman's "Mirror of Self-Knowledge," displays familiar pietistic themes: the call for experiential or "experimental" religion, the strong sexual imagery, and the emphasis on mystical introspection, known in the argot of eighteenth-century pietism as "self-knowledge."[3] On the other hand, such important pietists in the Middle Colonies as Peter Henry Dorsius and Guiliam Bertholf bequeathed little or nothing to historians, and the whole of John Henry Goetschius's sole published sermon has only recently been made available in English translation.[4] Accounts of contemporaries offer tantalizing glimpses of the lives and careers of Lars Tollstadius and Johann Bernhard van Dieren, but we have nothing from their own pens with which to render our judgments.[5]

The final obstacle is the general historiographical neglect of the Middle Colonies and the rich fabric of ethnic diversity therein. We are just now beginning to understand the variegated texture of ethnic life in the mid-Atlantic colonies—the Scots, the Dutch, the Huguenots, the Swedes, the Germans. It is becoming more and more apparent that religion played an important role in shaping the responses of these various ethnic groups to an eighteenth-century culture defined increasingly by the English.[6]

Having cataloged the difficulties in coming to terms with this subterranean world of eighteenth-century pietism, what are the benefits of perseverance?

First, an appreciation of pietism has implications for our understanding of the eighteenth-century revival of religion generally known as the Great Awakening. Even if you are not prepared, with Jon Butler, to dispense with the term *Great Awakening*, the revival of religion, at least in the Middle Colonies, looks more like an eruption of longer-term pietistic impulses than the last gasp of Puritanism.[7] Even a cursory examination of the extant pietist literature, much of it published in the decades before the Awakening, reveals some recurrent themes generally associated with the revival—the necessity of spiritual rebirth, for instance, or insistent calls for probity. The pietist view of the world, moreover, had been sustained in America since the late seventeenth century by irregular preaching and mostly unaccompanied hymn singing, which directed pietist expressions of faith into nonformal, nontraditional channels and thus helped to propel the movement toward acceptance of itinerant preachers and lay leadership. At the same time that Solomon Stoddard reported "harvests" in the Connecticut Valley, Guiliam Bertholf enjoyed considerable success in organizing pietistic congregations in northern New Jersey, and Lars Tollstadius created schisms among Swedish Lutherans in the Delaware Valley because of his pietistic preaching.[8]

Indeed, a whole range of pietists tapped into popular discontent among the rural peoples of the Middle Colonies. In addition to Bertholf and Tollstadius, the list includes Freeman, Mühlenberg, and Frelinghuysen, but also such lesser-known figures as Peter Henry Dorsius, Cornelius Van Santvoord, and Samuel Verbryck, among many others. Even Gilbert Tennent, schooled in pietism at the feet of Frelinghuysen when the two men were colleagues in the Raritan Valley, must be included in this camp—witness his evangelical vigor, his emphasis on a warmhearted piety, and his assault on the settled clergy in *The Danger of an Unconverted Ministry.*[9]

Tennent's liaison with Frelinghuysen underscores another characteristic of pietism, namely its ecumenical character. This cross-fertilization was certainly present in the Old World. The works of such English Puritans as William Perkins and William Ames had been translated into Dutch; Perkins, in turn, had been influenced by the ideas of Willem Teelinck, Godfridus Cornelisz Udemans, and Gysbertus Voetius.[10] In New Jersey, Tennent openly acknowledged his debt to Frelinghuysen, and the two men regularly traded pulpits and often officiated jointly. Both George Whitefield and Jonathan Edwards praised Frelinghuysen's efforts in New Jersey. Mühlenberg frequently preached in Dutch churches, and Frelinghuysen's partisans supported Lutheran evangelicals in the Middle Colonies. By the 1750s the distinction between pietistic Dutch and New Light Presbyterians was so slight that William Livingston, publisher of the *Independent Reflector,* remarked that "the different languages are the only criteria to distinguish them from each other."[11] Even that barrier eroded as the Great Awakening pushed Dutch pietists into the mainstream of eighteenth-century evangelicalism. Henceforth, the line between pietism and evangelicalism in American religion becomes considerably blurred.

Pietism in the eighteenth century was very much a transatlantic movement. Unlike the Puritans, whose settlement in New England— despite their protestations about remaining members of the Church of England—represented a break with Old World institutions, colonial pietists maintained ties with their confrères on the Continent well into the eighteenth century. The Dutch Labadists, for instance, followers of a radical separatist named Jean de Labadie, sought to establish a colony in the New World; many among the colonial Dutch admired Jacobus Koelman, a sometime disciple, back in the Netherlands, of Labadie. When Frelinghuysen, who acknowledged his theological indebtedness to Koelman, sailed across the Atlantic toward his assignment in Raritan, New Jersey, he boasted that after he had worked "to secure a following" in America, "immediately many more would come from Holland to his support," as indeed they did.[12] Among German pietists, Halle supplied pastors to Pennsylvania under the loose supervision of Mühlenberg, while Württemberg emigrés created the congregations. The Moravians maintained a presence in both worlds.

American pietism, then, was not an indigenous movement. Instead, it had deep roots in the Old World and continued to draw its inspiration from those sources until New World pietists were able to develop indigenous leadership through individual tutorials, small "kitchen seminaries" like that of Peter Henry Dorsius in Bucks County, Pennsylvania, and, eventually, pietistically inspired institutions such as the Dutch Reformed Coetus (1747) and Queen's College (1766) in New Brunswick.

That is not to say, however, that pietism on the western shores of the Atlantic was identical to that back on the Continent. The possibility of keeping "orthodox" doctrinal churches and pietist renewal groups together was difficult enough in the European context, but once disparate groups of immigrants arrived in America the spectrum of pietism tilted sharply toward a more radical version of the movement, witness, for example, Johann Conrad Beissel's Ephrata Community in Pennsylvania, which combined pietistic impulses with a sort of Catholic mysticism and monasticism, or Samuel Verbryck's insistence on dispensing with the forms of prayer and preaching a sermon on the crucifixion for Easter Sunday in order to demonstrate his disregard for ecclesiastical holidays.[13] Some pietists, like Mühlenberg among the Lutherans, continued to insist on a balance between orthodox doctrine and pietist renewal. More often than not, however, what would have been regarded as somewhat daring in a European context was more or less unexceptional in the American setting, where radicalism of a sort almost nowhere tolerated in Europe took root and flourished.

Eighteenth-century pietism's most profound effect was certainly on the inner life of believers, who found religious renewal and assurance amidst the ferment of revival. For historians, however, especially at a remove of more than two centuries, those effects are incalculable. We can point to certain heroic individuals—Gilbert Tennent, for instance, or John Wesley—whose lives and ministries were profoundly influenced by pietistic ideals, or we can identify congregations in the throes of revival, but we shall never know the full effects of pietism on the lives of individual "ordinary" colonists.

We do know, however, that pietism profoundly influenced the institutional life of eighteenth-century America, although its effects were oddly divergent because, once again, pietism, by its nature a very elastic movement, took on various characteristics within different traditions. Among the Dutch and the New Light Presbyterians, pietistic impulses reshaped colonial ecclesiastical structures and served as an almost iconoclastic movement. Pietism, however, generally did not serve the same radical function among the Germans, Reformed or Lutheran, as it did among the Dutch. There are only scattered references to the disruptions of pietism among the Germans. In 1709, for instance, the Governor's Council in New York learned that nineteen of the forty-seven Palatines along the Hudson River had "changed their religion become pietists and withdrawn themselves from the Communion of the Minister and ye Rest of ye said Germans."[14]

On the whole, however, pietism among the Germans was a source of unity, not division, and when the Lutherans finally organized their ministerium (or synod) in 1748, that body was controlled by Halle Pietists.[15] For the Lutherans, the influence of Mühlenberg and the Halle connection may have been critical. This influence domesticated pietism and made it both vibrant and a source for organizing congregations and promoting a deep personal and communal piety. But at the same time it was respectable and sustained by the transatlantic charities and pastoral supply at Halle that were disbursed through London. Those connections were hardly calculated to produce radical protesters against prevailing norms.

Among the German Reformed, pietist tendencies seem never to have been very pronounced, with the exception, perhaps, of Peter Henry Dorsius. The German Reformed were sustained by support from the Swiss and the Dutch and, unlike the Lutherans, never enjoyed the money or the clerical density of their fellow Germans. Moreover, there were so many free church and sectarian groups to their left that German pietists had little inclination or reason to be associated with those sorts of people. Moravians in particular were regarded with disdain, especially by the Lutherans, and those feelings were reciprocated. Furthermore, since the Moravians were thoroughly steeped in an emotional pietism, the Lutherans and Reformed had ample cause to maintain their distance.

Unlike the Dutch, moreover, the Germans had an entire spectrum of ethnic religious options available to them to accommodate theological and ecclesiastical differences—the Amish, Mennonites, Schwenck-felders, Moravians, Lutherans, Reformed—whereas the pietistic Dutch, locked within the confining orbit of the orthodox Dutch Reformed Church, had fewer choices. Either they would join forces with the Presbyterians (as many threatened to do) or they would recast the Dutch Reformed Church in their own image. As their numbers and influence increased, the latter option grew more and more attractive.

Among the Dutch, then, pietism functioned as a theology of the people, a protest against the clerical establishment. Although pietism certainly had its own positive agenda—revitalization of liturgy and worship, closer attention to personal probity—it also represented a challenge to the ecclesiastical hierarchy. Pietists first organized them-selves into conventicles, which, like John Wesley's "methodist" gath-erings, sought the infusion of spiritual ardor into religious traditions that had grown stuffy and cold. In the Netherlands, pietists had challenged the corruptions of wealth attending the growth of Holland's commercial empire and the arid scholasticism into which seventeenth-century Reformed theologians had fallen. Indeed, pietism among the Dutch both in the Netherlands and in the New World issued in a rural protest against the urban elite and the urban clergy as well as the ecclesiastical hierarchy of the Dutch Reformed Church.[16] The Classes of Middleburg, Schieland, and Lingen, for instance, were pietistic, whereas the Classis of Amsterdam sought to frustrate the spread of pietism on both sides of the Atlantic. The universities of Utrecht and Groningen turned out pietists, who then very often clashed with graduates of the University of Leiden.

Frustrated in their attempts to dislodge the traditionalist clergy, who opposed the pietist renewal, Dutch pietists unleashed an attack against the ecclesiastical hierarchy in New York and especially against the Classis of Amsterdam, which sought to thwart the spread of pietism in the New World. Indeed, Dutch pietists regarded Amsterdam as the mortal enemy of true religion. Guiliam Bertholf, a cooper from New Jersey and a lay reader for some of the fledgling Dutch con-gregations on the frontier, knew that the Classis of Amsterdam would never pass on his ordination because of his pietistic leanings and his lack of formal education, so he circumvented Amsterdam completely and was ordained by the Classis of Middleburg. Upon his return to

New Jersey in 1694, Bertholf worked tirelessly to organize pietistic congregations on the New Jersey frontier.[17]

Bernardus Freeman, another pietist, also nursed a grudge against the Classis of Amsterdam. When the Dutch church at Albany needed a new minister in 1699, Freeman, a tailor by trade, submitted his name. The Classis, however, denied his application and belittled him as someone "who had only just come down from his cutting board, and who had neither ability for his own craft, much less for that demanded of a pastor."[18] With the help of Willem Bancker, an Amsterdam merchant and patron to pietists in the Netherlands, Freeman sought and received ordination from the Classis of Lingen and sailed for the New World to claim the pastorate at Albany. Amsterdam's candidate, Johannes Lydius, prevailed in that initial ecclesiastical skirmish, but Freeman took the church in nearby Schenectady; several years later, through a series of perfidious maneuvers, he insinuated himself into the Dutch churches on Long Island. Freeman steadfastly refused to submit to the Classis of Amsterdam, and he summarily dismissed those consistories that opposed him. His obstinacy precipitated a bitter schism that lasted the better part of a decade and markedly diminished the Classis of Amsterdam's grip on the colony's churches.[19]

Although Theodorus Jacobus Frelinghuysen came to the New World with Amsterdam's formal approbation, he made no secret after his arrival of his intention to flout his independence from the Amsterdam ecclesiastical authorities. Within days of disembarking in New York, Frelinghuysen insulted—and alienated—the traditionalist clergy in New York, declared his disdain for the Classis of Amsterdam, and announced his intention to flood the Middle Colonies with pietistic clergy. His clerical career in New Jersey was marked by bitter disputes between his evangelical followers and his generally more prosperous detractors both in New Jersey and New York. Because of Amsterdam's suspicions about pietism, morever, Frelinghuysen's agenda for the New World implied a circumvention of Amsterdam's ecclesiastical prerogatives. He eagerly took that step. Frelinghuysen, moreover, together with Bertholf and Freeman, supported the incursion of other pietists in the Middle Colonies, once again over Amsterdam's objections.

Dutch pietists in general and Frelinghuysen in particular used the language of piety to assail the ecclesiastical establishment and their theological opponents. Frelinghuysen regularly taunted his adversaries. He restricted access to Holy Communion in his Raritan churches, excommunicated dissenters, and angered the more affluent of his auditors when he suggested that "it has been very true that the largest portion of the faithful have been poor and of little account in the world."[20] Despite debilitating bouts of mental illness and unrefuted allegations of homosexuality, Frelinghuysen persisted in his attacks on the Classis of Amsterdam and the non-pietist Dutch ministers. When disaffected members of his congregations drafted a bill of particulars against him and took their case to the New York clergy, Frelinghuysen and his consistory became defiant; they resolved unanimously "that we will never suffer any church or pastor in the land to assume dominion over us."[21]

When his mental incapacities finally disabled him, Frelinghuysen's struggle against the ecclesiastical establishment was taken up by an entire cohort of younger men, including his sons and John Henry Goetschius, who became minister on Long Island, over the strenuous objections of the Dutch Reformed establishment. Once installed there, Goetschius vigorously assailed his ecclesiastical adversaries. On 22 August 1742, he preached a sermon entitled "The Unknown God," in the course of which he reviled the mere practice of religion, which he contrasted with true spirituality, and he warned his adversaries that "you will experience your religion in hell, and not in heaven, as you had hoped." When called before the New York ministers to account for his attacks, Goetschius remarked that his opponents "were plainly godless people" and that were it not for the Netherlands church authorities, "this country had long ago been filled with pious ministers."[22]

As the number of pietistic clergy increased, these desultory attacks on the ecclesiastical establishment evolved into an orchestrated assault on the Classis of Amsterdam in the Netherlands and the traditionalist clergy in New York. Freeman, Frelinghuysen, Goetschius, and other Dutch pietists openly defied the Classis of Amsterdam on matters of ordination, church polity, and ecclesiastical discipline. In the 1740s, amidst the fervor of the Great Awakening, they began agitating for an independent, indigenous ecclesiastical body, a *coetus*, that would govern the American churches. When gavelled to order on 8 September 1747, the Coetus consisted almost entirely of pietist clergy, all of whom were eager to distance themselves from the Classis of Amsterdam. Within a very few years, members of the Coetus circulated proposals for the formation of an American classis and an American academy for the training of pietistic clergy, and after the American Revolution they declared their formal independence from the Netherlands church authorities.[23]

This protest against the religious establishment among the Dutch soon took on political overtones, as contemporaries recognized. After the pietists had banded together to form their Coetus in 1747, one anti-pietist predicted that if "we should complain about anything to the Classis or the Synod, that our Dutch churches were not regulated after the manner of the churches of the Fatherland, it would be said, 'Oh, the people of Holland govern *their* churches in *their* own way, and *we* find no fault with them; and *we* govern our churches, and we are no longer under obligations to give account of our doing to them.'" Others detected that "a spirit of independence is clearly manifest" in the pietists' machinations. In the 1750s, when Theodore Frelinghuysen of Albany proposed the establishment of a pietist American seminary independent of the Netherlands authorities, his conservative opponents asked if his next step was to "rebel against the king."[24]

Indeed, not long after the pietistic clergy in the Middle Colonies asserted their ecclesiastical independence from the Classis of Amsterdam by forming the Coetus, many of these same ministers—notably Theodore Frelinghuysen, Archibald Laidlie, Johannes Leydt, Dirck Romeyn, and Eilardus Westerlo—joined the chorus calling for political independence as well. During the throes of the Stamp Act crisis, for instance, Laidlie preached what at least one auditor considered a "sed[i]t[iou]s sermon" for the purpose of "exciting people to Reb[e]ll[io]n."[25] The rhetoric about ecclesiastical "liberty" and the aversion to "subordination" that saturated the pietists' communications with the Netherlands very easily transferred to the political sphere.[26]

Even among more conservative German congregations, the discussions about ecclesiastical liberty and suspicions about the motives of wealthy and learned people, lay and clerical, erupted in the late 1750s and early 1760s, just as the imperial crisis was breaking. For these congregations, steeped in a pietist tradition, suspicious of church authorities, and controlled by the laity, the language of piety with its anti-authoritarian overtones served as a training ground for thinking in political terms—a first among a largely apolitical people.[27]

Pietism in the Middle Colonies, then, as articulated by those alienated in some way from the religious establishment, provided a radical critique of eighteenth-century authority structures, first religious and then political. The exercise of lay initiative and a suspicion of clerical prerogative were deeply imbedded in the pietist tradition, and words like *liberty* and *subordination* in the lexicon of piety became highly charged after mid-century. For Dutch pietists, at least, the assertion of ecclesiastical independence led quite logically, almost seamlessly, to the assertion of political independence. Pietism, then, the earliest harbinger of eighteenth-century revival, provides a new

paradigm for understanding both ecclesiastical and political activism
in the Middle Colonies of the eighteenth century.

What happened to pietism in America? Along about the middle
of the eighteenth century the trail turns cold and we begin to lose
the scent. Aside from enclaves of intentionally insular Germans and
the periodic influx of pietistic immigrants from Scandinavia and the
Netherlands, Continental pietism largely disappears into the mainstream of American religious life, much the way that the Mohawk
River flows into the Hudson or the Schuylkill into the Delaware.

These examples are not random. What we know today as evangelicalism in America traces its origins to the confluence of Continental pietism and New England Puritanism in the eighteenth century.
This combustion (to shift the metaphor once more) erupted spectacularly in what historians have come to call the Great Awakening.
The Middle Colonies, moreover, served as the tinder box for this new
religious expression. Frelinghuysen's machinations in the Raritan Valley had produced both revival and reaction in the 1720s, and his
friendship with Gilbert Tennent introduced the Presbyterian minister
to pietistic traditions, disciplines, and techniques. Tennent then carried the message throughout the Middle Colonies and to New England
during his several missionary sorties there.[28] The influences were
reciprocal. Pietist congregations in the Middle Colonies welcomed
Tennent and George Whitefield, and when Theodore Frelinghuysen
of Albany, son of the redoubtable New Jersey pietist, preached a
sermon to New England troops during the French and Indian War,
it sounded for all the world like a Puritan jeremiad, full of lamen-
tations and apocalyptic warnings.[29]

The Great Awakening, together with a number of circumstances
and cultural changes thereafter, conspired to obfuscate the influence
of Continental pietism on American religion. For the Dutch, internal
conflicts, the desire to enjoy the commercial advantages of assimi-
lation, and the general desuetude of the Dutch language combined
to drive them away from their hereditary culture toward either Anglicanism or Presbyterianism, depending on their previous disposition
toward pietism. Later, and on a larger scale, the importation and
rapid success of Methodism in America largely co-opted pietistic expressions of faith (with the exception, once again, of the Germans).
John Wesley himself had been influenced by such Continental pietists
as Johann Albrecht Bengel, and he greatly admired the Moravians
for their "faith and love and holy conversation in Christ Jesus."[30]
Methodist itinerants in America, moreover, had come into contact

with pietist preachers. Late in the eighteenth century, then, the pietistic cudgels of protest against deficient personal morality, intransigent ecclesiastical establishments, and worldly elites were taken up by the Methodists and by other evangelical, populist groups in the early republic.[31]

What is the legacy of eighteenth-century pietism to American religion? Many pietists of German descent continue, against great odds, to retain their ethnic particularity, their cultural insularity, and their rootedness in Old World traditions. That is surely the most visible legacy of pietism in America. Evangelical fervor has also benefited from time to time from the continued infusion of pietistic groups from the Old World, witness, for example, the nineteenth-century immigration of Dutch Seceders who formed the Christian Reformed Church, the Janssonists from Sweden who settled Bishop Hill, Illinois, and the late nineteenth-century Scandinavians who eventually formed the Evangelical Covenant Church and the Evangelical Free Church denominations.[32]

But pietism has insinuated itself into the pastische of American religion, especially evangelicalism, in other, less tangible ways. The evangelical prayer meeting today looks quite similar to the "methodist" gathering and the pietist conventicle of the eighteenth century or to the nineteenth-century prayer and Bible study conducted in a Scandinavian *Bede Hus* (prayer house).

The most profound influence of pietism is, once again, incalculable—its effect upon ordinary believers. For anyone reared within the evangelical subculture in America, with its parietal rules, its emphasis on personal piety, its proscriptions against alcohol, tobacco, and dancing, and its sabbatarian scruples, the continued influence of pietism is self-evident. Countless evangelists have summoned their auditors to exacting standards of personal probity and spiritual piety, even when they themselves, like Frelinghuysen, fell shy of those standards. The rubric of self-examination as prelude to conversion or rededication is common to both traditions, and in the hands of such acknowledged masters as Charles Grandison Finney, Dwight Lyman Moody, Billy Graham, and even Jimmy Swaggart, it has served as a powerful tool for revival.

The literature of colonial pietism and American evangelicalism also bears many similarities. Both pietistic and evangelical sermons are replete with graphic descriptions of the torments of hell and the perils of unbelief or, more subtly, the consequences of a false security among those who merely practice religion in its outward forms and never know the experience of conversion. When Frelinghuysen implored, "O Sinner! abandon your Way which seemeth so right unto you, your careless and secure Tranquility, your own Righteousness, your Sins and Lusts, your own Thoughts and turn to the Lord," he might have been writing a script for Finney, Moody, Graham, Swaggart, or any one of a thousand other evangelists.[33] The devotional literature of both nineteenth- and twentieth-century evangelicalism also echoes the introspective mode of eighteenth-century pietistic treatises. The potent sexual imagery of Beissel or Frelinghuysen reverberates in such staples of the evangelical hymnal as "Blessed Assurance," "Jesus, Lover of My Soul," "Just as I Am," and "Rock of Ages, Cleft for Me."

In America, moreover, evangelicals continue to use the argot of piety as a protest against ecclesiastical establishments. The fundamentalist-modernist controversy of the 1920s comes to mind, as does Carl McIntire's rhetoric directed against the "godless" Federal Council of Churches. Fundamentalists, frustrated in their attempts to reverse the drift toward modernism in mainline denominations, abandoned those institutions and built their own denominations, Bible institutes, colleges, and seminaries. Those actions would not be at all alien to the eighteenth-century progenitors of New Side Presbyterianism, the Dutch Coetus, Queen's College, or the College of New Jersey, nor would it surprise leaders of the Cumberland Presbyterians or the holiness movement. Throughout its history, evangelicalism, with its roots in pietism, has mounted strident—and quite effective—attacks on recalcitrant and unresponsive ecclesiastical bureaucracies.

Those attacks, very often, have been personal, directed against "unconverted" or "liberal" clergy. In that way, the rhetoric of McIntire or Billy Sunday or J. Gresham Machen recalls Gilbert Tennent's *Danger of an Unconverted Ministry,* Frelinghuysen's relentless verbal assaults on his clerical adversaries (as when he criticized them as "unprofitable sickmaking Physicians"), and John Henry Goetschius's *The Unknown God,* which lambasted the opponents of true piety as those who impose "their old, rotten, and stinking routine of religion."[34]

In its various guises, pietism in America, from the eighteenth century to the present, has assiduously sought to avoid the "routine of religion," preferring instead a vibrant, experiential piety. That characteristic, in turn, has meant that pietistic impulses almost by definition transcend institutional, confessional, and ethnic boundaries. Just as Frelinghuysen and Gilbert Tennent crossed those boundaries in the eighteenth century (much to the scandal of their antirevivalist contemporaries), so too have evangelicals managed at various points in their history to submerge their differences. The ecumenicity of the Second Great Awakening comes to mind, as does the Evangelical United Front, the urban revivals of 1858, and the interfaith cooperation that attends Billy Graham crusades.

The confluence of Contintental pietism and Great Awakening revivalism in the eighteenth century renders nearly impossible the task of tracing specific influences in the myriad tributaries of American evangelicalism. The currents, however, are unmistakable: ecumenicity; exacting standards of morality; a suspicion of liturgical formalism, theological scholasticism, and ecclesiastical structures; the insistent, plaintive calls for conversion juxtaposed with warnings about the torments of hell. Both traditions have insisted on a warm-hearted piety as the basis for salvation and the sign of regeneration. Without "true and experienced knowledge God is still unknown and all religion is idle," John Henry Goetschius preached in 1742.[35]
Billy Graham could not have said it better.

### NOTES

1. See Martin H. Prozesky, "The Emergence of Dutch Pietism," *Journal of Ecclesiastical History* 28 (1977): 29–37; F. Ernest Stoeffler, *The Rise of Evangelical Pietism* (Leiden: E. J. Brill, 1971), especially 109–79; F. Ernest Stoeffler, s.v., "pietism," in *Dictionary of Christianity in America*, ed. Daniel G. Reid (Downers Grove, Ill.: Inter-Varsity Press, 1990).

2. Henry Melchior Mühlenberg, *The Journals of Henry Melchior Mühlenberg*, trans. Theodore G. Tappert and John W. Doberstein, 3 vols. (Philadelphia: Evangelical Lutheran Ministerium of Pennsylvania and Adjacent States, 1942–53); Theodorus Jacobus Frelinghuysen, *Sermons by Theodorus Jacobus Frelinghuysen*, trans. William Demarest (New York, 1856).

3. A translation of Beissel's works appears in Peter C. Erb, ed., *Johann Conrad Beissel and the Ephrata Community: Mystical and Historical Texts* (Lewiston, N.Y.: Edwin Mellen Press, 1985); a manuscript translation of Freeman's "Mirror of Self-Knowledge" is at the New York Historical Society, New York City; Freeman, for example, enjoined his readers to examine themselves and then "to lead a humble, virtuous, and Godly life." On pietistic introspection, see Carl J. Schindler, "The Psychology of Henry Melchior Mühlenberg's Pastoral Technique," *Lutheran Church Quarterly* 16 (1943): 54–55.

4. Randall Balmer, "John Henry Goetschius and *The Unknown God:* Eighteenth-Century Pietism in the Middle Colonies," *Pennsylvania Magazine of History and Biography* 113 (1989): 575–608.

5. Regarding Tollstadius, see Suzanne B. Geissler, "A Step on the Swedish Lutheran Road to Anglicanism," *Historical Magazine of the Protestant Episcopal Church* 54 (1985): 39–49; on van Dieren, see Douglas Jacobsen, "Johann Bernhard van Dieren: Protestant Preacher at Hackensack, New Jersey," *New Jersey History* 100 (1982): 15–29.

6. See, for example, Jon Butler, *The Huguenots in America: A Refugee People in New World Society* (Cambridge: Harvard University Press, 1983); Ned C. Landsman, *Scotland and Its First American Colony, 1683–1765* (Princeton: Princeton University Press, 1985), especially chapter 8; Randall Balmer, *A Perfect Babel of Confusion: Dutch Religion and English Culture in the Middle Colonies* (New York: Oxford University Press, 1989).

7. Jon Butler, "Enthusiasm Described and Decried: The Great Awakening as Interpretive Fiction," *Journal of American History* 69 (1982): 305–25. On the subtle differences between Puritanism and pietism, especially on the issue of assurance, see Baird Tipson, "How Can the Religious Experience of the Past Be Recovered? The Examples of Puritanism and Pietism," *Journal of the American Academy of Religion* 43 (1975): 695–707.

8. Once again, the lack of literary records frustrates any certain conclusions about the ministries of Bertholf and Tollstadius. When Bertholf returned to the Netherlands to seek ordination, however, he went to the Classis of Middleburg rather than Amsterdam, most likely because he believed that Amsterdam would look askance at his pietistic leanings; Bertholf also endorsed other pietist ministers such as Freeman and Frelinghuysen. Tollstadius is even more shadowy, but it is clear that his appeal lay in great measure in his warmhearted preaching and in his willingness to challenge the Swedish Lutheran hierarchy (see also Geissler, "Step on the Swedish Lutheran Road").

9. On Tennent's relationship with Frelinghuysen, see Milton J Coalter, Jr., *Gilbert Tennent, Son of Thunder: A Case Study of Continental Pietism's Impact on the First Great Awakening in the Middle Colonies* (Westport, Conn.: Greenwood Press, 1986), especially chapter 1. Tennent's sermon, first preached at Nottingham, Pennsylvania, 8 March 1740, appeared in print as *The Danger of an Unconverted Ministry* (Philadelphia, 1740).

10. James Tanis, "Reformed Pietism in Colonial America," in *Continental Pietism and Early American Christianity*, ed. F. Ernest Stoeffler (Grand Rapids: Wm. B. Eerdmans, 1976), 34–35.

11. Quoted in Edward T. Corwin, ed., *Ecclesiastical Records: State of New York*, vol. 5 (Albany, 1901–16), 3460 (hereafter *Ecclesiastical Records*).

12. Ibid. 3:2182–83.

13. See Erb, ed., *Johann Conrad Beissel*; *Ecclesiastical Records*, 6:3928.

14. *Ecclesiastical Records* 3:1742.

15. Theodore G. Tappert, "The Influence of Pietism in Colonial American Lutheranism," in *Continental Pietism and Early American Christianity*, ed. F. Ernest Stoeffler (Grand Rapids: Wm. B. Eerdmans, 1976), 17.

16. Prozesky, "Emergence of Dutch Pietism," 29–37; Stoeffler, *Rise of Evangelical Pietism*.

17. On Bertholf, see Randall Balmer, "The Social Roots of Dutch Pietism in the Middle Colonies," *Church History* 53 (1984): 187–99; Howard G. Hageman, "William Bertholf: Pioneer Dominie of New Jersey," *Reformed Review* 30 (1976): 73–80.

18. *Ecclesiastical Records* 2:1349.

19. For an account of this schism, see Randall Balmer, "Schism on Long Island: The Dutch Reformed Church, Lord Cornbury, and the Politics of Anglicization," in *Authority and Resistance in Colonial New York*, ed. William Pencak and Conrad Edick Wright (New York: New York Historical Society, 1988), chapter 4.

20. Quoted in James Tanis, *Dutch Calvinist Pietism in the Middle Colonies: A Study in the Life and Theology of Theodorus Jacobus Frelinghuysen* (The Hague: Martinus Nijhoff, 1967), 54.

21. Joseph Anthony Loux, Jr., trans. and ed., *Boel's Complaint against Frelinghuysen* (Rensselaer, N.Y.: Hamilton Printing Co., 1979), 53.

22. Balmer, "Goetschius and *The Unknown God*," 604; *Ecclesiastical Records* 4:2896, 2881.

23. *Ecclesiastical Records* 5:3493, 3541. *Coetus* is pronounced SEE-tus.

24. *Ecclesiastical Records* 5:3533, 3499, 3649.

25. *Journals of Capt. John Montressor, 1757–1778*, New York Historical Society, *Collections*, Publication Fund Ser., 14 (New York, 1881), 350.

26. The word "subordination" became highly charged among the Dutch Pietists at mid-century; see, for instance, *Ecclesiastical Records* 6:3945, 3950, 4005, 4021.

27. Anthony G. Roeber has developed these ideas and posited a connection between legal and charitable concerns and the American Revolution in "Germans, Property, and the First Great Awakening: Rehearsal for a Revolution?" in *The Transit of Civilization from Europe to America: Essays in Honor of Hans Galinsky*, ed. Winfried Herget and Karl Ortseifen (Tübingen: G. Narr, 1986), 165–84.

28. In one form or another, Isaac Backus, the Separate leader in Connecticut, imbibed pietist ideas; see William G. McLoughlin, *Isaac Backus and the American Pietist Tradition* (Boston: Little, Brown, 1967).

29. Theodorus Frielinghuysen [sic], *Wars and Rumors of Wars, Heavens Decree over the World: A Sermon Preached in the Camp of the New-England Forces* (New York, 1755).

30. Richard M. Cameron, *The Rise of Methodism: A Source Book* (New York: Philosophical Library, 1954), 204.

31. This point is made persuasively by Nathan O. Hatch, *The Democratization of American Christianity* (New Haven: Yale University Press, 1989).

32. See Paul Elmen, "Bishop Hill: Utopia on the Prairie," *Chicago History* 5 (1976): 45–52; James D. Bratt, *Dutch Calvinism in Modern America: A History of a Conservative Subculture* (Grand Rapids: Wm. B. Eerdmans, 1984); David Nyvall, *The Evangelical Covenant Church* (Chicago, 1954);

Arnold Theodore Olson, *The Search for Identity* (Minneapolis: Free Church Press, 1980).

33. Tanis, *Dutch Calvinistic Pietism*, 175.

34. Ibid., 169; Balmer, "Goetschius and *The Unknown God*," 599.

35. Balmer, "Goetschius and *The Unknown God*," 591.

# 2

# Revival and Enlightenment in Eighteenth-Century England

✦

## David Bebbington

The Evangelical Revival in eighteenth-century England has frequently been seen as hostile to the Enlightenment. Preachers of the gospel, in this view, were stern opponents of the *philosophes* and their English equivalents. The revival has been described as "a reaction against certain features of the orthodox theology and religious outlook of the early Enlightenment."[1] According to this analysis, contemporary churchmen appealed only to the head. The attraction of the revival for the heart was a response to the deficiencies of their cerebral approach. Piety challenged reason. The revival was an emotional protest against the intellectual hegemony of the age.

This plausible thesis rests on two premises. First, there is the contention that the Enlightenment was intrinsically antagonistic to spiritual religion. The grand sweep of eighteenth-century thought is normally depicted as irreligious in tendency.[2] Voltaire, Hume, and Gibbon are treated as representative figures. The elimination of religion, at least in its revealed and institutional forms, is presented as the ultimate goal of their endeavors. The Deists of the early eighteenth century were certainly part of such a secularizing trend. Its influence was also felt within the churches. The dominant Latitudinarians in the Church of England and the Socinians who proliferated among the Dissenters were alike in wishing to make the Christian religion more palatable to educated opinion.[3] Accordingly, it is suggested, traditional orthodoxy was cast to the winds. "Reason," wrote an evangelical critic of Gibbon in 1781, "has impertinently meddled with the Gospel."[4] It seems natural to cast the Enlightenment in the role of a liberalizing body of thought at odds with the revival's firm grasp of biblical teachings.

The second premise is that the revival was conspicuously unen-

lightened. The "emotional transports" of its Methodist dimension
have been censured as deluding the common people about their true
interests.[5] And there is a great deal of evidence suggesting that evangelicalism was a matter of heat rather than light. "The dales are
flaming," reported one Methodist to another in 1798 about a spate
of conversions. "The fire hath caught, and runs from one dale to
another."[6] Young converts would open the Bible at random for guidance; an ex-corporal on the fringe of Methodism claimed to be more
perfect than the unfallen Adam; and the leading evangelist George
Whitefield, who rarely preached without weeping, had his first sermon complained of to the bishop on the ground that it had driven
fifteen people mad.[7] A catalog of apparent irrationalism, what the
century decried as "enthusiasm," could be charged against the movement. The Evangelical Revival seems an anomalous intrusion into
the Age of Reason.

Both premises, however, are open to question. Enlightenment
thought may have been as good a medium for vital Christianity as
it was for more secularizing tendencies; and the Evangelical Revival
may have shared the characteristic worldview of progressive eighteenth-century opinion to a far greater extent than has normally been
supposed. After all, the metaphor of light was regularly used by
evangelicals to describe conversion, the central experience of the
revival. Thomas Gibbons, an Independent minister aligned with the
revival, spoke of regeneration as enlightenment or illumination.[8]
George Whitefield corresponded with others who had been "enlightened" and his first biographer wrote of Whitefield's mind, following
conversion, as "being now happily enlightened."[9] Charles Wesley, as
so often, incorporated this central idea in his hymnody:

> Expand thy wings, celestial Dove,
> Brood o'er our nature's night:
> On our disorder'd spirits move,
> And let there now be light.[10]

The metaphor, as Wesley's elaboration illustrates, had roots in biblical
imagery, and it had been reinforced by the Platonic tradition of
illumination. Nevertheless, there is significance in the evangelicals'
attraction to the notion of the dawning of light on the soul. Revival
in England, as much as in America or among Scottish Dissenters,
was perceived as the spread of "New Light." It is worth exploring
how far revival and Enlightenment were bound up in the same cultural
nexus.

What were the various strands in the English Evangelical Revival?

First, there were the Methodists, the spiritual offspring of John Wesley. The movement was almost unique among evangelicals in abandoning Calvinist teaching for the sake of Arminianism. Wesley consciously rejected the doctrine of predestination in 1725, at an early stage in his intellectual development, and never saw cause to reconsider.[11] After the pivotal Aldersgate Street experience on 24 May 1738, when he trusted in Christ for salvation, his preaching insisted that all are free to respond to the gospel. Although disputation on the subject was not of his own seeking, in the 1770s a Calvinistic controversy sharpened the boundaries between Methodists and other evangelicals.[12] Methodists were also distinguished by their discipline. Wesley remained a loyal clergyman of the Church of England until his death in 1791, and most of the members of the religious societies he supervised were faithful attenders of their parish churches. But Methodists were expected to maintain rigorous standards of Christian behavior and so grew into a people apart. Wesley enforced the standards by personal visits and by correspondence with the traveling preachers stationed in the various circuits up and down the land. And all the time he and his helpers devoted themselves to fanning the flame of revival. "You have nothing to do," Wesley commanded his traveling preachers, "but to save souls. Therefore spend and be spent in this work."[13] By 1800 there were some 88,000 Methodists in England.[14]

Second, there were the Calvinistic Methodists. George Whitefield was converted and entered a career of field preaching before Wesley. As early as 1739–40 he diverged from Wesley on the question of God's decrees, and his teaching remained resolutely, if unobtrusively, Calvinist.[15] His evangelistic zeal raised societies in several parts of England, and particularly Gloucestershire. By 1747 there were thirty-one of them.[16] Although he organized a Calvinistic Methodist Association in 1743,[17] his seven visits to America and a failure to exercise central control led to the virtual disintegration of this connection even before his death in 1770. In addition, Selina, Countess of Huntingdon, established seven places of worship where her chaplains exercised a gospel ministry. Between fifty-five and eighty additional congregations became loosely associated with the Countess of Huntingdon's Connection.[18] There the revival message continued to be preached in a Calvinist form. Like Whitefield's societies, however, they became virtually indistinguishable from Independent churches. The smallness of the institutional legacy of Whitefield and his circle to the nineteenth century must not disguise their major role in the evangelical movement of the eighteenth century.

Third, there was the band of gospel clergymen in the Church of

England. The established church, though riddled with anomalies such as nonresidence and pluralism, was by no means moribund in the eighteenth century. Public worship, especially in the north and west, was properly maintained, and attendance was probably higher than bare figures for Easter communion would suggest.[19] Thomas Secker, Archbishop of Canterbury from 1758 to 1768, urged his clergy "to preach fully and freely" the doctrines that evangelicals accused them of neglecting.[20] Yet the neglect was real. The tradition of Reformed teaching had virtually died out as broader theological views had come into fashion.[21] Individual clergymen wrestled through to evangelical convictions in isolation, commonly helped chiefly by books.[22] Most eventually reached Calvinist conclusions. The boundary between such men and the Calvinistic Methodists was blurred: Thomas Haweis, for instance, combined the care of a Northamptonshire parish with itinerant preaching on behalf of the Countess of Huntingdon.[23] A few beneficed clergymen, notably John Fletcher of Madeley and William Grimshaw of Haworth, cooperated closely with Wesley.[24] Increasingly, however, evangelical clergymen avoided the itinerant work that the ecclesiastical hierarchy stigmatized as "irregularity" and confined themselves to a parish ministry.[25] For them, revival was tempered by respect for the discipline of the church.

Fourth, there was the impact of the revival on the Old Dissent, the inheritors of the Puritan traditions of the seventeenth century. In many congregations, especially among the Baptists, entrenched ways of thinking and behaving proved resistant to evangelical influences, although from the earliest days of the revival the leading Independent, Philip Doddridge, favored the new movement.[26] The great upsurge of Dissenting zeal, carrying the gospel in a mildly Calvinistic form into the villages of England, did not begin until the 1780s.[27] One stimulus was the outflow from Calvinistic Methodism. On hearing Whitefield preach, Samuel Brewer, a candidate for the Independent ministry, immediately recognized "the difference between that *frigid orthodoxy* which depopulates congregations, and the attractive eloquence zeal inspires, collecting and animating the breasts of thousands."[28] Another stimulus was the theology of Jonathan Edwards. His combination of the evangelistic imperative with Reformed principles inspired Baptist classics such as Andrew Fuller's *The Gospel Worthy of All Acceptation* (1785).[29] Fuller and his circle supplied the rationale for the Baptist Missionary Society (the first in the modern wave of Anglo-American overseas missions), and for the spread of the gospel at home. The revival of the Old Dissent was

primarily a result of the attractions of evangelical thought and practice from outside its borders.

It was estimated in 1800 that in the four strands of the evangelical
movement there were by that year some 2,000 gospel ministers and
some 600,000 hearers.[30] Despite their differences on doctrinal matters,
and especially in the debate over Calvinism, they formed a self-
consciously united movement. The message of justification by faith
bound them together. Whitefield delighted to agree with others in
"the old Protestant Doctrine of Justification in the sight of God, by
Faith alone in the imputed righteousness of *Christ*."[31] Four characteristics marked all evangelicals in England during the eighteenth
century, just as they have marked evangelicals throughout the world
ever since. They insisted that conversion, whether conscious or not,
is the essential entrance to the Christian life. For most it was a crisis
of experience such as that reported by Thomas Hanson, an early
Methodist preacher: "My heart, with a kind, sweet struggle, melted
into the hands of God."[32] Evangelicals were equally united in emphasizing the atoning work of Christ as the agency of salvation. "There
is but one central point, in which we must all meet," wrote the
Anglican clergyman William Romaine, "Jesus Christ and him cru-
cified."[33] A further characteristic was devotion to the Bible. From the
scriptures, Evangelicals took their message, their authority, their guidance. John Nelson, another Methodist pioneer, was accused of making
his Bible his god.[34] And evangelicals were typically activist. The
tireless preaching of Wesley, Whitefield, and a host of lesser figures
turned isolated experiences into a mass movement. "We can admire
their energy," wrote a caustic nineteenth-century critic of the early
Anglican Evangelicals, "though we cannot read their books."[35] Con-
versionism, crucicentrism, biblicism, and activism were the defining
qualities of those associated with the revival.

Of these qualities, activism was new. The Puritans of the seventeenth century had been conversionist, crucicentric, and biblicist,
but rarely had they devoted themselves to spreading the gospel where
it was not yet known. Protestant missionary activity was remarkably
slight before the evangelical impetus of the eighteenth century.[36] Puritans typically cultivated an introspective piety that wrestled with
doubt about the destiny of their souls. Could they be confident that
God had elected them to salvation?[37] They lacked the buoyancy that
inspires to mission. Eighteenth-century Evangelicals, by contrast,
turned their attention from their own state to the message that was
to be proclaimed. "The proper object of saving faith," wrote Andrew

Fuller, "is not our being interested in Christ, but the glorious gospel of the ever-blessed God."[38] The Christian life was a matter not of self-doubt but of confidence in God. The overriding task was not to establish one's own salvation but to bring salvation to others. White-field expressed the novel attitude in a letter of 1739: "We have nothing to do but to lay hold on him by faith. . . . Not but we must be workers together with him; for a true faith in JESUS CHRIST will not suffer us to be idle. —No, it is an active, lively, restless principle; it fills the heart, so that it cannot be easy, till it is doing something for JESUS CHRIST."[39] A new spirit of mission had been born.

The transition from Puritan introspection to evangelical activism was founded on an altered attitude to the knowledge of God. It was a shift in the doctrine of assurance. Puritans held that certainty of being in a state of grace, though desirable, is normally late in the experience of believers and attained only after struggle. "This infallible assurance," according to the Westminster Confession, "doth not so belong to the essence of faith, but that a true believer may wait long, and conflict with many difficulties before he be partaker of it."[40] Evangelicals, by contrast, held that assurance is usually given to all believers at conversion. There was difference of opinion over whether assurance necessarily accompanies saving faith. James Hervey and William Romaine, two early evangelicals of the Church of England, taught that there is no faith without assurance; John Newton insisted, on the contrary, that assurance is "not essential to the being of faith."[41] Wesley held a robust view of the need for assurance, contending that it is the normal possession of a believer. His followers—and occasionally he—doubted if a person could be a Christian without certainty of acceptance by God. "Nay, if you know not," declared John Nelson, "that Christ is in you, you are now in a state of reprobation."[42] Calvinists believed that "the witness of the Spirit" testified to the eventual attainment of salvation guaranteed by God's decrees, while Arminians supposed it evidence only of a present state of grace from which declension is possible. Yet evangelicals in both camps, unlike their Puritan predecessors, understood assurance as, in Wesley's words, the "common privilege of the children of God."[43]

Evangelicals were confident that they possessed self-evident knowledge. "For these five or six years," Whitefield wrote to Wesley in 1740, "I have received the witness of GOD's Spirit; since that, blessed be GOD, I have not doubted a quarter of an hour of a saving interest in JESUS CHRIST."[44] Whitefield was expressing in the field of religion what contemporaries were starting to express in other fields. He was claiming the reliability of a certain type of knowledge. John Locke had inaugurated an era of special attention to epistemology in his *Essay Concerning Human Understanding* (1690). His denial of the existence of innate ideas cleared the ground for greater confidence in the powers of the mind to grasp knowledge through experience. Human beings, he insisted, understand the external world through the five senses.[45] Others pressed Locke's analysis further in various directions. In the field of epistemology, George Berkeley argued that the external world has no real existence unless perceived by the senses.[46] In ethics, Francis Hutcheson asserted that alongside the five natural senses there is a moral sense for identifying right and wrong.[47] The philosopher Peter Browne, bishop of Cork and Ross, claimed that God, as spirit, cannot be known directly by the senses, but only indirectly by reasoning about data provided by the material external world.[48] The status of knowledge was keenly debated. This was the intellectual climate inhabited by the early evangelicals. Inevitably the literati among them shared the preoccupations of their contemporaries, especially as they impinged on religion. Educated evangelicals were part of an Enlightenment cultural milieu.

Wesley and Edwards, the movement's towering intellects, clearly display the traits of the times. In his pre-evangelical days, Wesley wrestled with the thought of Peter Browne. Wesley craved the immediate knowledge of God that Browne believed was not possible. It was not until Wesley met the Moravians that he discovered, to his immense relief, a way to know God directly.[49] Thereafter he spoke of awareness of God as a new sense, analogous to hearing or sight. Faith, he explained, "is with regard to the spiritual world what sense is with regard to the natural."[50] Jonathan Edwards echoes Wesley in his identification of a new sense as the means by which God is known. Christian truths, he explains, are "seen, tasted, and felt" by new converts.[51] Edwards was recasting Reformed doctrine in terms of Lockean discourse. Wesley and Edwards were both Enlightenment thinkers.[52] The "Holy Club," the group around Wesley at Oxford in the 1730s, shared both his intellectual and his spiritual concerns, and from that matrix sprang the earliest evangelical leaders.[53] The popularity in England of Edwards's *Faithful Narrative* (1737) and his *Religious Affections* (1746) reinforced the tendency to analyze religious knowledge in contemporary terms. The result was that there arose a fresh awareness that God could be immediately known. That was the spark that ignited revival.

The rank and file of the movement, instructed by the revival leaders, formulated their experience in the same way. "By the eye of

faith," wrote an early Methodist about his sense of pardon through
the work of Christ, "I had as real a view of His agony on Calvary
as ever I had of any object by the eye of sense."[54] The understanding
of faith in terms of self-validating sense impressions was a striking
novelty. Received Protestant piety dictated questioning, not confidence. "I was very fearful of being deceived," recalled a later convert
of his early contacts with Methodists, "reasoning and doubting for
several years whether the knowledge of pardon was attainable here.
I thought God did forgive men their sin; but that none could know
it for himself."[55] Yet Methodists—humble class leaders as well as
eminent preachers—insisted that an individual can be sure that he
or she possesses God's pardon.[56] "I saw," said one of Wesley's hearers,
"I could never be saved without knowing my sins were forgiven."[57]
It was a matter, as Whitefield put it, of tasting the good word of
God.[58] In accounts of the last days of early Methodist women, assurance is overwhelmingly the chief theme recounted.[59] The realization
that God allows human beings to know that they are numbered
among the saved—what Wesley called "the witness of the Spirit"—
provided a deep-seated psychological release. It was the dynamic of
the revival; and it was a product of the Enlightenment.

The characteristics of the Evangelical Revival therefore reflect
those of the Enlightenment. Both were dedicated to empirical method.
The prestige of John Locke in philosophy and, even more, of Isaac
Newton in natural science, set a premium on the technique of investigation. It was high praise to call preaching "experimental," that is,
"explaining every part of the work of God upon the soul."[60] In argu-
mentation, evangelical leaders such as Henry Venn, Vicar of Hud-
dersfield, habitually appealed for authority not to scripture alone but
"to observation, and scripture."[61] The evidences of Christianity were
valued as much by evangelicals as by divines of broader schools.[62]
Wesley encouraged the Methodists to use medical remedies he had
himself investigated,[63] and he approached spiritual experience in
exactly the same scientific spirit. Thus, for example, in 1760 at Leeds
he undertook a careful scrutiny of claims to entire sanctification.[64]
A corollary of respect for empiricism was contempt for more traditional modes of analysis. Disputation was thought an unproductive
exercise. Wesley dismissed ancient ecclesiastical debates as "subtle,
metaphysical controversies."[65] Likewise, fine Puritan distinctions were
criticized by John Newton since they were "not Scriptural modes of
expression, nor do they appear to me to throw light upon the subject."[66] Metaphysics, scholasticism, systematization—these belonged

to the darkness of the past. The spirit of inquiry was illuminating religion as much as other fields of knowledge.

The optimism of the Enlightenment was also shared by evangelicals. Happiness was treated as the proper goal of individuals and of society.[67] Wesley went further than the Calvinists in his estimate of the attainability of happiness on earth. According to his *Plain Account of Christian Perfection* (1766), believers may progress to a state where they are free from all voluntary transgressions of known laws. They are then in a state of "perfect love."[68] All evangelicals, however, believed that the ultimate welfare of believers, together with that of society at large, is guaranteed by divine providence. "If we be sincere in intention," avowed John Newton, "we cannot make a mistake of any great importance."[69] For many, millennial expectations reinforced their optimism. Millennialism, merged with the beginnings of the idea of progress, was a widespread concern in the eighteenth century.[70] Not all evangelicals embraced millennial notions: Whitefield, for example, professed to have no interest in the subject.[71] Others, however, especially as the century advanced, were animated by high hopes. The progress of the gospel was certain. "Slavery and war shall cease," announced the Baptist John Ryland. *"In fine, the whole earth shall be full of the knowledge of Jehovah, as the waters that cover the depths of the seas!!!"*[72] A sanguine temper undergirded the evangelical movement as it developed its momentum.

Doctrinal moderation, a feature of the Latitudinarianism that prevailed in the eighteenth-century Church of England, was also evident in the theology of the evangelicals. Arminianism has been seen as a revolutionary creed because it propagated belief in human free will.[73] What has been less widely appreciated is that the Calvinism upheld by non-Methodist evangelicals was of a similar stamp. The Calvinistic Controversy was a relatively brief episode of the 1770s, fought only, on the Reformed side, by extremists.[74] Thomas Haweis wrote a biblical commentary as a Calvinist, but hoped "there is not a line I have written at which a spiritually minded Arminian need stumble."[75] "That man is a free agent," wrote the Baptist Robert Hall, Sr., "cannot be denied, consistently with his being accountable for his own actions."[76] The statement was possible from a Calvinist because Hall, like many of the evangelicals in the Reformed tradition, embraced Jonathan Edwards's distinction between natural and moral inability. Naturally human beings are free, but morally they are unable to obey God. Hence they are culpable and condemn themselves to divine judgment. Since nobody is predestined to reprobation, all have a duty to believe, and the gospel should be preached to all. This theological position, often called "moderate Calvinism," was normal among evangelical Anglicans.[77] Its wide embrace, its benevolent tone, were symptomatic of the age.

An ethical emphasis was a further symptom. Evangelicals themselves commonly denounced ordinary clergymen for preaching mere morality. They were censuring the idea that salvation can be by works: "it was *faith* alone that did everything without a grain of morality."[78] Yet their own insistence that salvation is by faith alone did not preclude moral instruction. Haweis's *Evangelical Principles and Practice* (1762) gives far more space to practice than to principles.[79] The idea of sanctification dominates Wesley's theology.[80] Whitefield used to define true religion as "a universal morality founded upon love of God, and faith in the Lord Jesus Christ."[81] Evangelicals repeatedly repudiated the slander that they denied the duty of the believer to observe the moral law. A few higher Calvinists in both Church of England and Dissent made remarks that veered toward antinomianism, but only a handful on the fringe of the movement, such as Robert Hawker of Plymouth and the eccentric William Huntington, actually taught it.[82] Faith, according to Henry Venn, "is not understood, much less possessed, if it produce not more holiness, than could possibly be any other way attained."[83] Evangelicals, like their contemporaries, were eager to enforce the duties of morality.

While they did not apply utilitarian principles to ethics, leaders of the revival adopted the criterion of utility in many areas of policy. Field preaching, the grand strategy of the movement, was justified on pragmatic grounds: it led to the salvation of souls. To be "useful" was the highest ambition of a preacher.[84] In a similar spirit, Martin Madan, a London evangelical clergyman, actually recommended polygamy as a remedy for prostitution, though others hastened to disavow his views.[85] This was not the only question of expediency where there was a division of opinion. There were some clergymen, notably Samuel Walker of Truro, whose respect for church order prevented them from endorsing Wesley's employment of laymen as preachers. Even Walker, however, rejoiced that there were "good men of all persuasions, who are content to leave each other the liberty of private judgment in lesser things, and are heartily disposed to unite their efforts for the maintaining and enlarging Christ's kingdom."[86] Wesley was prepared to go much further. "What is the end of all ecclesiastical order?" he asked. "Is it not to bring souls from the power of Satan to God, and to build them up in His fear and love? Order, then, is so far valuable as it answers these ends; and if

it answers them not, it is nothing worth."[87] Hence, Wesley was prepared to undertake ordinations of clergy for America even though
that responsibility was restricted to bishops by the Church of England.[88] Hence, too, he was willing to turn a blind eye to female
preaching.[89] The climax of the pragmatic spirit came with the foundation, in 1795, of "The Missionary Society," later the London Missionary Society, designed to unite evangelicals of all types in the
furtherance of the gospel.[90] "*Expediency*," declared Charles Simeon,
a leading Anglican evangelical by the turn of the century, "is too
much decried."[91] It was another Enlightenment attitude that evangelicals upheld.

Their taste was similarly adjusted to the spirit of the age. "The
commencement of this century," wrote Haweis in 1800, "has been
called the *Augustan age*, when purity of stile added the most perfect
polish to deep erudition, as well as the *belles lettres*. A Newton, an
Addison, need only be mentioned, out of a thousand others, whose
works will be admired to the latest posterity; and afford the noblest
specimens in the English language."[92] What Haweis most approved
about the Augustans was their union of "conciseness with precision,"
the goal he aimed for in writing his own history.[93] Wesley shared the
same ideal in his "Thoughts on Taste" (1780), and the exemplar was
again Joseph Addison.[94] The classical principles of order, balance,
and harmony appealed to the early evangelicals as much as to the
Augustan *littérateurs*. They formed even Wesley's eye for the natural
world, so that he attributed to the Creator an earth before the flood
that was "without high or abrupt mountains, and without sea, being
one uniform crust."[95] Dissenters adopted the same criteria. Cornelius
Winter, a disciple of Whitefield, quotes with approval William
Cowper's identification of elegance with simplicity.[96] The Baptist John
Ryland imitated Horace and Virgil in English verse.[97] The greatest
monument, however, to evangelical taste is the hymnody of John
Wesley's brother Charles. Disciplined emotion, didactic purpose, clar-
ity, and succinctness are qualities for which he is preeminent among
hymnwriters. A single line can exhibit all his traits: "Impassive he
suffers, immortal he dies."[98] Charles Wesley turned contemporary
literary idiom into a powerful vehicle for revival.

It is evident, therefore, that evangelical religion was firmly
embedded in the progressive cultural milieu of the eighteenth century.
It shared assumptions with the mainstream of educated opinion. Its
substantial appeal to the elite is often disguised by its numerically
larger impact on the common people. Yet the gentry of England were
sometimes attracted. Sir Nevil Hickman opened the Great Hall at

Gainsborough in Lincolnshire as a preaching place for Wesley and his followers. William Lambe of Aubourn Hall in the same county became a class leader in Methodism. Robert Carr Brackenbury of Raithby Hall, again in Lincolnshire, became a Methodist preacher at large.[99] There were eight "gentlemen" and twenty-one "gentlewomen" among the 790 class members of Bristol Methodism in 1783.[100] Whitefield, perhaps because of his histrionic skills, drew an even higher social echelon to hear him. At Bath in 1766 he preached "to the most numerous assembly of the nobility he had ever seen attend there." In earlier years he had preached in the home of the Countess of Huntingdon to "very brilliant auditories" including several peers.[101] The Earl of Dartmouth, and apparently the Earl of Buchan, professed conversion.[102] There were rumors that Frederick, Prince of Wales, intended, on his succession to the throne, to make Whitefield a bishop.[103] Evangelicals could also find their way into the highest circles of literature and art. Hannah More, an evangelical bluestocking, moved easily among such luminaries as Sir Joshua Reynolds, Samuel Johnson, David Garrick, and Edmund Burke. "I made such a figure lately," she playfully reported to her family in 1777, "in explaining Arianism, Socianism, and all the isms, to Mr. Garrick."[104] Although most of the fashionable world shunned revivalism as a species of enthusiasm, there were points of intersection with those fired by vital Christianity. The evangelical leaders were not divorced from elite culture.

It was typical of Enlightenment thinkers to wish to bring knowledge from the elite to the masses. The French *Encyclopédie*, itself modeled on an English precedent, is the classic case of an enterprise designed to propagate the wisdom of the age. The people were to be enlightened. The English Enlightenment in particular produced not eminent philosophical systematizers but popularizers in many fields.[105] The evangelicals should be numbered in their ranks. Their primary aim was to fit their hearers for heaven, but they also wished to bring the barbarous within the pale of civilization. Dissenting evangelists desired to refine the boorishness of remoter parts; and Whitefield, dismayed by the absence of cultivation among the colliers of Kingswood, near Bristol, gave priority to "the civilizing of these people" as well as to their evangelization.[106] The darkness of rude ways had to be dispelled. Wesley, like other arbiters of taste, supposed laughter to be a sign of ill breeding. Accordingly, with his usual briskness, he directed that his preachers must avoid laughing.[107] He expressed satisfaction with the success of his civilizing mission at Nottingham: "although most of our society are of the lower class,

chiefly employed in the stocking manufacture, yet there is generally
an uncommon gentleness and sweetness in their temper, and something of elegance in their behavior, which, when added to solid, vital
religion, make them an ornament to their profession."[108] Manners had
been softened. Evangelicals were promoting an Enlightenment program for the improvement of the people.

The chief dimension of this program—other than the imparting
of vital faith—was education. The revival was often charged with
deprecating learning, since it flourished among the illiterate and
uncritical, and it is true that books were sometimes suspect as sources
of error.[109] Whitefield and Wesley concurred that Latin, the foundation
of polite culture, was "of little or no use" for the preacher.[110] Yet this
judgment was part of the Enlightenment preference for the vernacular,
and is no evidence for a low estimate of learning. On the contrary,
Wesley created a publication industry for his followers. He issued
grammars of English, French, Latin, and Greek, short histories of
England and of the Christian church, an outline of Roman history,
a compendium of natural philosophy in five volumes, and a "Christian Library" of practical divinity in fifty volumes.[111] The first lay
connectional officials were appointed to run the Book Room, and
when, in 1778, Wesley launched the *Arminian Magazine* he acquired
his own printing presses.[112] By 1791, 7,000 monthly copies of the
magazine were circulating, in comparison, for example, with 4,550
of the *Gentleman's Magazine* six years later.[113] Wesley prepared a
"Female Course of Study, intended for those who have a good Understanding and much Leisure," entailing five or six hours' work a day
for three to five years.[114] But he concentrated his educational efforts
on his traveling preachers, since they were expected to transmit what
they learned. At least one claimed to have read every one of Wesley's
more than four hundred works.[115] "I trust," wrote Wesley of the
preachers, "there is not one of them who is not able to go through
such an examination, in substantial, practical, experimental divinity,
as few of our candidates for holy orders, even in the university . . .
are able to do."[116] Every preacher, in turn, was to be a book agent.[117]
Wesley thus undertook a campaign of systematic enlightenment.

His efforts were duly rewarded. The connection produced prod-
igies of learning. A Lowestoft class leader knew Latin, Greek, and
Hebrew; a child of Methodist parents read the greater part of the
Bible before the age of four; and an older girl composed her journal
in faultless French. Humbler Methodists would meet on weekday
evenings to instruct their unlettered friends in how to sing the Sunday
hymns, and by such means literacy spread.[118] Other evangelicals,

though in less dragooned fashion than the Methodists, were equally dedicated to fostering elementary education, since literacy was a condition for reading the Bible. Hence they gave powerful support to the Sunday school movement as it gathered momentum from the 1780s. The instruction was frequently undenominational, in part a corollary of the policy of pragmatic cooperation in furtherance of the gospel. In the early days, in fact, Unitarians and others frequently participated alongside the various types of evangelicals, a sign that in educational work a common allegiance to the Enlightenment ideal of propagating useful knowledge took precedence over the preservation of gospel purity.[119] It has been estimated that by 1801 there were over 200,000 regular attenders at the Sunday schools, chiefly drawn from the poor.[120] Literary societies and libraries in churches and chapels helped carry education to a higher level. Evangelicalism generated at least its fair proportion of scholars at the turn of the nineteenth century. Isaac Milner, subsequently president of Queen's College, Cambridge, for instance, had his degree result starred *"incomparabilis."*[121] The revival did not turn its adherents into ignorant bigots. On the contrary, it proved effective in spreading a thirst for knowledge.

The revival challenged popular culture in the name of reason and religion. The customary ways of the eighteenth century added color to humdrum lives, but they were shot through with roughness, cruelty, and paganism. Traditional holidays gave scope for drunkenness, torturing animals, or indulging in relics of nature worship, like the Abbots Bromley horn dance. Evangelicalism, as is often stressed, opposed overt sexuality, and so denounced occasions of customary sexual license.[122] Thus William Grimshaw, the rugged incumbent of Haworth in the West Riding of Yorkshire, attended local feasts to preach the gospel and protested to his parishioners against the annual races. But his normal behavior was not that of a religious professional, let alone an obsessional fanatic. "A stranger might be in company with him from morning to night," commented John Newton, "without observing anything that might lead him to suppose he was a minister; he would only think he saw and heard a pious, plain intelligent man."[123] Reason dictated his attitudes. William Romaine, a scholarly but angular clergyman, would have claimed the same for his response to the custom of conversing after church. "He not only spoke against such conversations from the pulpit," according to his biographer, "but frequently interrupted them, when he came out, by tapping the shoulders of those who were engaged in them; and once, if not oftener, by knocking their heads together, when he found them particularly close."[124] Those associated with the revival were taking the offensive against the improprieties of popular habits. It is hardly surprising that there was a bitter response, whether (at a higher social level) by means of vituperative satire or (at a lower) by mob violence.[125] Much of the persecution suffered by gospel preachers must be seen as retaliation against the threat their civilizing mission posed to custom.

Those aroused to serious concern for the welfare of their souls formed a counterculture shunning worldliness. Wesley formed "awakened sinners" into classes, admission being regulated by quarterly ticket. The classes were not designed for converts only: indeed, their purpose was to encourage conversions. Yet their members were subject to strict discipline, having to avoid evils such as taking God's name in vain, sabbath-breaking, and drunkenness, to do good by charity, visiting the sick, and to attend the divine ordinances.[126] "Give no ticket," Wesley enjoined his preachers, "to any that wear . . . enormous bonnets."[127] Even higher standards were expected of members of bands, which consisted of those professing conversion.[128] Evangelical Anglicans established similar groups, with Grimshaw, for instance, holding a parish class.[129] The group was sharply demarcated from the ways of the world. Before conversion, John Iredale, a grocer in a village near Halifax, used to fill the baskets of customers while they attended church on Sunday; after conversion under the ministry of Henry Venn, he refused to desecrate the sabbath and so lost business.[130] Elizabeth Evans, the prototype of Dinah Morris in George Eliot's *Adam Bede*, was converted in about 1797. "I had entirely done with the pleasures of the world," she wrote, "and with all my old companions. I saw it my duty to leave off all my superfluities in dress; hence I pulled off all my bunches—cut off my curls—left off my lace—and in this I found an unspeakable pleasure. I saw I could make a better use of my time and money, than to follow the fashions of the vain world."[131] Early Methodists, driven together for mutual support, generated a strong community spirit. Ten soldiers in a regiment, for example, "were joined in such love for one another that we had in effect all things in common."[132] The result was a new cultural ambience, the religion of the cottage, where there was particular scope for women to act as counselors and exhorters.[133] If the revival confronted traditional folkways, it created fresh and (it may be suggested) more enlightened patterns of life.

The appeal of evangelical religion was by no means uniform across the population of England. Women were attracted in larger numbers than men. At Bristol in 1783 there were two women for every man in Methodism.[134] More than half the Methodists of East

Cheshire were female, and, interestingly, nearly half of them were unmarried.[135] The other group to be consistently overrepresented consisted of the artisans, the working men with a particular trade. They were more than twice as numerous in Methodism as in society at large.[136] That statistic helps explain the fact that the greatest initial impact of Wesley's followers was in Yorkshire. In 1760 nearly a quarter of all Methodists lived in that county.[137] Yorkshire, and especially its West Riding, contained a high proportion of the early industrial settlements that employed artisans in large numbers. The West Riding, furthermore, contained parishes that were often immense in comparison with their counterparts in the south of England. In the vast upland tracts the traditional social discipline of squire and parson could rarely be exerted to any effect. By contrast, in the south and east of England, where parishes were often smaller and land ownership was more concentrated, evangelical nonconformity could be resisted successfully. It was planted only in the settlements where social control was in decay.[138] Unmarried women, masterless men, and areas of weaker deference were favorable to evangelicalism. The common element here is independence. Wherever people were free to think for themselves, some saw the new light of the gospel.

The Enlightenment frequently generated a spirit of reform, but it must be admitted that the revival did not foster a common mind on political affairs. There was a strong tendency for evangelicals to avoid politics altogether as worldly entanglement—"Satan's most tempting and alluring baits."[139] If evangelicals did make pronouncements on public issues, they could be diametrically opposed. Thus when in 1775 John Wesley called upon the Americans to submit to the royal government, the Baptist Caleb Evans retorted with a defence of the colonists' case.[140] There was greater unanimity about the "Reformation of Manners," which entailed pressure on local Justices of the Peace for the enforcement of statutes against vice.[141] In general there were more calls by evangelicals for loyalty to the existing order, especially in the wake of the French Revolution, than for reform of its inadequacies. That, however, was true of most privileged contemporaries.[142] In some fields the Enlightenment imperative to eliminate abuses did emerge among evangelicals. There was a commitment to toleration, natural among Dissenters but shared by Wesley and many Anglicans. Thomas Scott, for instance, acknowledged "the vast obligation which the whole religious world is under" to Locke for his *Letters Concerning Toleration*.[143] And there was the campaign against the slave trade that was spearheaded by Wilberforce and his associates. The antislavery ideology, founded on benevolence, happiness, and liberty, was a creation of the Enlightenment. Evangelicals added their characteristic zest for activity.[144] In doing so, however, they demonstrated once more their affinity for Enlightenment ideals.

The relationship between revival and Enlightenment was therefore remarkably close. John Fletcher, Wesley's longtime lieutenant, argued "not only that feeling and rational Christianity are not incompatible, . . . but also that such feelings, so far from deserving to be called madness and enthusiasm, are nothing short of the actings of spiritual life."[145] Emotion, fervor, even irrationality, are inseparable from the human condition, but progressive opinion in the eighteenth century kept them bridled. So did evangelicals, investigating them in a dispassionate spirit of scientific enquiry. Such analysts were firmly bound up in the Enlightenment. It follows that the Age of Reason was by no means necessarily heading in an irreligious direction. England could bring forth a John Toland, the Deist writer, but equally it produced John Wesley, a zealous propagator of scriptural Christianity. Evidence has been accumulating in recent years that England was by no means alone. In Wales a literary efflorescence was largely stimulated by a Great Awakening that was intimately allied with the English revival.[146] In Scotland, alongside the skeptical Hume there was a group of cultivated ministers of religion who stood at the pinnacle of intellectual achievement.[147] In north Germany the *Aufklärer* were anticipated in many of their attitudes by the Pietists.[148] In south Germany there was a movement of Catholic reform appealing to the simplicity of the early Christians against the inherited legacy of scholastic intricacies, Jesuit intrigue, and Baroque piety.[149] And the list could go on.[150] Evangelicals were part of an eighteenth–century trend in western civilization to promote a Christianity that was at once purer and more rational than what had gone before.

If the Enlightenment was by no means intrinsically hostile to spiritual religion, no more so was the revival a reaction against the Age of Reason. It is simply wrong to suppose that Wesley intended to debunk the Enlightenment or that the "burgeoning Evangelical revival anathematized rational religion."[151] On the contrary, the epistemological concern of the age was itself responsible for the stronger doctrine of assurance that was to become the hallmark of evangelicalism. The characteristics of the eighteenth-century evangelicals— empiricism, optimism, moderatism, moralism, utilitarianism, and Augustanism—were also features of the rising cultural mood. And evangelicals, as much as the *philosophes* across the English Channel, wished to propagate their brand of elite culture to the masses, but they achieved their aim far more effectively. There was born a popular counterculture that by the mid-nineteenth century had grown to dominate England.[152] The alignment of evangelicalism with the Enlightenment has been noticed by a number of historians, but their insight has been inadequately appreciated.[153] It is not just that there were points of contact between the two movements. Rather, a central cultural significance of the revival is that it spread Enlightenment assumptions throughout the land. "We join with you then," wrote John Wesley to "men of reason and religion" in 1743, "in desiring a religion founded on reason, and every way agreeable thereto."[154]

## NOTES

1. Geoffrey Best, "Evangelicalism and the Victorians," in *The Victorian Crisis of Faith*, ed. Anthony Symondson (London: Society for Promoting Christian Knowledge, 1970), 38. Such a view has been questioned by John D. Walsh, "Origins of the Evangelical Revival," in Gareth V. Bennett and John D. Walsh, *Essays in Modern English Church History in Memory of Norman Sykes* (London: Adam & Charles Black, 1966), 148–53.

2. Paul Hazard, *European Thought in the Eighteenth Century* [1946] (Harmondsworth, England: Penguin, 1965); Peter Gay, *The Enlightenment: An Interpretation* (London: Weidenfeld and Nicholson, 1967).

3. Roland N. Stromberg, *Religious Liberalism in Eighteenth-Century England* (Oxford: Oxford University Press, 1954).

4. Joseph Milner, *Gibbon's Account of Christianity Considered . . .* (London, 1781), 154, quoted in Stromberg, *Religious Liberalism*, 168.

5. Edward P. Thompson, *The Making of the English Working Class* [1963] (Harmondsworth, England: Penguin, 1968), 402.

6. Thomas Vasey to Mary Barritt, in Mary Taft, *Memoirs of Mary Taft, Formerly Miss Barritt* (London: Stevens, 1827), 65, quoted by Leslie F. Church, *The Early Methodist People* (London: Epworth Press, 1948), 122.

7. James Lackington, *Memoirs of the Forty-Five First Years of the Life of James Lackington* (London: for the author, 1795), 62; Stanley Ayling, *John Wesley* (London: Collins, 1979), 211–12; John Gillies, *Memoirs of the Life of the Reverend George Whitefield, M.A.* (London: Dilly, 1772), 10.

8. Thomas Gibbons, *Sermons on Evangelical and Practical Subjects*, vol. 1 (London: for J. Blackland, 1787), 81, 86.

9. Whitefield to Rev. Mr. ———, 18 July 1739, in John Gillies, ed., *The Works of the Reverend George Whitefield, M.A.*, vol. 1 (London: Dilly, 1771), 52; Gillies, *Whitefield*, 8.

10. Charles Wesley, "Come, Holy Ghost, Our Hearts Inspire," in John Wesley, ed., *A Collection of Hymns for the Use of the People Called Methodists* [1780] (London: Wesleyan Conference Office, n.d.), 88.

11. Martin Schmidt, *John Wesley: A Theological Biography*, vol. 1 (London: Epworth Press, 1962–73), 88.

12. Rupert Davies, "The People Called Methodists," in *A History of the Methodist Church in Great Britain*, ed. Rupert Davies and Gordon Rupp, Vol. 1: *Our Doctrines* (London: Epworth Press, 1965–88), 176–79.

13. *The Journal of the Rev. John Wesley, A.M.*, ed. Nehemiah Curnock and John Telford, vol. 3 (London: Robert Culley, 1909–16), 517 (27 Mar. 1751).

14. Robert Currie et al., *Churches and Churchgoers: Patterns of Church Growth in the British Isles since 1700* (Oxford: Clarendon Press, 1977), 139.

15. Arnold Dallimore, *George Whitefield: The Life and Times of the Great Evangelist of the Eighteenth-Century Revival*, vol. 2 (London: Banner of Truth, 1970–80), chapters 1, 3.

16. C. E. Watson, "Whitefield and Congregationalism," *Transactions of the Congregational Historical Society* 8 (1922): 175.

17. Dallimore, *Whitefield* 2:157–58.

18. John Walsh, "Methodism at the End of the Eighteenth Century," in *Methodist Church*, ed. Davies and Rupp, 1:292.

19. Stephen J. C. Taylor, "Church and State in England in the Mid-Eighteenth Century: The Newcastle Years, 1747–1762," (Ph.D. diss., University of Cambridge, 1987), chapter 2.

20. Thomas Secker, "Charges," in *The Works of Thomas Secker*, ed. Beilby Porteous, vol. 5 (London: Rivington, 1811), 480, quoted in Norman Sykes, *From Sheldon to Secker: Aspects of English Church History, 1660–1768* (Cambridge: Cambridge University Press, 1959), 222.

21. Walsh, "Origins," 154–56.

22. A classic account is given by Thomas Scott, *The Force of Truth* [1779] (Edinburgh: Banner of Truth, 1984).

23. Arthur Skevington Wood, *Thomas Haweis, 1734–1820* (London: Society for Promoting Christian Knowledge, 1957), 18.

24. Patrick P. Streiff, *Jean Guillaume de la Fléchère, John William Fletcher, 1729–1785: Ein Beitrag zur Geschichte des Methodismus* (Frankfurt am Main: Peter Lang, 1984); Frank Baker, *William Grimshaw, 1708–1763* (London: Epworth Press, 1963).

25. Charles Smyth, *Simeon and Church Order* (Cambridge: Cambridge University Press), chapter 6.

26. Geoffrey F. Nuttall, "Methodism and the Older Dissent: Some Perspectives," *Journal of the United Reformed Church Historical Society* 2 (1981): 271–73.

27. Deryck W. Lovegrove, *Established Church, Sectarian People: Itinerancy and the Transformation of English Dissent, 1780–1830* (Cambridge: Cambridge University Press, 1988).

28. *Evangelical Magazine* (1797): 7, quoted by Walsh, "Methodism at the End of the Eighteenth Century," 297.

29. John Ryland, *The Work of Faith, the Labour of Love and the Patience of Hope Illustrated in the Life and Death of the Reverend Andrew Fuller* (London: Button, 1816), 9n, 44, 56, 58.

30. Thomas Haweis, *An Impartial and Succinct History of the Rise, Declension and Revival of the Church of Christ*, vol. 3 (London: for J. Mawman, 1800), 331.

31. Gillies, *Whitefield*, 31.

32. John Telford, ed., *Wesley's Veterans: Lives of Early Methodist Preachers Told by Themselves*, vol. 4 (London: Robert Culley, n.d.), 227.

33. William B. Cadogan, "The Life of the Rev. William Romaine, M.A.," in *Works of the Late Reverend William Romaine*, vol. 7 (London: for T. Chapman, 1796), 101.

34. Telford, ed., *Wesley's Veterans* 3:57.

35. Leslie Stephen, *History of English Thought in the Eighteenth Century*, vol. 2 (London: Smith, Elder, 1876), 428.

36. Stephen Neill, *A History of Christian Missions*, 2d ed. (Harmondsworth, England: Penguin, 1986), 187–92.

37. Peter G. Lake, *Moderate Puritans and the Elizabethan Church* (Cambridge: Cambridge University Press, 1982), 150–68.

38. Andrew Fuller, "The Gospel Worthy of All Acceptation," in *The Complete Works of Andrew Fuller*, vol. 2 (London: Holdsworth and Ball, 1831), 9.

39. Whitefield to Mr ———, 8 February 1739, in *Works of Whitefield*, ed. Gillies, 1:47.

40. *The Confession of Faith* (Edinburgh: Blair and Bruce, 1810), chapter 18.3, 106.

41. Abner W. Brown, *Recollections of the Conversation Parties of the Rev. Charles Simeon, M.A.* (London: Hamilton, Adams, 1863), 320. John Newton, "Of the Assurance of Faith," in *The Works of the Rev. John Newton*, vol. 2 (London: for the author's nephew, 1808), 586.

42. Telford, ed., *Wesley's Veterans* 3:125. Wesley's own view is discussed by Arthur S. Yates, *The Doctrine of Assurance with Special Reference to John Wesley* (London: Epworth Press, 1952), but Yates exaggerates Wesley's early commitment to the essentiality of assurance to faith.

43. Robert Southey, *The Life of Wesley*, vol. 1 (London: Longman, 1820), 295.

44. Whitefield, "A Letter to the Reverend Mr. John Wesley: in answer to his sermon, entitled, Free-Grace," in *Works of Whitefield*, ed. Gillies, 4:66.

45. Richard I. Aaron, *John Locke*, 3d ed. (Oxford: Oxford University Press, 1971).

46. Geoffrey J. Warnock, *Berkeley* (Harmondsworth, England: Penguin, 1953).

47. Hutcheson, *Illustrations on the Moral Sense* [1728], ed. Bernard Peach (Cambridge: Harvard University Press, 1971).

48. Arthur R. Winnet, *Peter Browne: Provost, Bishop, Metaphysician* (London: Society for Promoting Christian Knowledge, 1974).

49. J. Clifford Hindley, "The Philosophy of Enthusiasm," *London Quarterly and Holborn Review* 182 (1957).

50. Wesley, "An Earnest Appeal to Men of Reason and Religion" [1743] in *Works of John Wesley*, ed. G. R. Cragg, vol. 11 (Oxford: Clarendon Press, 1975), 46.

51. Edwards, "A Narrative of Surprising Conversions," *Select Works*, vol. 1 (London: Banner of Truth, 1965), 42.

52. Frederick Dreyer, "Faith and Experience in the Thought of John Wesley," *American Historical Review* 88 (1983); Richard E. Brantley, *Locke, Wesley, and the Method of English Romanticism* (Gainesville: University of Florida Press, 1984), chapters 1, 2, appendix A. Although Perry Miller's classic study, *Jonathan Edwards* (New York: William Sloane Associates, 1949), exaggerates the extent of Locke's specific influence on Edwards, it remains true that the framework for Edwards's thought was erected by Locke.

53. Richard P. Heitzenrater, ed., *Diary of an Oxford Methodist: Benjamin Ingham, 1733-1734* (Durham, N.C.: Duke University Press, 1985), 14.

54. Telford, ed., *Wesley's Veterans* 7:140 (James Rogers).

55. Ibid., 4:225 (Thomas Hanson).

56. Church, *Early Methodist People*, 115.

57. Silas Told, *Life of Mr. Silas Told* (London: Methodist Conference Office, 1789), quoted in Church, *Early Methodist People*, 111-12.

58. Whitefield to Rev. Mr ———, 18 July 1739, in *Works of Whitefield*, ed. Gillies, 1:52.

59. Earl K. Brown, *Women of Mr. Wesley's Methodism* (New York: Edwin Mellen Press, 1983), 235.

60. Telford, ed., *Wesley's Veterans* 2:147 (John Pawson on Alexander Mather).

61. Venn, *The Complete Duty of Man*, 3d ed. (London: for S. Crowder and G. Robinson, 1779), 2.

62. John H. Pratt, ed., *The Thought of the Evangelical Leaders: Notes of the Discussions of the Eclectic Society, London, during the Years 1798-1814* [1856] (Edinburgh: Banner of Truth, 1978), 230-32.

63. Wesley, *Primitive Physic* [1747] (London: Epworth Press, 1960).

64. *Journal of John Wesley* 4:372 (12 Mar. 1760).

65. Wesley to Charles Wesley, 8 June 1780, in *The Letters of the Rev. John Wesley*, ed. John Telford, vol. 7 (London: Epworth Press, 1931), 21.

66. Newton, "Of the Assurance of Faith," 587.

67. Roger Anstey, *The Atlantic Slave Trade and British Abolition, 1760-1810* (London: Macmillan, 1975), 163.

68. Harold Linström, *Wesley and Sanctification* (London: Epworth Press, 1946), chapter 4.

69. Pratt, ed., *Thought of the Evangelical Leaders*, 77.

70. Ernest L. Tuveson, *Millennium and Utopia* (Berkeley: University of California Press, 1949).

71. Whitefield to ———, 17 June 1739, in *Works of Whitefield*, ed. Gillies, 1:51.

72. John Ryland, Jr., *Salvation Finished, as to its Impenetration at the*

*Death of Christ; and with Respect to its Application at the Death of the Christian* (London, 1791), 21.

73. Bernard Semmel, *The Methodist Revolution* (London: Heinemann Educational, 1974).

74. Walsh, "Methodism at the End of the Eighteenth Century," 290.

75. Wood, *Haweis*, 116.

76. Hall, *Help to Zion's Travellers* (Bristol: William Pine, 1781), 236.

77. John D. Walsh, "The Yorkshire Evangelicals in the Eighteenth Century: with especial reference to Methodism" (Ph.D. diss., University of Cambridge, 1956), chapter 1; George C. B. Davies, *The Early Cornish Evangelicals, 1735-1760: A Study of Walker of Truro and Others* (London: Society for Promoting Christian Knowledge, 1951), 154-56.

78. Lackington, *Memoirs*, 48.

79. Thomas Haweis, *Evangelical Principles and Practice*, 4th ed. (London: Dilly, 1762).

80. Lindström, *Wesley and Sanctification*, 217-18.

81. Gillies, ed., *Whitefield*, 287.

82. John Williams, "Memoirs of the Rev. Robert Hawker, D.D.," in *The Works of the Rev. Robert Hawker, D.D.*, vol. 1 (London: Ebenezer Palmer, 1831); Thomas Wright, *The Life of William Huntington, S.S.* (London: Farncombe and Son, 1909).

83. Venn, *Complete Duty*, xi.

84. Telford, ed., *Wesley's Veterans* 7:23 (Thomas Taylor).

85. Wood, *Haweis*, 159-60.

86. Davies, *Early Cornish Evangelicals*, 71.

87. Wesley to "John Smith," 30 December 1745, in *Letters of John Wesley* 2:77-78.

88. Frank Baker, *John Wesley and the Church of England* (London: Epworth Press, 1970), chapter 15.

89. Brown, *Women of Mr. Wesley's Methodism*, 92.

90. Roger H. Martin, *Evangelicals United: Ecumenical Stirrings in Pre-Victorian Britain, 1795-1830* (Metuchen, N.J.: Scarecrow Press, 1983), chapters 3 and 4.

91. Brown, *Conversation Parties*, 93.

92. Haweis, *Impartial and Succinct History* 3:221.

93. Ibid. 1:v.

94. J. L. Golden, "John Wesley on Rhetoric and Belles Lettres," *Speech Monographs* 28 (1961): 252-53.

95. *Journal of John Wesley* 5:351 (17 Jan. 1770).

96. William Jay, *Memoirs of the Life and Character of the Late Rev. Cornelius Winter*, 2d ed. (London: for William Baynes, 1812), 279.

97. John Ryland, *Pastoral Memorials*, 2 vols. (London: B. J. Holdsworth, 1826-28), 2:422-23.

98. Charles Wesley, "Invitation to Sinners," in *The Poetical Works of John and Charles Wesley*, ed. George Osborn, vol. 4 (London: Wesleyan

Methodist Conference Office, 1868–72), 371. See James Dale, "The Theological and Literary Qualities of the Poetry of Charles Wesley in Relation to the Standards of his Age" (Ph.D. diss., University of Cambridge, 1961).

99. Leslie F. Church, *More about the Early Methodist People* (London: Epworth Press, 1949), 44, 117–25; Church, *Early Methodist People*, 164.

100. John Kent, "Wesleyan Membership in Bristol, 1783," in, *An Ecclesiastical Miscellany*, ed. David Walker et al., vol. 11 (Bristol: Archeological Society Records Section, 1976), 111.

101. Gillies, ed., *Whitefield*, 249, 174–75.

102. Brown, *Women of Mr. Wesley's Methodism*, 103.

103. Dallimore, *Whitefield* 2:544–45.

104. William Roberts, *Memoirs of the Life and Correspondence of Mrs. Hannah More*, 2d ed., vol. 1 (London: R. B. Seeley and W. Burnside, 1834), 54–55, 104.

105. Roy Porter, "The Enlightenment in England," in *The Enlightenment in National Context*, ed. Roy Porter and Mikulas Teich (Cambridge: Cambridge University Press, 1981), 3, 5.

106. Lovegrove, *Established Church, Sectarian People*, 70; Gillies, ed., *Whitefield*, 37.

107. Beverly Sprague Allen, *Tides in English Taste (1619–1800)*, vol. 1 (Cambridge: Harvard University Press, 1937), 94–95; Church, *Early Methodist People*, 19.

108. *Journal of John Wesley* 6:156 (18 June 1777).

109. E.g., Telford, ed., *Wesley's Veterans* 2:247 (George Story).

110. Jay, *Winter*, 70.

111. Church, *More about the Early Methodist People*, 47.

112. Horace F. Mathews, *Methodism and the Education of the People, 1791–1851* (London: Epworth Press, 1949), 171.

113. Brantley, *Locke, Wesley, and the Method of English Romanticism*, 118.

114. Brown, *Women of Mr. Wesley's Methodism*, 51.

115. Telford, ed., *Wesley's Veterans* 6:148 (Thomas Rankin).

116. Wesley, "A Farther Appeal to Men of Reason and Religion, Part III" [1745], in *Works of John Wesley*, ed. Cragg, 11:296.

117. Mathews, *Methodism and the Education of the People*, 32–33.

118. Church, *Early Methodist People*, 12, 243; Church, *More about the Early Methodist People*, 49, 46.

119. William Reginald Ward, *Religion and Society in England, 1790–1850* (London: B. T. Batsford, 1972), 12–20; Philip B. Cliff, *The Rise and Development of the Sunday School Movement in England, 1780–1980* (Nutfield, Redhill, England: National Christian Education Council, 1986), chapter 4.

120. Thomas W. Laqueur, *Religion and Respectability: Sunday Schools and Working Class Culture, 1780–1850* (New Haven: Yale University Press, 1976), 44.

121. Doreen M. Rosman, *Evangelicals and Culture* (London: Croom Helm, 1984), 217, 205, and chapter 9A generally.

122. Roy Porter, *English Society in the Eighteenth Century* (Harmondsworth, England: Penguin, 1982), 167–71, 325–26.

123. George G. Cragg, *Grimshaw of Haworth* (London: Canterbury Press, 1947), 98.

124. Cadogan, "Romaine," 80.

125. Albert M. Lyles, *Methodism Mocked: The Satiric Reaction to Methodism in the Eighteenth Century* (London: Epworth Press, 1960); John Walsh, "Methodism and the Mob in the Eighteenth Century," in *Popular Belief and Practice*, ed. Geoffrey J. Cuming and Derek Baker, *Studies in Church History*, vol. 8 (Cambridge: Cambridge University Press, 1972).

126. John Lawson, "The People Called Methodists," in *Methodist Church*, ed. Davies and Rupp, *Vol. 2: Our Discipline*, 192–94.

127. "The Large Minutes," *Works of John Wesley* 8:307.

128. Lawson, "People Called Methodists," 196–97.

129. Church, *Early Methodist People*, 157.

130. Ibid.

131. Church, *More about Early Methodist People*, 160.

132. Telford, ed., *Wesley's Veterans* 1:73 (Sampson Staniforth).

133. Deborah M. Valenze, *Prophetic Sons and Daughters: Female Preaching and Popular Religion in Industrial England* (Princeton: Princeton University Press, 1985).

134. Kent, "Wesleyan Membership," 107.

135. Gail Malmgreen, "Domestic Disorder: Women and the Family in East Cheshire Methodism, 1750–1830," in *Disciplines of Faith: Studies in Religion, Politics, and Patriarchy*, ed. James Obelkevich et al. (London: Routledge and Kegan Paul, 1987), 60.

136. Clive D. Field, "The Social Structure of English Methodism: Eighteenth-Twentieth Centuries," *British Journal of Sociology* 28 (1977): 202.

137. Walsh, "Yorkshire Evangelicals," 144.

138. Alan Everitt, *The Pattern of Rural Dissent: The Nineteenth Century* (Leicester, England: Leicester University Press, 1972), chapter 2.

139. Thomas Jones, in John Owen, *Memoir of the Rev. T. Jones, Late of Creaton* (London, 1851), 160.

140. Semmel, *Methodist Revolution*, 63–66.

141. John Pollock, *Wilberforce* (London: Constable, 1977), chapter 7.

142. See Richard B. Sher, *Church and University in the Scottish Enlightenment: The Moderate Literati of Edinburgh* (Edinburgh: Edinburgh University Press, 1985), 187–212, 305.

143. Scott, *Force of Truth*, 44n. For Wesley, see Semmel, *Methodist Revolution*, 88–90.

144. Ansley, *Atlantic Slave Trade*.

145. *The Works of the Rev. John Fletcher*, vol. 9 (London: Wesleyan Conference Office, 1877), 425, quoted by Streiff, *Fletcher*, 241.

146. Derec L. Morgan, *The Great Awakening in Wales* (London: Epworth Press, 1988).

147. Sher, *Church and University.*

148. Joachim Whaley, "The Protestant Enlightenment in Germany," in *Enlightenment in National Context,* ed. Porter and Teich, 111.

149. Timothy C. W. Blanning, "The Enlightenment in Catholic Germany," in *Enlightenment in National Context,* ed. Porter and Teich, 119–20.

150. See also Sheridan Gilley, "Christianity and Enlightenment: An Historical Survey," *History of European Ideas* 1 (1981).

151. Porter, "Enlightenment in England," 16–17, quoting Ford K. Brown.

152. David W. Bebbington, *Evangelicalism in Modern Britain: A History from the 1730s to the 1980s* (London: Unwin Hyman, 1989), chapter 4. Chapter 2 of the book develops most of the themes sketched in this essay.

153. Among those who have identified the alignment are Haddon Willmer, "Evangelicalism, 1785 to 1835," Hulsean Prize essay, University of Cambridge, 1962; Ward, *Religion and Society,* 17–20; Anstey, *Atlantic Slave Trade,* chapter 7; Semmel, *Methodist Revolution,* 87–96; Rosman, *Evangelicals and Culture.*

154. Wesley, "Earnest Appeal," 55.

# 3

# Christian Revivalism and Culture in Early America: Puritan New England as a Case Study

———————◆———————

GERALD F. MORAN

IN 1741, AT THE HEIGHT of the Great Awakening in Boston, Massachusetts, William Cooper articulated a theme common to our understanding of the role of Christian revivalism in Puritan America. "What a dead and barren time it has now been, for a great while, with all the churches of the Reformation," the minister to the Brattle Street Church declared. "The golden showers have been restrained; . . . few sons have been born to God; and the hearts of Christians not so quickened, warmed and refreshed under the ordinances, as they have been." But now, "Behold!," Cooper continued, "The Lord whome we have sought has suddenly come to his temple. The dispensation of grace we are now under is certainly such as neither we nor our fathers have seen; and in some circumstances so wonderful, that I believe there has not been the like since the extraordinary poring out of the Spirit immediately after our Lord's ascension." Surely, he went on to say, "the apostolical times seem to have returned upon us."[1]

From Cooper's time to today, Christian revivalism in Puritan New England has often been described as Cooper described it, as a sudden, dramatic break from "a dead and barren time" and a harbinger of a new age of spiritual vitality. As Charles Spalding said in 1832, the church, which had been in a state of protracted declension, was "saved from utter extinction" by the Great Awakening.[2] Perry Miller has argued that, even before the Puritans stepped foot on American soil, "their piety was on the wane," and the covenant theology, which had once served "the cause of their creed," became in America "of most lasting importance as an aspect of the political and social order."[3] Only with Jonathan Edwards and the Great Awakening was this process of "declension" halted, but Edwards had to revise Calvinism and break from the Puritan past to do it. Miller's student, Edmund S. Morgan, picked up the theme of declension and gave it his own peculiar emphasis, ascribing it to the domestication of piety and Puritan tribalism. "Before the end of the century," Morgan argued, "the Puritan system was tottering . . . though Increase Mather was still mumbling his phrases about the loins of Godly parents in 1721, it was long since clear, to anyone with eyes to see, that grace was not hereditary."[4]

In recent years new versions of the theme of declension and of the culture's recovery through revival have appeared in social histories of the New England ministry and church. Paul Lucas has argued that in the eighteenth century the authority of the Puritan clergy "collapsed," "the influence of the churches in the town deteriorated," and parish dissension became "a way of life," a culture.[5] In a study of a New England town, Dedham, Massachusetts, Kenneth Lockridge has argued that as the first Puritan planters of the town "dwindled and died away, the rule of love dwindled and died with it. In this sense . . . the New England preachers of the 1670s and 80s could take some satisfaction in being right. Their famous laments over the decline of the spirit of the founders were justified by events in Dedham." In Dedham and elsewhere, people were beginning to break free "of the last ties of the old community," and were moving toward an age in which free choice "would be enshrined as a new kind of God."[6]

William McLoughlin, on the other hand, sees the Great Awakening as a rather dramatic break with the past. Before New Englanders could free themselves from the last ties, McLoughlin argues, "the individual villagers had to break free of the picture they carried in their heads of the ideal social order and its relationship to God. . . . The tremendous cultural reorientation that this required is the movement historians have called the Great Awakening." Borrowing terminology from Richard Bushman's study of the social-psychological effects of the Great Awakening in Connecticut, McLoughlin maintains that the revival was nothing less than a "psychic earthquake," produced by a crisis of modernization and the accompanying shift from *Gemeinschaft* to *Gesellschaft*. Rapid social change had "made it impossible for the existing institutional structure to sustain . . . 'a minimally fluctuating, life supporting matrix for individual members of the social organism.' Individual stress increased to the point of cultural distortion." The significance of the Great Awakening was its role in providing for people a route through the blocked mazeways of society to a new ideological orientation. By calling the Awakening "a work of God," McLoughlin says, the people excused their "rebellion against traditional authority; it was out of their hands."[7]

Yet statements such as "the collapse of clerical authority," congregational "deterioration," "psychic earthquake," and "rebellion against traditional authority" little resemble the historical situation of the New England ministry and church at the time of the Great Awakening. The Awakening, in fact, was less an act of cultural defiance than an adaptation of vital orthodoxy to changing cultural and demographic circumstances. While there are reasons to believe that the Puritan ministry occupied a precarious position in the decades before 1690, primarily because of "changing patterns of employment,"[8] after 1690 it strengthened its position within the church in several ways, especially in providing parishes with new and better-trained preachers who were willing to experiment with received devotional forms to achieve a revival of religion. At the same time, church membership, which David Hall has called "the crux of the matter" in the declension debate, showed little evidence of deterioration on the eve of the Great Awakening. To be sure, the church membership roles that historians have only begun to exploit do point to some weakness in admissions before 1690, but after that date church membership in general was strong. Moreover, new evidence on the religious and institutional activities of the laity both before and during the Great Awakening makes it difficult to interpret that event as an act of cultural defiance. Rather, evidence concerning the people who were establishing and joining churches demonstrates that the Great Awakening represented not a dramatic break from the Puritan past but a popular reaffirmation of it. That the cultural meaning of Christian revivalism in Puritan America cannot be found in the theme of religious declension is a point fully confirmed by the history of the ministry, church membership, and the laity.

For the New England ministry, the period before the Great Awakening—the so-called "glacial era" of Puritan history—was a time not of religious decline but of rapid growth, occupational stability, and pastoral experimentation. Both Harvard College and Yale College, the latter of which was founded in 1701 for the purpose of "upholding and Propagating . . . the Christian Protestant Religion by a succession of Learned and Orthodox men," produced increasing numbers of well-trained ministers for Connecticut and Massachusetts parishes.[9] The supply of college graduates qualified to preach the gospel increased tenfold from 1700 to 1740, and of the 1,252 students graduated in that period, 558 (42 percent) found jobs in the ministry.[10] Moreover, by 1740 only 3 percent of ordained ministers were non-graduates, as opposed to 12 percent in 1700.[11] While the 1700 to 1740 clerical cohort was increasingly embroiled in disputes with their parishioners, particularly over salaries and doctrine, their pastoral careers were yet remarkably long and stable.[12] In Connecticut, which has had an especially notorious reputation for parish dissension, the rate of clerical dismissals remained steady throughout the period, never rising above 5 percent of all pulpits per five-year interval. In addition, more than 90 percent of New England clergymen stayed with the same church for their entire careers, averaging over twenty-six years in office compared to sixteen years for their seventeenth-century predecessors. Despite the contentiousness of the Great Awakening, surprisingly few ministers were dismissed, and average ministerial tenure remained the same as previous decades.[13] To one recent student of the New England ministry in the period 1750–1850, "The extent of permanence among the established Congregational clergy in New England during the eighteenth century is indeed significant," especially when viewed "from the standpoint of the extraordinary rate of pastoral turnover of the early nineteenth century."[14]

As their numbers grew, and as support from the state shrank, New England ministers turned to county associations and consociations to manage their internal affairs, a development that to many historians has smacked of clerical elitism and formalism. Yet clerical associationalism, which had firm roots in the Puritan tradition, gave ministers new opportunites for developing solutions to problems at the local level of their affairs, and thus provided contexts for pastoral innovation. As Charles Hambrick-Stowe has demonstrated, second- and third-generation Puritan pastors were the legatees of a vast and rich repertoire of devotional themes, on which they played variations as they sought to adapt to new, rapidly shifting local circumstances. The Half-Way Covenant was one such adaptation, sacramental evangelism was another. A third was the covenant renewal, which had been used in the 1630s, but came into its own only after 1670, as a "preparation for renewed life in Christ." Through these and other devotional rituals, New Englanders aimed "to create a form through which God would work powerfully and popularly," and "hoped to engender mass religious feeling, so that the majority of the population would know once more, as they had earlier in the century, God's claim on their lives."[15] While pastoral ceremonialism often fell short of expectations, it was not for want of effort or even struggle, such was the conservatism of the local laity. "Not, in fact, until the preachers of another generation came upon revivalism," David Hall has argued, "did the clergy have the weapon that they needed to play upon a fluid, pluralistic culture. But renewal of covenant was a step in that direction."[16]

The close, yet generally ignored connection between clerical professionalism and pastoral innovation and adaptation finds vivid confirmation in the history of the idea of the revival. Congregational clericalism involved New England ministers in two primary regional networks, one originating at Northampton, Massachusetts, and radiating south along the Connecticut River valley, the other beginning at Boston and branching out north and south along the Atlantic coast. Solomon Stoddard's innovative practices at Northampton, especially his promotion of the gospel over law after 1710, found quick converts among ministers tied to him through neighboring associations or through his extensive kin network.[17] At the same time, Cotton Mather's "New Piety," which he developed after 1700 in the midst of mounting frustration over the failure of moral reformation, found fertile soil for cultivation among ministers who were his close clerical colleagues in Boston and surrounding communities. As Robert Middlekauff has written about this crucial development, Mather's "Pietism was not something he picked up to repair the sagging authority of the ministry in New England. It expressed the intensity of his own spirit, and the spirits of his followers." It was, in addition, "a strategy, and a well-conceived one, to produce the reformation which virtually every minister in New England had cried out for over the past two generations."[18] The sermons of Mather's group, and also those of the Connecticut River valley preachers, "constituted a concerted campaign," a movement to produce revivals of religion, and when their sermons finally bore fruit in regional and then colonial harvests of souls, their professional networks provided the context for the revivals' surprisingly rapid transmission.[19]

Puritan professionalism also involved ministers in a transatlantic evangelical network, one with deep roots in the seventeenth-century Dissenting network thrown up by the Puritan "community of saints." Through this network evangelical ministers shared ideas and news about revival activity that, in the 1740s, crystallized into the modern notion of the great and general revival. Jonathan Edwards, Benjamin Colman, and Thomas Prince, Sr. of New England entered into "a letter-writing network" with James Robe, William McCulloch, John M'Laurin, and John Erskine of Scotland, and Isaac Watts, George Whitefield, and Philip Doddridge of England. By encouraging the exchange of information on revival techniques and outcomes, this "new international epistolary circuit" promoted a "process of convergence within evangelicalism" and also common organizational initiatives.[20] As Susan O'Brien writes,

> The major contrast that historians have drawn between the spontaneity of the mid-eighteenth-century revivals and the professionalism of those in the nineteenth century is misleading. . . . Instead, the eighteenth-century revivals should take their place on a continuum of Protestant evangelical development. The real significance of the mid-eighteenth-century revivals was not their wondrous spontaneity or their primary role in the formation of a national consciousness, but rather their combining of traditional Puritan practices with fresh evangelical techniques and attitudes.[21]

This was the combination that produced what historians refer to as the Great Awakening.

All movements, especially in their initial phase, are susceptible to ironic outcomes. So it was with the mid-eighteenth-century evangelical movement, which released unanticipated forces for change that exploded in the ministry's face. Religious enthusiasm, lay and clerical itinerancy, popular separatism, all were innovations of the Great Awakening, all posed profound threats to clerical authority, and all, according to some historians, divided and then conquered the ministry.[22] But the established ministry weathered the storm surprisingly well. While they did initially divide over the relative merits of emotional and rational preaching, they quickly forgot their differences in the face of radical challenges to their authority, using what got them there in the first place, the professional network, to adapt to the new circumstances imposed on them by the revival. The major adaptations entailed combining old pastoral practices, which they used to guide the revival and counsel their stricken parishioners, with fresh attitudes toward the proper role of the people in the church and the propriety of the pure church. Their willingness to adapt and innovate in the face of change—a suppleness lost on many contemporary historians—enabled most of them to maintain their pulpits, despite the turmoil of the Great Awakening, and to retain the loyalty of the great majority of the people, despite the growth of the Anglican, Baptist, and Presbyterian communions.[23] Not until the American Revolution and the sacralization of popular sovereignty did the established ministry begin to lose its grip on the evangelical culture. According to Harry Stout, by the early decades of the nineteenth century "new 'Christian movements,' proclaiming an 'egalitarian

religion,' replaced Congregationalism as the driving force in the evangelical tradition," and "this transition to an antihistorical individualistic faith . . . marked the start of 'modernization' in religion that
would be every bit as transforming as the changes taking place in
politics and society."[24]

"Ministers were all ambassadors of God," Donald Scott writes,
"but they were ambassadors to a specific place."[25] Even as Puritan
ministers immersed themselves in the concerns and affairs of their
profession, they remained forever tied to the parish, for it was the
parish that bestowed their position upon them, not the profession.
It was also the parish that gave them their self-image as preachers,
for within the parish their training as preachers was put to the ultimate
test—the people. Even before the Great Awakening strengthened the
ties between pastors and people, the final arbiter of an individual's
ministry was the laity of his parish. Ministers could gauge the extent
of their pastoral progress among the people in a variety of ways,
but the most important measure of clerical evangelism was church
membership. As David Hall has said, "Every minister blessed the
day when he could present someone to his congregation as a prospective member in full communion."[26]

Church membership also offered a time of popular, collective
celebration, because it centered "on a reaffirmation of the covenant
by the entire church," and was thus in fact "a reenactment of the
first founding of the church," when the first members were "grafted"
into the line of descent from Abraham.[27] As Richard Mather states,
"Members are admitted as the church state was first erected, viz.,
by solemn confession publicly before the whole church and by joining
with the church in the covenant, in which the church was joined at
her first gathering together."[28] Every admission ceremony thus represented a new beginning for the church and its people as well as a
renewal of their covenantal obligations *and* promises. Depending on
their range and frequency, such popular, celebratory occasions were
fraught with revival potential.

As church membership records indicate, the Awakening of the
1740s deserves the epithet *great*. In Connecticut, for example, more
churches admitted more than the mean number of new members than
in any other recorded five-year interval. In several instances, churches
filled up with new converts with surprising speed, adding more than
100 communicants in less than a year. In over half of the churches of
the colony, more people became members than at any other five-year
period in their history. In terms of the numbers of people presenting

themselves for communion and "grafting" onto the old stock of the church, the Great Awakening was truly "a surprising work of God."[29]

Yet the Great Awakening gained sustenance from and was made possible by a number of prior local and regional revivals in church membership, which derived in turn from seventeenth-century revivals. As extant church membership records demonstrate, as early as the 1630s and 1640s New England experienced a great religious revival, and many of the newly gathered churches ended up filled with new communicants. But then the well of potential converts ran dry, the flow of new members into churches slowed to a trickle, and the ratio of church members to inhabitants in some parishes dipped to as low as one to three. Even as preachers generally struggled to refill their churches with new communicants, some ministers managed to produce local revivals, drawing upon the resources available to them in the generations of church members coming to maturity. The generational revivals of the 1660s and 1670s quickly gave way to cohort revivals, as several generations began to unite in producing rising numbers of new members for the church. So it was in Solomon Stoddard's Northampton church, which had "harvests" of religion in 1679, 1683, 1696, 1712, and 1718. By the time of the fourth "harvest," which was among the most "plentiful" in terms of "the ingathering of souls," and among the most important in terms of Stoddard's development of the idea of the local revival, regional revivals were beginning to break out. In 1712-13 a Hampshire county "harvest" took place, followed in the early 1720s by the "Thames River Valley Awakening," and in the late 1720s by "the earthquake revival."[30] Following the route laid out by clerical and church networks, regional revivals expanded their range throughout the next decade, moving back and forth along the Connecticut River valley in the mid-1730s and then through all of New England in 1741-42. In 1743, however, the Great Awakening already began to run out of steam, and for at least a decade, amidst declining admissions, the Standing Order struggled, with some success, to keep new adherents from converting to dissenting communions. By the 1760s church membership began to revive out of a whole new generation of church children, and regional revivals broke out anew, thus preparing the way for another great revival, the "New Light Stir" of 1776-83.[31]

Even as revivals broadened their range after 1690, and especially after 1720, however, popular participation in them remained generally parish based. Even the Great Awakening, which tended to leap beyond the boundaries of the parish, drew its popular support mainly from the "natural" constituency of individual churches, which local preachers had worked on cultivating for many years, and which had produced the generational and cohort revivals of church membership. Without such an active, local tradition of popular participation in the church and its rituals, New England revivalism would have been impossible, notwithstanding the exertions of the evangelical ministry. The social sources of the revival movement and of New England Congregationalism thus were in the main one and the same, and were based not on class, as some historians have argued, but rather on family and gender.[32]

A key factor in the expansion of New England Congregationalism was the Puritan family. While Edmund Morgan fixed the blame for Puritan declension on the tribal nature of the religion, historians who have recently reconstituted church membership have discovered that Puritan tribalism was actually a vehicle of religious revitalization. As Cotton Mather once observed, "The Continuation of churches is ordinarily to depend on the Addition of Members out of the Families already incorporated therinto," and local church records testify to the accuracy of Mather's observation.[33] The History of Milford First Church, which underwent a series of dramatic generational revivals from its founding in 1639 through the Great Awakening and beyond, offers a case in point of the family's role in sustaining the life of a church. Over a period of 130 years, a mere thirty-six family groups contributed 693 members to the Milford church, or 72 percent of the total. From one decade to the next, at least three out of every four new members came from the same thirty-six families, and of these core families, 83 percent had appeared in town before 1660, and 78 percent before 1650. During times of revival these families participated even more fully in the church than at any other times. When the Great Awakening struck the town, for example, over 90 percent of the new membership came from the old family groups.[34]

While Morgan assigned responsibility for Puritan tribalism to the ministry, it was actually the product of the local laity. As David Hall noted, the people tended to confuse church membership with family well-being and safety, and the confusion "did not originate with the ministers, though they would more or less acknowledge it. Ordinary people imposed their own needs on the church."[35] Many of the circumstances accompanying popular participation in the church had little if anything to do with the needs of ministers, but everything to do with their parishioners' tribal and conjugal values. This lay tribalism found expression in various popular religious practices, including the common tendency of people to join the church at marriage or parenthood; the intermarriage of church children; the joint membership of spouses, siblings, and parents and their children; and the church membership of eldest sons.[36] It was also a source of the common, generational patterns of church membership revivals.

But lay tribalism could constrict as well as expand opportunites for popular participation in the church, denying some people, especially newcomers unknown to the brethren, access to church membership. Ministers were well aware of the restrictive aspects of local church practices, and it deeply troubled those of an evangelical mind. As early as the late 1640s Thomas Hooker complained about the "curious inquisitions and niceties" of the laity at admission, and during the 1660s John Woodbridge criticized the brethren for being "such a heavy stone at the ministers leggs that they cannot fly their own course."[37] By the early eighteenth century Solomon Stoddard decided to scrap the law for the gospel in an attempt to circumvent the local fraternity.[38] Perhaps, he felt, religious revivalism could unite all parishioners, old and new, behind the church.

But as was the case with Milford, the Great Awakening in the towns studied by historians did nothing to weaken the hold of the local tribe on the church. Despite its broad and general nature, the Great Awakening brought to the church mainly people from well-established, traditionally church-oriented families. Adults from local church families often responded first to the revival, and then were followed into the church by their children, as the enthusiasm for the event percolated down through the age structure of revival-prone families.[39] Even in trading towns, with highly differentiated and mobile populations, the Great Awakening had a traditional appeal. As Christine Heyrman has argued about the Great Awakening in the commercial towns of Gloucester and Marblehead, Massachusetts, "it was the major merchant families of these ports that played a leading role in the outpouring of religious piety and the reaffirmation of traditional Calvinist theology." The Great Awakening did not accelerate the secularization of the towns, but had the opposite effect, strengthening the local tribal values of traditionalism, insularity, and intolerance of dissent and outsiders.[40]

From Puritan tribalism there developed a second social source of New England Congregationalism and revivalism, a group of people whom Cotton Mather referred to as "The Hidden Ones," those "who make no Noise at all in the World; People hardly known to be in the World; Persons of the Female Sex, and under all the Covert imaginable."[41] Yet these "Hidden Ones," Mather realized years before he used the phrase, were proving to be the church's salvation from religious declension. When in 1691 Mather observed that "there are far more *godly Women* in the World, than there are *godly Men;* and our *Church Communions* give us a little Demonstration of it," he was taking notice of a development, the feminization of church membership, well under way since the 1660s, when women began outnumbering males in the church two to one.[42] By the early eighteenth century, churches in Mather's Boston and other New England ports were admitting as high as 80 percent women, and churches in the rural areas of the region as high as 70 percent women.[43] Thus, increasingly, Puritan churches were becoming numerically dominated not only by certain families but also by the women of those families. As Mary Beth Norton observes about this development, "women could no longer automatically turn to their husbands for spiritual guidance; they were forced into a condition of religious independence. . . . In individual women's minds, religious and familial roles appear to have been closely linked, perhaps because a woman facing a career of repeated pregnancies (and thus the constant risk of death in childbirth) had reason to be concerned about her spiritual well-being."[44]

Mather and other ministers often discussed the rise of the godly woman in the context of a related development, the declining religious zeal of men, which Carol Karlsen has attributed to the rise of a new commercial order, but which also probably derived from fraternal intolerance of outsiders, especially males.[45] Even as ministers reacted to the increasingly feminine composition of their churches by employing domestic imagery in their sermons and preaching on the female role, the regeneration of males remained a priority for them. To solve the problem of male apostasy, ministers encouraged wives to proselytize their husbands, to use those "Vast Opportunites," as Mather put it, "that a woman has to bring over her husband unto real and serious godliness."[46] If godly women, though, were confined to the home, where piety itself now seemed also confined, and men to the marketplace, where there lurked the greatest threats to piety, how could wives accomplish the conversion of their husbands? Men could be encouraged, as some were, to employ their "Talents for the Glory of GOD" in the world, but as long as the world remained unconverted, many men would remain unchurched.[47] Maybe a great revival of religion would succeed where all else had failed.

But in many towns affected by the Great Awakening, women continued to outnumber men at admission. In Connecticut, for example, well over two-thirds of the churches admitted 55 percent women or above in 1740–44, and one-fifth of them added 66 percent or more. In addition, in over half of the churches the proportion of women at admission increased from previous levels or remained in line with

the church's historical appeal.[48] Moreover, in some New England parishes, women, for the first time, assumed public religious roles, organizing separate women's meetings for devotion and speaking publicly
to large assemblies of both sexes.[49] But this was only a temporary
phase of the Great Awakening, and women receded as quickly from
public view as they had entered it, returning to their traditional
religious roles in the home and the church. This quick retreat of
women from public life was partly the product of lay tribalism, which
the revival mobilized, and also the symptom of "an increasing cir-
cumspection of acceptable female social roles within the wider culture," as Christine Heyrman argues.[50] In the aftermath of the Great
Awakening, women increased their dominance in church membership,
and during the nineteenth century they went on to play a critical
role in the Second Great Awakening.[51]

On occasion, however, the Great Awakening did redress the severe
imbalance of females over males in new membership, and in several
towns even tipped it decidedly in the latter's direction. Noteworthy
here were a number of second-generation Connecticut churches,
which emerged from the Great Awakening with a preponderance of
male church members. One such church was Woodbury First, which
was among the Connecticut churches most affected by the Great
Awakening. From its founding in 1670 until the Great Awakening,
First Church always admitted far more women than men, but the
revival changed that, albeit temporarily. In 1740–44 the church
brought in six males for every four females, reversing the customary
ratio. Sixty-six men joined the church during the Great Awakening
in Woodbury, more than double the number added the previous
decade.[52] Why did the Woodbury First and other churches in its cohort
suddenly attract males?

From Woodbury's local records comes a likely answer to this
question, one rooted in the social-religious history of the town's outlying regions. In the decade before the Great Awakening, all of the
town's peripheral neighborhoods were involved in the creation of
communities where none had existed before. Several areas had
received "winter privileges" to conduct religious services, but still
retained quasi-corporate status until they attained legal incorporation
as parishes. The first neighborhood to achieve society status was
Southbury in 1731, followed by Bethlehem in 1739, Judea in 1741,
and Roxbury in 1743. In each instance, the formation of a church
was a crucial part of the process, either preceding or coinciding with
the creation of the society.[53]

During the revival in Woodbury, residents from several of these

outlying neighborhoods produced for the First Church a number of
new members, many of whom were male. They included the sons of
families that had participated actively in the First Church, but were
now moving to the periphery and starting their own churches. From
their position on the edges of town, these and other families were
exposed to abrupt changes in local life that strengthened their commitment to the church; for during the 1730s, fifty new families, or
five times the number recorded in any previous decade, entered the
outlying areas, introducing a hitherto unknown element of transiency
into the community.[54] In the context of these changes, the church
became a source of continuity at a time when community, while
being recreated, had become problematic.

One of the regions of New England that was hardest hit by the
Great Awakening and that was also involved in the kinds of changes
that mobilized men behind the revival in Woodbury was eastern
Connecticut. Settled during the second half of the seventeenth century
by a second generation of New Englanders, eastern Connecticut was
increasing rapidly in population during the period of the Great Awakening and its towns were quickly subdividing into parishes when the
first regional revivals erupted. As communities in the area continued
to subdivide, a sense of urgency was added to a phase of parish life,
the "first planting" of a church, that required broad male participation. By tradition, men wrote and adopted the church covenant,
selected the church pillars, and elected and helped ordain the first
minister. In the course of rapid parish development, men were being
called upon to organize their communities into churches, and this
was reflected in the rising rates of male participation that affected
the churches of the region at the time of the Great Awakening.[55] Both
new, satellite churches and their parent parishes were involved in the
process, for networks of communication had been created among old
and new parishes in the course of the expansion, and these were the
networks that united men from old, church-oriented families around
developing churches. The creation of interparish networks was part
of a larger process, as Harry Stout indicates, by which eighteenth-
century towns were drawn "into widening webs of interdependence
and intercommuication" that "paved the way for religious movements
that could transcend local boundaries and mobilize groups from
neighboring communities into a united revival."[56]

When evidence on the growth of the church in all regions of
Connecticut and Massachusetts is gathered up, it becomes apparent
that the Great Awakening was a part of the most constructive phase

in New England history, a fact that casts doubt on recent efforts to locate religious revivalism in acts of cultural defiance. New Englanders at the time of the Great Awakening were not struggling to break free of the standing order, but were rather involved in efforts to expand the church to keep pace with the expanding population. That their efforts met with considerable success is revealed in data on church foundings. In the period 1710–40, the number of churches in Massachusetts increased from 87 to 207, and the number of churches in Connecticut from 46 to 120. In the span of one generation, 194 churches were founded in the two colonies, more than quadruple what each of three generations had averaged.[57] So phenomenal was the growth rate of the church that it actually exceeded the growth rate of the population, which itself was phenomenal. In Connecticut, for example, the ratio of churches to people was 1:696 in the 1730s, way down from the ratio in the 1690s, 1:981.[58] To be sure, in certain areas new churches lagged behind population growth, leaving in the spaces between settlements pockets of unchurched inhabitants vulnerable to the lure of separatism.[59] Nevertheless, the rate of expansion when contrasted to other periods was remarkable, and at the very least raised the kind of expectations normally accompanying the "first planting" of churches.

It was this root of live orthodoxy that George Whitefield tapped upon his arrival in New England in 1740. The broad popular response to his ministry, while certainly a reflection of his charisma, was also an expression of the church's inner vitality, periodically renewed and revived by preachers and their people. In the capacity of the Puritan system for self-renewal is to be found the central meaning of Christian revivalism in colonial New England.

## NOTES

1. William Cooper, "Preface," Jonathan Edwards, *The Distinguishing Marks of a Work of the Spirit of God*, in C. C. Goen, ed., *The Works of Jonathan Edwards*, 4 vols. (New Haven: Yale University Press, 1972), 4:216–17.

2. Charles Spalding, ed., *Edwards on Revivals* (New York, 1832), ix.

3. Perry Miller, *The New England Mind: The Seventeenth Century* (New York: Macmillan, 1939), 396–97.

4. Edmund S. Morgan, *The Puritan Family: Religion and Domestic Relations in Seventeenth-Century New England*, rev. ed. (New York, 1966), 185.

5. Paul Lucas, *Valley of Discord: Church and Society along the Connecticut River Valley, 1636–1725* (Hanover, N.H., 1976), xiii, 205.

6. Kenneth Lockridge, *A New England Town: The First Hundred Years: Dedham, Massachusetts, 1636-1736* (Hanover, N.H., 1970), 90, 159.

7. William G. McLoughlin, *Revivals, Awakenings, and Reform: An Essay on Religion and Social Change in America, 1607-1977* (Chicago: University of Chicago Press, 1978), 52-58.

8. David D. Hall, *The Faithful Shepherd: A History of the New England Ministry in the Seventeenth Century* (Chapel Hill: University of North Carolina Press, 1972), 194.

9. Richard Warch, *School of the Prophets: Yale College, 1701-1740* (New Haven: Yale University Press, 1973), 31.

10. See Table 1 in James W. Schmotter, "Ministerial Careers in Eighteenth-Century New England: The Social Context, 1700-1760," *Journal of Social History* (Winter 1975): 250.

11. James W. Schmotter, "The Irony of Clerical Professionalism: New England's Congregational Ministers and the Great Awakening," *American Quarterly* 31 (Summer 1979): 157.

12. Ministers' chances of engaging in a serious dispute with their parishioners rose from 22 to 47 percent in 1700-1740. Schmotter, "Ministerial Careers," 256; "Irony of Clerical Professionalism," 159.

13. At five-year intervals in 1700-1740, the rate of clerical dismissals as a percentage of existing pulpits was as follows: 0.0, 2.5, 0.0, 1.2, 3.1, 2.5, 4.3, and 1.0. Frederick Lewis Weis, *The Colonial Clergy and the Colonial Churches of New England* (Baltimore: Genealogical Publishing Co., 1977). For the average tenure of ministers, see J. William T. Youngs, Jr., *God's Messengers: Religious Leadership in Colonial New England, 1700-1750* (Baltimore: Johns Hopkins University Press, 1976), appendix.

14. Donald M. Scott, *From Office to Profession: The New England Ministry, 1750-1850* (Philadelphia, 1978), 3, 158 n. 11.

15. Charles E. Hambrick-Stowe, *The Practice of Piety: Puritan Devotional Disciplines in Seventeenth-Century New England* (Chapel Hill: University of North Carolina Press, 1982), 132, 255.

16. Hall, *Faithful Shepherd*, 244.

17. Lucas, *Valley of Discord*; Kevin M. Sweeney, "River Gods in the Making: The Williamses of Western Massachusetts," in Peter Benes, ed., *The Bay and the River* (Boston: Boston University, 1982), 101-16.

18. Robert Middlekauff, *The Mathers: Three Generations of Puritan Intellectuals, 1596-1728* (New York: Oxford University Press, 1971), 306.

19. Michael J. Crawford, "The Invention of the American Revival: The Beginnings of Anglo-American Religious Revivalism, 1690-1750" (Ph.D. diss., Boston University, 1978), 40.

20. Susan O'Brien, "The Great Awakening and the First Evangelical Network, 1735-1755," *American Historical Review* 91 (Oct. 1986): 811-32.

21. O'Brien, "Great Awakening," 815.

22. Schmotter, "Irony of Clerical Professionalism."

23. Youngs, *God's Messengers*, 129-37.

24. Harry S. Stout, *The New England Soul: Preaching and Religious Culture in Colonial New England* (New York: Oxford University Press, 1986), 316.

25. Scott, *From Office to Profession*, 17.

26. Hall, *Faithful Shepherd*, 204 n. 20.

27. Hambrick-Stowe, *Practice of Piety*, 129.

28. Quoted in Hambrick-Stowe, *Practice of Piety*, 129–30.

29. Information on church membership in Connecticut comes from the records of the following churches, almost all of which are in manuscript or on microfilm in the Connecticut State Library, Hartford, or the Connecticut Historical Society, Hartford: New London, Stonington, North Stonington, Preston, Suffield, Norwich, Bozrah, Colchester First and Second, Groton, Woodstock, Voluntown, Wethersfield, Lisbon, Thompson, Southington, Kent, Meriden, Hampton, Bolton, New Milford, Middletown, West Hartford, Old Lyme, Hartford, Branford, Windham, Woodbury, Franklin, Canterbury, East Haddam, New Canaan, Brooklyn, Fairfield, Westfield, Cromwell, Mansfield, Trumbull, Redding, Lebanon, Milford, Portland, Somers, Griswold, Scotland, New Haven, Putnam, New Hartford, Bloomfield, Bethlehem, Columbia, Cheshire, and Stratford.

30. See preceding note, and also Crawford, "Invention of the American Revival," chapter 2.

31. For an analysis of the "New Light Stir," see Stephen A. Marini, *Radical Sects of Revolutionary New England* (Cambridge: Harvard University Press, 1982), 38–39, 43–48.

32. For an interpretation of the Great Awakening in terms of class, see Gary B. Nash, *The Urban Crucible: Social Change, Political Consciousness, and the Origins of the American Revolution* (Cambridge: Harvard University Press, 1979), especially chapter 8.

33. Cotton Mather, *Companion for Communicants* (1690), quoted in E. Brooks Holifield, *The Covenant Sealed: The Development of Puritan Sacramental Theology in Old and New England, 1570–1720* (New Haven: Yale University Press, 1974), 200.

34. Milford First Congregational Church Records, Connecticut State Library, 1; Barbour Collection of Connecticut Records, Births-Marriages-Deaths, Connecticut State Library. See also Gerald F. Moran, "Religious Renewal, Puritan Tribalism, and the Family in Seventeenth-Century Milford, Connecticut," *William and Mary Quarterly*, 3d ser., 36 (Apr. 1979): 236–54.

35. David D. Hall, "Toward a History of Popular Religion in Early New England," *William and Mary Quarterly*, 3d ser., 41 (Jan. 1984): 54.

36. Gerald F. Moran, "The Puritan Saint: Religious Experience, Church Membership, and Piety in Connecticut, 1636–1776" (Ph.D. diss., Rutgers University, 1974), especially chapters 5, 8–10.

37. John Woodbridge, Jr., to Richard Baxter, 31 March 1671, "Correspondence of John Woodbridge, Jr., and Richard Baxter," *New England Quarterly* 10 (Sept. 1937): 574.

38. Lucas, *Valley of Discord*, 199–200.

39. Moran, "Puritan Saint," chapters 9–10.

40. Christine Leigh Heyrman, *Commerce and Culture: The Maritime Communities of Colonial Massachusetts, 1690–1750* (New York: W. W. Norton, 1984), 411.

41. Cotton Mather, *El Shaddi. A Brief Essay . . . Produced by the Death of . . . Mrs. Katharin Willard* (Boston, 1725), 21; Cotton Mather, *Bethiah. The Glory Which Adorns the Daughters of God. And the Piety, Herewith Zion Wishes to See her Daughters Glorious* (Boston, 1722), 34–35.

42. Cotton Mather, *Ornaments for the Daughters of Zion; or the Character and Happiness of a Virtuous Woman* (Cambridge, Mass., 1692), 48.

43. See note 29. See also Richard D. Shiels, "The Feminization of American Congregationalism, 1730–1835," *American Quarterly* 33 (1981): 46–62; Gerald F. Moran, "'Sisters' in Christ: Women and the Church in Seventeenth-Century New England," in Janet W. James, ed., *Women in American Religion* (Philadelphia: University of Pennsylvania Press, 1980), 47–65, and "'The Hidden Ones': Women and Religion in Puritan New England," in Richard L. Greaves, ed., *Triumph over Silence: Women in Protestant History* (Westport, Conn.: Greenwood Press, 1985), 125–49.

44. Mary Beth Norton, "The Evolution of White Women's Experience in Early America," *American Historical Review* 89 (June 1984): 608.

45. Carol F. Karlsen, *The Devil in the Shape of a Woman: Witchcraft in Colonial New England* (New York: W. W. Norton, 1987), chapter 5.

46. Mather, *Ornaments for the Daughters of Zion*, 96.

47. Thomas Prince, *A Sermon . . . upon the Death of the Honourable Samuel Sewall, Esq.* (Boston, 1730), 32.

48. See note 29.

49. Heyrman, *Commerce and Culture*, 375; Moran, "'The Hidden Ones,'" 142–43.

50. Heyrman, *Commerce and Culture*, 382.

51. Donald G. Mathews, *Religion in the Old South* (Chicago: University of Chicago Press, 1977), 47–48, 101–24; Mary P. Ryan, *Cradle of the Middle Class: The Family in Oneida County, New York, 1790–1865* (New York: Cambridge University Press, 1981), 76–83.

52. Woodbury First Congregational Church Records, Connecticut State Library.

53. For the ecclesiastical history of Woodbury, see William Cothren, *History of Ancient Woodbury, Connecticut . . .* 3 vols. (Waterbury, Conn., 1854–79), 1.

54. Since Woodbury's tax lists are divided by parishes, the movement of people from one neighborhood to the next can be traced. "Woodbury Town List for the Year 1731," "Woodbury List for the Year 1741," Woodbury Town Hall.

55. See note 29. In addition, see Shiels, "Feminization of American Congregationalism," 58. The best account of the active social and religious history

of eastern Connecticut is in Richard L. Bushman, *From Puritan to Yankee: Character and the Social Order in Connecticut, 1690–1765* (Cambridge: Harvard University Press, 1967).

56. Stout, *New England Soul,* 188.

57. *Contributions to the Ecclesiastical History of Connecticut; Prepared under the Direction of the General Association* . . . (New Haven, Conn., 1861); Harold Field Worthley, "An Inventory of the Records of the Particular Congregational Churches of Massachusetts, Gathered 1620–1805," *Harvard Theological Studies* 25 (1970).

58. For the population of Connecticut on which these ratios were based, see Bruce C. Daniels, *The Connecticut Town: Growth and Development, 1635–1790* (Middletown, Conn.: Wesleyan University Press, 1979), 47.

59. See, for example, Peter Onuf, "New Lights in New London: A Group Portrait of the Separatists," *William and Mary Quarterly,* 3d ser., 37 (Oct. 1980): 627–43.

# 4

# Revivalism, Renewal, and Social Mediation in the Old South

———————✦———————

JOHN B. BOLES

THE SOUTHERN COLONIES were left relatively untouched by the Great Awakening of the 1730s and 1740s, largely because the prerequisites for that kind of resounding religious revival did not yet exist in the South. Individual ministers in particular locations effected local upsurges in religious fervor—William Robinson's Presbyterian ministry in Hanover County, Virginia, in the early 1740s, for example[1]— and the visitation of George Whitefield to Savannah and Charleston created temporary excitement, some controversy, and, in the person of Hugh Bryan, a legacy of evangelical fervor.[2] But except for occasional hotspots associated with charismatic preachers or laypeople, the region as a whole remained cool to the religious dynamism that was creating a perception of general awakening in portions of the Middle Atlantic and New England colonies. Before anything like a general, regional awakening could occur, there had to be in place a network of churches and ministers, a widely accepted belief system about how God worked with mankind vis-à-vis salvation, and a perceived social-economic-cultural tension that lent itself to interpretation as a religious crisis that could only be resolved by a rebirth or revival of religious faith.[3] This rebirth, it was hoped, could be evoked by a combination of reinvigorated preaching and prayer that would result in divine intervention. These preconditions for a general awakening existed in New England and portions of Pennsylvania and New Jersey by the 1730s or earlier; they did not generally exist in the South until the mid–1790s, with the result that the South's First Great Awakening, often called the Great Revival, took place in the early years of the nineteenth century.[4]

The religious movement that came to fruition in 1800–1805 had its roots in the late colonial and Revolutionary-era South, and much of its character had been formed in response to the cultural and social conditions of that time.[5] Throughout the pre–Revolutionary South the Anglican church was established, and in close consort with colonial governments it stood for order, stability, and godliness, with civil and ecclesiastical officers working to the same effect. When for a variety of reasons in the middle of the eighteenth century dissenter sects began to emerge—the major ones being Presbyterianism, the evangelical Separate Baptists, who were a splinter group spawned by the New England Great Awakening,[6] and then, from England, the Methodist movement—they each met a degree of opposition and persecution from the established government and church. The Presbyterians, with their heritage of learned ministers, quickly worked out a rapproachement with the political and church establishment, but the more popular churches—the Baptist and Methodist (technically a wing of the Anglican church until 1784)—with their traditions of lay ministers and their strong lower-class appeal, seemed more of a threat to society and were more harshly treated. The Baptist and Methodist churches were countercultural in the sense that they stood outside the bounds of the established church and ignored traditional parish boundaries.[7] Partly as a cause and partly as a result of being excluded from acceptability, the Baptists and Methodists embraced and promoted lay leadership and emotionally demonstrative worship services; they opposed the materialism, competitiveness, and hauteur of the plantation aristocracy; and they tended both to attack slaveholding and to accept slaves as members of their churches. These attitudes were based on theological principles and grounded in the Bible—they were not a simple reaction against the ruling establishment. But the opposition of that establishment and its contrary attitudes helped to strengthen and validate the dissenters' countercultural self-identity because they quite naturally came in part to define themselves and their faith in terms of who they were not.

The established church saw itself in cooperation with the civil government as defining the capital "C" Community that was coterminous with the state. The dissenter churches rejected the corporate idea of the church-state society and saw themselves as a distinct community of fellow believers set apart from the larger Community.[8] The evangelicals' vision of community was not the entire society but rather the local fellowship of likeminded believers; theirs was a more private conception of religious responsibility, and their idea of religious discipline was congregational, not an aspect of civil government. Because they were evangelical churches, they interpreted church membership to be a matter of individual faith, not a status one was born into or assumed by residence or nominal practice. Again they exaggerated the contrast with the established Anglican church, but the emphasis on personal conversion was real and characterized the nature of their faith.[9] In the South, among comparatively less-educated settlers, this emphasis on a conversion experience that was fixed in time and space included the assumption that it was an emotionally charged moment and that it represented an individual's direct confrontation with God.

Ultimately the religious experience was private and emotional, and though it might lead to good works and a concern for the larger community, in the South the counterexample of the established church persuaded evangelicals to emphasize individual reformation and the perfection of the local congregation, not the larger society. The experience of the evangelical churches in the South convinced them that when a church defined its role in terms of the whole society the result was persecution and the corruption of the church by the state; when they attempted to criticize the institution of slavery, they again met official and popular opposition. The Methodist church in the South, for example, quickly realized it had to reconsider its original anti-slavery strictures if it was to have any chance to grow in the region. It could of course have decided to remain pure on the slavery issue, but to have done so would, as many of its leaders recognized, have greatly restricted its opportunity to spread its version of the gospel. That being the range of alternatives, southern Methodists opted to individualize and privatize their faith so it could be offered to southern whites and blacks with miminal fear of slaveholder opposition.

The Baptists made essentially the same compromise, defining a spiritual role for themselves that by compartmentalizing issues like slavery into a separate political sphere allowed them to evangelize the South without bringing down upon their heads the opprobrium of the state and public opinion. Persecuted in their early days as threats to the established order of society, the evangelical churches accommodated themselves to that society without at first either accepting or legitimating it. They sidestepped political and economic issues that divided civil society and carved out an arena of spiritual responsibility that—as compared with northern evangelicalism—was individualistic and privatistic.[10]

Such a set of compromises and emphases was well adapted to the South. For a complex of reasons, the late colonial Anglican church seldom touched the hearts of its parishioners. The dispersed pattern of settlement, and then the scope of the movement westward and southwestward, left many·people devoid of a sense of belonging to a viable community. The democratic nature of the evangelical churches also fit the needs of the rapidly expanding backcountry. The evangelical churches gave individuals a sense of purpose and provided a local community; without condescending to the plain people or attempting to favor the slaveowning aristocracy, the evangelicals empowered believers to organize and discipline local congregations and to take a degree of moral responsibility for their lives.[11] God's redeeming power was offered in the vernacular, and an emotion-filled ritual of conversion, whose very morphology enabled believers to understand their new status in concrete fashion, evolved. This conversion experience was held out as normative, and involved feelings of contrition and worthlessness leading to gradual acceptance of God's grace, and then an emotional high when a sense of redemption was achieved.

In the Great Revival of 1800–1805 the path from rejection to redemption was spelled out in vigorous and emotionally persuasive form, and the vogue of large outdoor worship services, soon called camp meetings, gave the hesitant seekers living examples of what was interpreted as redemptive grace: several ministers were preaching simultaneously, hundreds were moved to tears and repentance, then forgiveness and faith. In the midst of the crowds and the excitement and the emotion it was easier for people to overcome their inhibition and doubts and to accept the salvation being offered so vividly. The very size and novelty of the camp meetings seemed to legitimate God's miraculous power, as did the evident number of conversions being effected. In such settings, and among a people lacking in formal education or acculturation, there was little time for theological precision; what seemed important was emotional commitment. The lay-controlled evangelical churches—the Baptist and the Methodist—were already more concerned with portraying Jesus as the good shepherd seeking out those who were lost and God as a loving Father than in developing sophisticated theologies about atonement, or theodicies about slavery; emphasis on the individual's need to accept Christ personally became the primary point of every revival sermon.

The efficacy of the camp-meeting revival for effecting conversions was recognized long before it was seen as a human technique, and the patina of God's grace was never completely removed from the camp meeting even after the 1820s, when it had become the subject of printed manuals with diagrams for seating and sketches of preachers' stands. The Presbyterians first pulled away from the camp-meeting revival because it was deemed too emotional and disorderly, and the Baptists sought some distance from it in the early aftermath of the Great Revival, leaving it for a while as a characteristically Methodist

institution. But by 1820 the camp meeting became regularized: its
promoters learned to dampen some of the more extreme emotional
displays and to prohibit disruptions by rowdies and the sale of spirits
nearby.[12] In many southern counties the Methodists established camp-
meeting grounds with tenting sites, a covered preaching stand, and
an annually scheduled late-summer session that became an accepted
part of the social/religious season. The Baptists tended to have revivals centered in individual rural congregations, while in the scattered
towns Presbyterians and Baptists came to make use of what were
called protracted revivals, a concerted effort of several churches,
preceded by preparatory sermons and prayers and followed by efforts
to nurture new converts and situate them in supportive congregations.

Certainly by the middle of the antebellum period most evangelical
churches saw periodical revivals as a major means of augmenting
their membership. The high point of the church year became the
annual revival, and ministers and active laypeople redoubled their
efforts in advance of and during the season of intense preaching—
usually every night for a week or more, with two or three sermons
on Sundays. For many rural southerners the annual summer revival
was also a major social event, the occasion for seeing and talking
with neighbors, friends, and visitors who traveled to attend the special
worship services. The personal, social aspect of the revival enhanced
the sense of religious community.

The purpose of the revivals was to gain new converts, but seldom
were these people strangers to the church. Active laypeople almost
always had members of their families—perhaps a husband, or a son
or a daughter, or a brother—who had not professed his or her faith
and joined the church, and the letters and diaries of church members
were often filled with references to the hopes and prayers of believers
that some loved one would overcome hardness of heart or indifference
and join the church. Letters to relatives often included entreaties to
accept Christ, and parents especially were wont to write to grown-
up children urging conversion. The regularly scheduled revival was
often the occasion for intensifying these efforts, and church members
would bring the unconverted person to the services after already
attempting to prepare her or him for a moment of decision. Even
young people who by no means were reprobates or hardened sinners
but had only recently become old enough to think seriously about
religious matters were talked to and counseled by serious parents on
the eve of a revival, pointing toward their having an emotional
epiphany that was interpreted as the conversion experience. The

already converted increased the psychological pressure on the unconverted in advance of revival time, and those so cultivated (typically men who had been importuned by their wives or mothers) often were forced to think about their present state and the promise of eternal life. Although new members could and did join the churches throughout the year, the aura of the revival meeting—when congregational conversation turned to anticipation of new converts, and ministers and devout laypeople addressed with special attention and intensity those in their midst who were as yet undecided—almost always resulted in what was often called a new harvest of souls.

The revival also became an annual ritual to ceremonialize the local religious community's self-awareness of its faith commitment. That commitment was shown by a desire to bring others to a faith decision and to renew one's own commitment by a ritual reenactment of a prior conversion experience. As the minister ostensibly addressed the unconverted and attempted to awaken them to a recognition of their sinful behavior, then persuade them to ask God for forgiveness and receive his redemptive and guilt-removing love, those who were already members of the church appropriated the message for themselves and applied it to their own lives, in effect transforming the revival meeting into a kind of corporate confession. Here was a way to come to terms with one's ongoing sinfulness, silently and confidently request forgiveness, then either privately feel unburdened of one's sin and empowered to face the future or—an increasingly common development—publicly "rededicate one's life to Christ" as a means of renewing, strengthening, and sealing one's faith. In this sense the annual revival was at least as important for church renewal as for church growth, and it served the important function of letting church members see their faith in action. We underestimate the significance of the annual church revivals if we see them only as efforts to reach out to the unconverted; for most church members, the revival season was primarily a period of renewal of their faith—a battery-charging time.

The southern evangelical churches did not offer a quiet, contemplative religion but rather an energetic one whose annual revival-season focus on an emotionally felt conversion served to concentrate the mind and produce a period of annual renewal, recommitment, and redefinition of, and conformity to, the congregational community. Revivalistic religion fit the pace and frame of mind of an overwhelmingly agricultural society, and revivals usually occurred in late summer, after the crops had been "laid by" and when farmers were most conscious of how the yield of their labors and, by implication, their lives, lay ultimately in God's hand. Both farmers and preachers talked of "harvest" at this time, and the sudden violence of southern summer thunderstorms could remind everyone of how fragile human efforts were compared to the awesome displays of heaven.

The Presbyterians, Baptists, and Methodists—dissenter sects on the eve of the American Revolution—after the Great Revival became the dominant denominations in the South. Their personal theology, with its individualistic emphasis on a felt conversion experience, suited social conditions in the expanding South of cotton and slavery. The Presbyterians, who had formal educational requirements for the ministry and an elaborate ecclesiastical organization, were quickly able in the Piedmont, backcountry, and new plantation regions of the Old Southwest to replace the Episcopal (Anglican before the Revolution) church as the meeting house of most respectability. But the Baptists and Methodists, with ministers whose only requirement for ordination was an evident call to preach, and whose organizational scheme was perfectly suited to the often sparsely settled backcountry, overwhelmingly won the recruitment race and dominated southern church membership. The Baptist ministers throughout the period were, except in the cities and largest towns, farmers or small planters during the week, and with minimal financial support often served several churches in close proximity to one another. The early Methodist itinerant system allowed one minister on horseback to travel a circuit many miles in circumference, preaching at prearranged times at a number of sites. Both Baptists and Methodists depended on local deacons, elders, and "bands" (essentially a support group) to maintain church morale and discipline. By the middle of the antebellum period most Methodist ministers were stationary, preaching in one or several churches, but the itinerant system still operated in the least populated regions. It was not unusual for several denominations to share a common "union" church building on successive Sundays.

The Great Revival occurred at the beginning of a period of substantial population migration in the Deep South; in the generation that followed 1800, Alabama, Mississippi, and Louisiana all became states and the southern culture, economy, and labor system—slavery—expanded westward. The significant increase in church membership and ministers that resulted from the revival, and the growth in the churches' self-confidence, made possible the proliferation of the three dominant evangelical churches across what is now called the Old Southwest, and later into Texas and Arkansas. The Episcopal church, disestablished following the Revolution, declined in relative influence and prestige everywhere but in certain Tidewater areas of the Chesapeake and the Lowcountry of South Carolina and Georgia, but even there the Presbyterians began to compete for the fealty of the planter aristocrats. Elsewhere, as the Baptists and Methodists enjoyed great growth, gradually toned down the emotional excesses of the Great Revival, and began to include a much broader cross section of society among their members, their sense of being countercultural eroded and they began to reflect and shape many of the values of the larger society. In one sense the class location of the Baptists and Methodists moved upward in the antebellum era, but this was not necessarily accomplished at the expense of those at the bottom of society; rather, it represented a broadening of the churches' appeal. In the later years of the nineteenth century, new dissenter movements, the Holiness and Pentecostal sects, found a social niche among people at the bottom of society who had been partially abandoned by the then mainstream evangelical denominations.[13]

Essential to the growth of the evangelical churches in the South was their principled compromise with slavery. This was not simply a selling out to the forces of black exploitation for the sake of courting planter popularity. The spread of the gospel was the major evangelical goal, and the early antislavery ministers soon recognized that their abolitionist stance conflicted with their evangelical mission, for their freedom to preach in areas where there were significant numbers of blacks was severely restricted so long as the preachers criticized the institution of slavery. To provoke such restriction meant that the evangelicals would often be prevented from preaching the gospel of salvation to the slaves—or to the slaveholders. Even though slavery in the abstract was evil, the preachers reasoned, would not slaves be better off in the ultimate scheme of things if they could hear the gospel and thereby gain freedom from sin and hence eternal life?[14] Ministers who had also once questioned whether slaveholders could be Christians had since encountered many planters who in fact were Christians, an experience that in itself tended to defuse militant abolitionism. Hence both logic and human relationship persuaded many antislavery Baptist and Methodist ministers to squelch or soft-pedal their emancipationism in order that their basic evangelical mission could be advanced. Some ministers who could not accept that kind of compromise left the South and went to free states like Ohio and Illinois, while other ministers, who now often had slaveholding members in their churches, came to accept slavery as a fact of life and as a potential benefit to the slaves themselves. It came to seem more appropriate to attempt to ameliorate the institution of slavery of its abuses than to try to abolish it outright.[15]

Even those who still harbored doubts about slavery could take refuge in the evangelical demarcation of a spiritual realm of life and a political or civil sphere, placing slavery in the sphere over which the church supposedly had no responsibility. This dualist attitude toward appropriate responsibilities was one consequence of the eighteenth-century dissenter heritage of the churches and the tendency to reject the larger world in favor of the privatized spiritual fellowship of the local congregation; the reality of slavery as a part of the larger society that could not safely be criticized reinforced the inclination to compartmentalize religious responsibility. The net result of this combination of influences was that, in effect, the evangelical churches accepted the institution of slavery. Even so, the churches did not simply reflect societal attitudes toward slaves; instead they subtly changed how whites saw blacks.

In their initial decades in the South the Baptists and Methodists, whose first converts were disproportionately drawn from the lowest orders of white society and felt themselves despised by the planter aristocrats, and whose evangelical zeal was both robust and universalistic, welcomed slaves as members. This occurred even though, generally speaking, race relations were harsher in the mid-eighteenth-century South than they had been in the seventeenth century or would be in the antebellum period. The slave population had grown rapidly in the early decades of the eighteenth century, in part because of a significant increase in African imports, and the legal parameters of slavery had hardened in response to the ballooning number of blacks. Yet dissenter Baptists and Methodists, religious and to a degree social outcasts in their own right, eagerly accepted black worshipers at their meetings. The evangelical churches in the South were biracial from the very beginning, and this practice did not change appreciably during the antebellum period. White and black, slave and free, sat in the same buildings, heard the same sermons, responded verbally to the preacher with a chorus of "amens" and other words of approval, sang the same lively hymns, took communion together, participated in church disciplinary hearings, and were ultimately buried in the same cemeteries.

Gradually the presence of devout blacks in the church pews helped change evangelical attitudes toward slavery. It came to be seen as the process by which purportedly heathen Africans were introduced to Christianity. Thus the participation by blacks in the evangelical churches provided evidence to many whites that slavery was God's

way of bringing Africans to the gospel, and—in the minds of whites—
the presence of black worshipers stood as a convincing refutation of
abolitionist charges that southern churches had abandoned their
responsibilities to the blacks.[16] Throughout the antebellum period the
scriptural defense of slavery in the abstract and the visible religious
conversions of particular slaves constituted the foundation of the
defense of slavery. And this represented one important way that the
existing society helped move the evangelical churches from being
cultural dissenters in opposition to a major social institution to being
cultural defenders of that very institution.

But the presence of black Christians in the pews also to a degree
softened white attitudes toward blacks and helped create and solidify
the black community. One reason racial attitudes had grown more
harsh in the mid-eighteenth century was the increasing presence of
slaves directly from Africa, people often unable to speak English and
whose ritual scarification of their bodies symbolized their alien
nature; they were called "outlandish" slaves to distinguish them from
more fully acculturated "country-born" slaves of American nativity.
The reports of early Anglican missionaries to the bondspeople were
filled with references to the slaves' linguistic and cultural incompat-
ibilities with white religion.[17] But as time passed, the number of
American-born slaves soared and imports largely ceased, and significant numbers of slaves became fellow Christians. Slowly, almost
imperceptibly, in the several decades after 1790 or so, white churchgoers began to see slaves less as savages, as unknowable beasts of
burden, and more as people with souls, inferior it is true, but people
nonetheless who responded to Jesus' love and his indwelling spirit:
brothers and sisters in Christ who shared in the fellowship of believers. This is not to argue that slaves were seen as social or political
equals—though ministers and laity often said that all people were
morally equal in the eyes of God—or that slavery was disapproved;
rather, blacks were seen more as permanent children, inferior to
whites but not lacking in essential humanity. In church records blacks,
like whites, were referred to as Brother Sam or Sister Judy, using the
identical familial language of address that was employed with whites
and that subtly suggested all—black and white alike—were the children of a heavenly Father.[18] And this familial language both reflected
and reinforced the slaveholders' tendency to see their slaves as part
of their domestic household or family. As one Presbyterian minister
wrote, "Our servants constitute a part of our households. . . . It is
only on this ground that we can find any sanction in the word of
God for the institution of slavery. As members of the family-compact,

they have therefore the same claims for religious instruction that our children have."[19]

There is a great deal of evidence in the correspondence and diaries of antebellum southerners that whites recognized the depth of slave Christianity; there are numerous primary sources describing biracial religious conversation, whites witnessing to slaves, and vice versa, about the necessity of salvation, and many comments about the near sainthood of certain beloved slaves. This gathering together under the same church roof, experiencing a similar faith, and accepting blacks as genuine participants in the community of faith, fundamentally changed white attitudes about blacks from primarily revulsion and fear to condescending paternalism. The relationship was still one between unequals, and was marked by racism; but it was a far less hostile relationship than what had obtained in much of the eighteenth century, and it contributed mightily to what has been called the domestication of slavery in the nineteenth century.[20] The image of the slave kneeling in prayer, or worshiping with tears of joy streaming down his or her face, or singing heartfelt spirituals, was far different from the earlier image of the half-naked heathen who at best only partially understood English. The presence of at least some slaves who were irrefutably devout Christians contributed to the white self-delusion that because some blacks had accepted Christianity, almost all blacks were content to be slaves. Certainly the new image was self-serving for whites, but it helped shape their perception of blacks and affected their actions toward them. Even the occasional example of individual slave rebellions or the much rarer communal insurrections such as that led by Nat Turner in 1831 did not disabuse white southerners of their confidence in the essential contentment of the slaves. White southerners did not live racked by fear of slave rebellion.

There is also much evidence that slaves in their participation in the worship life of the evangelical churches were treated more equally than anywhere else in the slave society. Slaves heard the entire sermons, not just the pro-slavery homilies addressed directly to them almost in the fashion of a children's lesson, and slaves discovered in the full message grounds for self-respect and self-worth otherwise denied them in their everyday life. Slaves seized the concept of a chosen people who were enslaved but remained in special relationship to God and applied it to themselves; the role of Jesus as the suffering servant they found very attractive, as was the concept of Moses and the Israelites' eventual deliverance from bondage. From the evangelical message slaves found meaning for lives that were usually hard;

they found joy, forgiveness, a reason to keep on living and struggling. In church disciplinary proceedings—unlike the civil courts of the South—their testimony was valued and accepted, even when directed against whites, and in the church courts they were held to essentially the same moral codes as were whites. Slaves were not disciplined out of proportion to their numbers.[21] The church constituted an arena for slaves' self-growth and moral improvement, a place to practice leadership skills and even to feel morally superior to whites. But in addition to this wedge of humanity and personal accountability that the church drove into the institution of slavery, the church ironically helped nurture the black community that incorporated slaves from a variety of plantations.

It has often been pointed out that black worshipers sat apart from whites—is it supposed the slaves would have preferred to sit with their masters?—in balconies or at the rear of the church, and at outdoor revival meetings separate sections of the grounds were set aside for the use of the black worshipers. Today we tend to interpret such separation as examples of segregation that should be denounced, though in an age when both race and gender were widely employed to determine seating, it may not have attracted as much notice. But for slaves widely scattered on small farms and plantations across the southern rural landscape and living with restrictions against freedom of travel and visiting, the most accepted and un-regulated time for socializing with other slaves was at church and revival services. Here was a time to visit with friends and relatives, to court, to share information of all kinds, to help create the sense of a black community that was part of, but larger than, the church religious community. From the slave viewpoint, segregated seating offered a safe opportunity, beneath the very nose of whites, to engage in the kind of interactions with others of their race that strengthened the sense of racial solidarity and identity. In urban areas separate black churches often developed, usually associated with a patron white church but just as often completely independent.[22]

The evangelical churches, their growth bolstered by revivals, in addition to "domesticating" relations between blacks and whites, mediated between different social classes in white society as well. As the circle of evangelical influence widened to encompass most of southern society, whites of every economic and social level became members of Baptist, Methodist, and Presbyterian churches, and, particularly after 1800, the Episcopal Church developed a much warmer attitude toward revival preaching styles and the appropriateness of demonstrative emotion in worship services. No longer were Baptists, for example, the church almost exclusively of nonslaveholding whites and slaves. Slaveholders were a minority in the South, but in the evangelical churches they met, sat among, served on committees with, and otherwise were part of a community that crossed economic and social boundaries. Class conflict was surprisingly muted in the antebellum South, and the reasons are manifold: the presence of a black underclass of slaves united all whites in a kind of racial solidarity; there were real economic bonds between whites of all classes; they often were kin; they met as political equals at the court house and polling place; and they were fellow members of local congregations. The wealthy planter and the plain-folk farmer mutually addressed each other at church services as brother, and mutual suspicions toward one another decreased. Lower-class worshipers may very well have come to think more positively about themselves as a result of intermingling with worshipers of a higher economic class. Commonplace religious interactions, then, served to help mediate potential class tensions during the antebellum period. The ongoing democratization of southern political life in the nineteenth century was in part a reflection of the demographic success of the major evangelical denominations.

But the democratization of southern political life was not simply a matter of practice; its intellectual roots lay in the popularity during the Revolutionary era of what was called the country or republican ideology.[23] For several reasons (beyond the purview of this essay), southern aristocratic political leaders appropriated the ideas and vocabulary of an English political dissenter tradition with which to attack what they at first called Parliamentary abuse, then Royal tyranny. Juxtaposing their assumed values against those of the king and his corrupt advisers, the planter-patriots of the American Revolution attacked the idea of unrestrained power and the corrupting influence of wealth, luxury, and idleness; they praised, in opposition to British policy, the ideals of simplicity, plain living, and disinterested devotion to the common good. This emerging vocabulary of political virtue soon was used not simply to attack British officialdom but to prescribe the expected behavior of American political leaders. Thomas Jefferson, for example, was a democrat by intellectual persuasion, and this tradition of appealing to limited, frugal government, led by men who were not distanced by extravagant displays of wealth from the common voter, became a staple of southern public life. Wealthy planter aristocrats, in order to be elected, had to cultivate the common touch and not offend the democratic sensibilities of the plain, God-fearing folk, as one transplanted Virginia aristocrat in antebellum Mississippi, Thomas Dabney, learned to his chagrin when a yeoman farmer rejected Dabney's begloved offer to loan the use of his slaves.[24] This republican ideology had a British pedigree for learned readers of political discourse, but for the majority of southerners, the republican attacks on abuse of political power and the corrupting effects of wealth and extravagant living bore a close resemblance to the contemporary evangelical critique of planter dissipation and church-state infringements of the religious freedom of dissenters. Without claiming any causal relationship between the two, it is perhaps reasonable to argue that after 1800 the political language of republicanism and the moral language of evangelicalism merged together, and the confluence gave the imprimatur of the popular churches to a conception of political virtue that dominated the antebellum South. This is not to insist that evangelicals were overtly political—quite the contrary. It is, rather, to suggest that politics and religion represented parallel universes and reinforced each other in ways neither side appreciated.

Religious freedom, what the dissenters often called soul liberty, was also related to the republican idea of the independent man, uncontrolled by the influence of others. The point here is that the value system of the evangelicals, shaped by theology and practice, predisposed them to accept and appropriate certain ideas and emphases of the Revolutionary-era political leaders, gaining, as it were, mass American acceptance of a style of political rhetoric that had originated among a small group of elite British political dissenters. The emerging model of the political leader as a spokesman of the people rather than as a representative of the Crown, and the political inexpediency of an image of luxury and dissipation as compared to the beneficial image of being a man of the people—witness the devastating attacks on John Quincy Adams for supposed aristocratic pretensions and the victorious log-cabin-and-cider democratic image of William Henry Harrison—represented how evangelical attitudes toward acceptable behavior had replaced late colonial attitudes. Parenthetically, one should note how the Baptist and Methodist ministers—who were not set apart from the common run of people either by a clerical collar or any particularity of dress, nor by education, nor by how they often supported themselves financially—democratized the position of the minister. No religious elite ruled the dominant southern churches. It could hardly have been otherwise when, in the absence of state subsidies, churches had to depend upon popular support to survive and prosper. Disestablishment forced ministers to address the real needs of their parishioners, ascertain mass sentiment, and speak the language of the common people.[25] In the changed world of, say, 1825, the culture of the evangelicals had triumphed; they were no longer cultural dissenters; instead they lived in a world largely of their own making.

The evangelical opposition to extravagant wealth, luxurious living, and dissipation continued as a powerful motif in southern religious life, and while the churches effectively achieved what they felt to be a principled compromise with slavery, they never caved in to unchecked pursuit of wealth for its own sake.[26] There was a strong capitalist ethos in the South: the great staple crops were sold in an international market; slaveholders avidly speculated in land and slaves and calculated ways best to insure future prosperity; planters in their daybooks often kept careful records of expenses, sales, prices received, and the like. Correspondence reveals an intense concern with prosperity, with getting ahead, with achieving a comfortable standard of living, and young men debated with themselves, their wives, and their parents about the pros and cons of staying near their parent's homeplace or migrating west to improve their economic prospects.[27] Yet this constant preoccupation with prices and profits was moderated by an evangelical conscience that cautioned about overconcern with such matters. Older, precapitalist notions about debt, about usurious interest rates, and about raising the price of commodities in times of distress continued alongside the determination to prosper. The older notion of a just price, set by morality and tradition rather than the neutral calculus of the market, persevered and received legitimation in the pulpits.

Despite the pell-mell cotton boom, the land rush in the "flush times" of Alabama, and the spread of the Cotton Kingdom from Georgia to Texas, there remained in the public and private ethos of the South the understanding that Christianity puts limits on greed. As an Alabama planter wrote his son in 1851, "Don't let this world, or the honors of the world, yea I would add the Riches, too, cheat you out of the love, and of course the favour of your blessed Savior . . . watch and pray *much* in order to keep humble and devotional . . . or . . . you will backslide."[28] It was deemed un-Christian to drive one's slaves too hard, to charge exorbitant prices for corn in times of drought, to press creditors too hard for repayment, or to profane the Sabbath for the sake of gain. When natural or financial disasters struck, ministers were quick to see divine retribution for public and private greed. Many southerners, avoiding idleness, practicing thrift and hard work, and buying slaves to enlarge their harvests, struggled with flickers of guilt over their success. In fact, greed rather than the actual holding of slaves was often the concern of ministers, and one of the implicit functions of annual revival services, with their ritual of contrition, forgiveness, acceptance, and then rededication, was to empower people to engage fully in the struggle to prosper, to overcome their doubts about the morality of their efforts, and to be able to face life confidently, exuberantly, and, yes, profitably. Guilt is perhaps too strong a word, but many planters especially seemed vaguely uneasy about their involvement in the market economy—a phrase they never used, barely understood, and certainly never reified—for staple crops, land, and slaves; evangelical religion offered them a means of overcoming these tensions between practices and ideals.[29] While careful to mute their concerns about slavery, ministers often lamented the evil consequences of slave sales that separated black families, and they in effect toned down their strictures against divorce and remarriage to accommodate slave members whose marriages were disrupted through no fault of their own.

In addition to helping white southerners come to terms paradoxically with slavery and democracy, evangelical religion with its widening class influence and special appeal to women served to legitimate emotion in southern family and political life. In some historical situations, new ideas, outlooks, and behavior patterns trickled down from elites to find broad popular acceptance, but just as often new ideas, outlooks, and behaviors that first emerge among the folk bubble up to change the lives of the elites. Evangelical religion had that effect in the early nineteenth-century South. By 1825 or so, evangelical attitudes characterized not only the Baptist, Methodist, and Presbyterian churches but the Episcopal church as well, and an evangelical frame of mind—a personalistic, emotional, privatistic conception of religion—had become as common to upper-class whites as to those in the lower order of society, perhaps even more so.[30] In fact, there is some evidence that by that date evangelical conceptions of Christian behavior were more dominant among the better off, who now associated "proper" behavior—an aversion to profanity, anger, and violence; genteel notions of decorum; opposition to too much concern with making money; "feminine" concepts of meekness, gentleness, and sweetness of character—with role modeling that called for being Christlike. When, for example, during the Civil War southern men of all classes were forced to be together, those of the upper-class sometimes complained about the immorality, gambling, cardplaying, and general irreligion of the lower class—a real reversal of mid-

eighteenth-century class attitudes.[31] Christian precepts were far more
important than an abstract conception of honor in shaping the mores
of upper-class southerners, and even "honor" was often undergirded
and interlaced with openly Christian ideas and expressed with a
Christian vocabulary.

Significantly more women than men were members of the southern evangelical churches, and the influence worked in both directions:
so-called women's virtues helped shape and define the worship practice, and women modeled themselves after the church-defined pre-
scriptions of proper Christian behavior and accepted the role of moral
exemplars. In the rural, agricultural South, participation in the
churches offered southern women an opportunity to serve, organize,
and lead that existed nowhere else in rural southern society. In addition to raising funds for or teaching Sunday school, women served
on disciplinary and visitation committees, and on sewing or baking
committees to raise funds for a new church building, or bell, or
organ. In a male-oriented region, with few professions open to
women, the church represented most women's only opportunity to
be involved in important activities outside the household. The church
played an extraordinarily significant role in many women's lives, and
women constructed their images of the proper wife, mother, and
slaveholder in terms of religious precepts. Women were supposed to
be, and generally were, demonstrably more religious than men, and
the personalistic, privatistic, and emotional emphases of evangelical
religion found reinforcement in the household worlds of most
women.[32] The evangelical emphasis on demonstrable emotion contributed to a change in fundamental cultural attitudes about the
family and marriage.

Historians of the family have posited that the affectionate, child-
centered family and love-based companionate marriage were both
products of modernity—declining infant mortality rates and the like.
But both developments in the South seem to have been in advance
of what modernization theory would suggest, and the influence of
evangelical religion—authenticating the open display of emotion, of
love—might very well have been the motivating force for change. In
the mid-eighteenth century South, and especially for upper-class families, it was not fashionable to display affection openly. Marriages
were often arranged, children were kept at a comparative emotional
distance, and personal emotions were expected to be carefully controlled. The Anglican church projected the socially acceptable image
of restraint. Evangelical religion, on the other hand, was personal
and expressively emotional, and "touchy-feely" emotional displays—

footwashing, the kiss of brotherly or sisterly love, the right hand of fellowship, the holy embrace of new converts—authenticated one's faith community. A central emphasis of the preachers was God's all-forgiving love for sinners and Jesus' personal love for the converted. The emotional nature of evangelical religion also had a sentimental dimension, and this combination of characteristics made more accept-able the showering of affection on children. Love for children and between spouses became less something people were afraid to risk or were embarrassed to reveal and more the expectation. Restraint was out, open affection was in.

Older, patriarchal-style discipline was not forgotten. Many Chris-tian fathers associated strict, even harsh, discipline, with what might today be called "tough" love, and the discipline meted out to children, slaves, and even wives by Christian fathers/masters/husbands shocks modern sensibilities. The loving father often saw himself as the stern authority figure,[33] an image not altogether absent today in Christian households. Yet even the patriarchal model had come to assume that children's characters were plastic and could be shaped by attentive Christian parents. This meant that fathers should not be aloof and unconcerned with parenting but rather the reverse. Many stern fathers certainly had a "hands on" attitude toward their children, and the ostensible motivation was love.

Into the second quarter of the nineteenth century, considerations of family background and wealth still figured in the calculations both of young people contemplating marriage and their parents, but they were by no means the only desiderata. Detailed studies of familial correspondence and analysis of such factors as the order of marriage among maturing young adults in a family suggest that love and congeniality shaped marriage choice more than did calculations of inheritance.[34] Surely it was not the only cause, but evangelical reli-gion's positive emphasis on emotion, and its portrayal of love as a motivating factor in God's attitude toward his people, raised the acceptability level of love in the choice of marriage partners. To some extent companionate marriage elevated the expectations of conjugal happiness and might thereby have occasionally heightened frustra-tions and deepened disappointments when love faded or failed to materialize. In an age when divorce was practically impossible, reli-gion could also offer consolation and forgiveness to spouses unhappy in marriage.

In the eighteenth-century Great Awakening debates over the valid-ity of emotion as an appropriate response to religion and as a technique used by ministers to move listeners to a conversion experience, emotion was often denounced as "enthusiasm" devoid of intellectual content. The accepted pre-Awakening sermon style was a learned treatise explicating a biblical text, with an attempt at the conclusion to apply the text logically to the listeners' life situations. Demonstrable emotion was considered a phony sentiment, unrelated to true conversion. But the preachers who became revival supporters intuitively pioneered a new understanding of the role of emotion in the conversion experience and in the sermon style. Even before Jonathan Edwards provided a psychological justification, revival ministers used emotion as a persuasive tool in their sermons to "pierce" listeners' indifference and to motivate them to turn their minds and souls to the message of God's redemption that the ministers held out. A learned minister like Edwards could combine sophisticated biblical analysis with vivid, concrete imagery that affected listeners emotionally. Few if any evangelical ministers in the South (or elsewhere) had Edwards's learning, but they developed extraordinary skill in using emotion in their extemporaneously delivered sermons to cajole, to frighten, and ultimately to persuade their listeners to think seriously about religion. The whole range of emotions was appealed to, and the minister's voice rose and fell in pitch and volume as his eyes, hands, and body language were all employed to make every individual hearer feel that the message was aimed squarely at him or her. This use of emotion-filled rhetoric, intended to persuade listeners by touching their hearts more than their minds—though it was thought the heart was the path to the mind and understanding—was tremendously validated by the preaching successes of the Great Revival and the rapid growth of the most aggressively evangelical churches. The emergence into the mainstream of the evangelical churches with their revival-centered practices raised the acceptability level of emotion in public discourse.

The Baptist and Methodist revivalists in Virginia in the 1770s, for example, using plain language to speak to plain people, proved the efficacy of their rhetorical style—and Patrick Henry apparently learned from their success the secret of persuasive oratory appropriate to an emerging democracy.[35] Analogous to the older style of scholarly sermon, read from the pulpit with a minimum of feeling, the pre-Henry political address made few concessions to its listeners. Learned, laced with allusions to the classics and references to British and Continental political writings, the political speech was intended to appeal to the intellect of the well-educated assemblymen. The political essays (often masquerading as letters) printed in colonial newspapers, as well as the broadsides, were not "written down" to the common reader; they were not, in a democratic sense, reader friendly—the essays were intended to engage the intellect and convince the mind of the writer's peers. When Patrick Henry introduced the new fashion of persuasive rhetoric to the world of Virginia politics, employing the histrionic flourishes of the revival preacher, his politically sophisticated listeners were overwhelmed and almost hypnotized by the power of his words even though, as Jefferson once commented, after it was all over one might well wonder what Henry had really said—but he had already gained your consent.[36]

Disdaining the tidy rhetoric of older politics, Henry in oratory did what Thomas Paine did in pamphleteering—introduce pithy, vernacular language that addressed and persuaded the common person of the rightness of the speaker's conviction and invested that assent with the motivating power of emotion. A revolution in political discourse had occurred, and in no region was the vocabulary of emotion employed more universally than in the South. Southern political speech was consciously or unconsciously modeled on revival preaching: for most southerners, that was the only language of persuasion they knew, and they used it and expected others to do so as well. The southern political stump speech was a close cousin of the revival sermon, and when southerners thereafter sought to persuade their listeners, they used a sermonic style. The great Populist outdoor meetings of the late nineteenth century had the overtones of a political camp meeting, and when anti-hookworm campaigners in the early twentieth century cautioned against going barefooted in barnyards, they talked about parasites as if they were sin and tried to convert farm parents into shoeing their children.[37] Southern oratory today, whether it is delivered by Andrew Young of Atlanta, a black, or former Speaker of the House Jim Wright of Fort Worth, a white, often has the cadence, the form, the texture, of a revival sermon. No early revival preacher would have imagined such a secular influence from his heartfelt delivery of what he called God's holy message.

Southern religious spokesmen had from the 1790s a fatalistic bent, a tendency to explain the vicissitudes of life as the intent of Providence.[38] Indeed, this trait has made itself felt in a wide range of cultural responses, from the southern proclivity to avoid litigation[39] to a disinclination to accept the idea of medical malpractice—one's fate was ultimately in the hands of God, not a medical practitioner.[40] Southerners have been noted to have a disproportionately high death rate from tornadoes, because, the meteorologists and psychologists conjecture, southerners' religious fatalism leads them to disdain building storm cellars.[41] Surely, then, there can be no understanding of southern history unless the dimension of religion is included, for the South has been a region that, in Flannery O'Connor's words, has been haunted by God.

## NOTES

1. Wesley M. Gewehr, *The Great Awakening in Virginia, 1740–1790* (Durham, N.C.: Duke University Press, 1930), 40–67.

2. Alan Gallay, "The Origins of Slaveholders' Paternalism: George Whitefield, the Bryan Family, and the Great Awakening in the South," *Journal of Southern History* 53 (Aug. 1987): 369–94.

3. John B. Boles, "Evangelical Protestantism in the Old South: From Religious Dissent to Cultural Dominance," in *Religion in the South*, ed. Charles R. Wilson (Jackson: University Press of Mississippi, 1985), 14–21.

4. Jon Butler, "Enthusiasm Described and Decried: The Great Awakening as Interpretative Fiction," *Journal of American History* 69 (Sept. 1979): 305–25, cautions against too expansive interpretations of the North's Great Awakening.

5. My discussion of the Great Revival is based primarily on John B. Boles, *The Great Revival, 1787–1805: The Origins of the Southern Evangelical Mind* (Lexington: University Press of Kentucky, 1972), and Dickson D. Bruce, Jr., *And They All Sang Hallelujah: Plain-Folk Camp-Meeting Religion, 1800–1845* (Knoxville: University of Tennessee Press, 1974).

6. William L. Lumpkin, *Baptist Foundations in the South: Tracing through the Separates the Influence of the Great Awakening, 1754–1789* (Nashville, Tenn.: Broadman Press, 1961), and C. C. Goen, *Revivalism and Separatism in New England, 1740–1800* (New Haven: Yale University Press, 1962).

7. The best discussion of the evangelical revolt is in Rhys Isaac, *The Transformation of Virginia, 1740–1790* (Chapel Hill: University of North Carolina Press, 1982), chapters 8, 11, and 13.

8. Ibid., and Donald G. Mathews, *Religion in the Old South* (Chicago: University of Chicago Press, 1977), chapter 1, especially 26–28.

9. Boles, *Great Revival*, 131–34, emphasizes the centrality of the conversion experience. See also Susan Juster, "In a Different Voice: Male and Female Narratives of Religious Conversion in Post-Revolutionary America," *American Quarterly* 41 (Mar. 1989): 34–62. Her evidence, despite the article's misleading title, is drawn entirely from New England, but her rich analysis can be provocatively extended to the South.

10. Boles, *Great Revival*, chapters 11 and 12, and John W. Kuykendall, *Southern Enterprise: The Work of National Evangelical Societies in the Antebellum South* (Westport, Conn.: Greenwood Press, 1982), 159–70.

11. Mathews, *Religion in the Old South*, 39–80.

12. Charles A. Johnson, *The Frontier Camp Meeting: Religion's Harvest Time* (Dallas: Southern Methodist University Press, 1955); and John B. Boles,

*Religion in Antebellum Kentucky* (Lexington: University Press of Kentucky, 1976), 127–30.

13. David Edwin Harrell, Jr., "The South: Seedbed of Sectarianism," in Harrell, ed., *Varieties of Southern Evangelicalism* (Macon, Ga.: Mercer University Press, 1981), 45–58.

14. See, for example, Elmer T. Clark et al., ed., *The Journal and Letters of Francis Asbury*, vol. 2 (Nashville, Tenn.: Abingdon Press, 1958), 591 [5 Feb. 1809].

15. Boles, *Religion in Antebellum Kentucky*, chapter 6.

16. See "Introduction" to John B. Boles, ed., *Masters and Slaves in the House of the Lord: Race and Religion in the American South* (Lexington: University Press of Kentucky, 1988), 1–18.

17. John C. Van Horne, ed., *Religious Philanthropy and Colonial Slavery: The American Correspondence of the Associates of Dr. Bray, 1771–1777* (Urbana: University of Illinois Press, 1985), 99–100, 129, 219, and passim.

18. Larry M. James, "Biracial Fellowship in Antebellum Baptist Churches," in *Masters and Slaves*, ed. Boles, 37–57.

19. Quoted in Jack P. Maddex, Jr., "A Paradox of Christian Amelioration: Proslavery Ideology and Church Ministries to Slaves," in *The Southern Enigma: Essays on Race, Class and Folk Culture*, ed. Walter J. Fraser, Jr., and Winfred B. Moore, Jr. (Westport, Conn.: Greenwood Press, 1983), 107.

20. Willie Lee Rose, "The Domestication of Domestic Slavery," in *Slavery and Freedom*, ed. William W. Freehling (Oxford: Oxford University Press, 1982), 18–36.

21. See Randy J. Sparks, "A Mingled Yarn: Race and Religion in Mississippi, 1800–1861" (Ph.D. diss., Rice University, 1988).

22. See Elizabeth Hayes Turner, "Equality in Christ: A Social History of the First Baptist Church of Galveston, 1840–1861" (unpublished paper, Rice University, Sept. 1984).

23. The literature on republican ideology is enormous and growing like kudzu. For a good early survey of its importance see Robert E. Shalhope, "Toward a Republican Synthesis: The Emergence of an Understanding of Republicanism in American Historiography," *William and Mary Quarterly*, 3d ser., 29 (Jan. 1972): 49–80.

24. Susan Dabney Smedes, *Memorials of a Southern Planter*, ed. Fletcher M. Green (Jackson: University Press of Mississippi, 1981), 53.

25. Sidney E. Mead, "The Rise of the Evangelical Conception of the Ministry in America: 1607–1850," in *The Ministry in Historical Perspectives*, ed. H. Richard Niebuhr and Daniel D. Williams (New York: Harper & Bros., 1956), 212–18; and Winthrop S. Hudson, *The Great Tradition of the American Churches* (New York: Harper & Row, 1953).

26. See Kenneth More Startup, "Strangers in the Land: The Southern Clergy and the Economic Mind of the Old South" (Ph.D. diss., Louisiana State University, 1983).

27. Jane Turner Censer, *North Carolina Planters and Their Children* (Baton Rouge: Louisiana State University Press, 1984), chapter 6.

28. Quoted in James Oakes, *The Ruling Race: A History of American Slaveholders* (New York: Alfred A. Knopf, 1982), 103-4.

29. Ibid., 96-122.

30. Jan Lewis, *The Pursuit of Happiness: Family and Values in Jefferson's Virginia* (Cambridge: Cambridge University Press, 1983), 40-68.

31. Drew Gilpin Faust, "Christian Soldiers: The Meaning of Revivalism in the Confederate Army," *Journal of Southern History* 53 (Feb. 1987): 77, 78.

32. Suzanne Lebsock, *The Free Women of Petersburg: Status and Culture in a Southern Town, 1784-1860* (New York: W. W. Norton, 1984), 214-18; Elizabeth Fox-Genovese, *Within the Plantation Household: Black and White Women of the Old South* (Chapel Hill: University of North Carolina Press, 1988), 43-45, 250-52; Jean E. Friedman, *The Enclosed Garden: Women and Community in the Evangelical South, 1830-1900* (Chapel Hill: University of North Carolina Press, 1985).

33. See William G. McLoughlin, "Evangelical Child-Rearing in the Age of Jackson: Francis Wayland's View of When and How to Subdue the Willfulness of Children," *Journal of Social History* 9 (Fall 1975): 21-34; John B. Boles, "John Hersey: Dissenting Theologian of Abolitionism, Perfectionism, and Millennialism," *Methodist History* 14 (July 1976): 226-30; and Jay Fliegelman, *Prodigals and Pilgrims: The American Revolution against Patriarchal Authority, 1750-1800* (Cambridge: Cambridge University Press, 1982).

34. Censer, *North Carolina Planters*, chapter 4.

35. Isaac, *Transformation of Virginia*, 267-69.

36. Bernard Mayo, *Myths and Men: Patrick Henry, George Washington, Thomas Jefferson* (Athens: University of Georgia Press, 1959), 9.

37. Robert C. McMath, Jr., *Populist Vanguard: A History of the Southern Farmers' Alliance* (New York: W. W. Norton, 1977), 75-76; John Ettling, *The Germ of Laziness: Rockefeller Philanthropy and Public Health in the New South* (Cambridge: Harvard University Press, 1981), 162-64. Southern demagogues like Theodore G. Bilbo also made effective use of revivalistic oratorical technique. See Jerry A. Hendrix, "Theodore G. Bilbo: Evangelist of Racial Purity," in *The Oratory of Southern Demagogues*, ed. Cal M. Logue and Howard Dorgan (Baton Rogue: Louisiana State University Press, 1981), 156-57. For a moving analysis of the role of revivals in the popular culture of the South into the early twentieth century, see Lillian Smith, *Killers of the Dream* (New York: Anchor Books, 1963), 83-96. Educators in Louisiana used evangelistic techniques to garner support for public school reform in the early nineteenth century. See Clarence L. Mohr, "Public Schooling, Modernization, and Collective Identity: The Dilemmas of Educational Reform in Progressive Era Louisiana," paper presented at the Southern Historical Association annual meeting, Lexington, Kentucky, 10 November 1989.

38. See Boles, *Great Revival*, 25-35.

39. Carol J. Greenhouse, "Interpreting American Litigiousness," paper delivered at the Wenner-Gren Foundation for Anthropological Research sym-

posium, "Ethnohistorical Models for the Evolution of Law in Specific Societies," Bellagio, Italy, 10–18 August 1985, 12–27. For a perceptive analysis of southern religion and conflict resolution, see Greenhouse, *Praying for Justice: Faith, Order and Community in an American Town* (Ithaca: Cornell University Press, 1986).

40. Kenneth Allen De Ville, *Medical Malpractice in Nineteenth-Century America: Origins and Legacy* (New York: New York University Press, 1990), 131–36, especially 134–35.

41. Charles P. Roland, "The Ever-Vanishing South," *Journal of Southern History* 48 (Feb. 1982): 9.

# 5

# The Second Great Awakening in Comparative Perspective: Revivals and Culture in the United States and Britain

RICHARD CARWARDINE

IN THE EARLY DECADES of the nineteenth century, successive tremors of religious revival rearranged the contours of the social and ecclesiastical landscape of the United States. Evangelical Protestant churches, on the defensive against Deism and rational religion through the Revolutionary era, recovered their confidence during what is known as the Second Great Awakening and established themselves as the primary religious force in the country. During the urgent later stages of the Awakening, in the 1830s and 1840s, hundreds of thousands of new converts became full members of Protestant churches, many of them convinced that the Kingdom of God was at hand. By mid-century evangelical Protestantism was the principal subculture in American society. Although the decade of the 1840s marks something of a fault line, the awakening's influence persisted in a variety of ways, including the renewed outcropping of revivals in 1857–58.[1]

The historiography of the Awakening, with varying emphases, has tended to explain it as a response to changes in the wider culture and also to a new momentum within the churches themselves.[2] The general story line traces the movement of evangelicalism from political empowerment to economic progress to cultural integration. In the first place, this burgeoning, self-confident evangelicalism can be seen as only one expression of profound social changes that occurred between the Revolution and the Jacksonian period. The accelerating development of a national market economy and the geographical mobility of a rapidly growing population, both aided by a revolution in transportation networks and technology, inevitably eroded traditional social relationships. Families broke up, servants ceased to live in the households of their masters, systems of patronage were eroded, and established routes of social progress were closed as new ones opened up. A Revolutionary spirit of egalitarianism challenged—if it did not exactly remove—old social distinctions, eroded eighteenth-century patterns of deference, and fashioned new democratic and republican codes of manners and behavior. New certainties, new communities, new social networks, and new patterns of living were needed in this world of flux and disintegration. For thousands of Americans evangelical religion provided the answer.

That religion was itself changing. Unable to depend on formal state support in the fashioning of a Christian society, enterprising evangelicals turned with formidable energy to the tasks of church-building and soul-saving, reshaping their theology and methods in the process. Influenced by the extraordinary success of a precocious Methodism, many in the older Protestant denominations sought to enhance their popular appeal by neutralizing "the repulsive force of the Calvinist doctrines of election and reprobation," the symbols— in this culture—of an elitist, aristocratic society, and shifted toward a democratic Arminianism that for many presented a "system that seemed to harmonize with itself, with the Scriptures, with common sense, and with experience."[3] "New measure" revivalists emphasized the sinner's free will and ability actively to seek his or her own salvation, and sought to introduce God's kingdom through the systematic application of the laws of religious psychology.

Until very recently, American historians have remained remarkably unimpressed by what was in fact one of the most profound popular movements in the whole of their country's history, and their neglect undoubtedly deserves an essay in itself. For, as Gordon Wood has remarked, the power and range of the Awakening deserves comparison with the religious upheavals of seventeenth-century England and even with the European Reformation itself.[4] Our understanding of the Awakening derives largely from a variety of local and regional studies, geographically ranging from John B. Boles's treatment of its southwestern frontier phase, to the studies by Whitney Cross, Paul Johnson, and Mary Ryan of its manifestations in upstate New York communities at a more mature stage of economic development; from Randolph A. Roth's and Richard Shiels's analyses of established historic communities in New England to Terry Bilhartz's study of urban revivals in early nineteenth-century Baltimore.[5] In their focus on the local and the particular, the most recent historians of the Awakening have typified much of the best of "new social history," with its painstaking reconstruction of community and social context, and conviction that broad generalizations are best challenged and constructed at the local or regional level. This "rush to the localities,"[6] as it has been described in another context, would seem to be vindicated by the fact that there was not one experience of revival, but several; the revivalism of Cane Ridge was not that of Finney's Rochester, and both could claim only a distant relationship to the institutionalized camp meetings of the Old South of the 1850s or to the prayer-meeting revivals of 1857–58.

Local studies, however, through the very closeness of their focus, tend to the celebration of characteristics that are particular and unique to the immediate culture; but the Awakening in its origins and cultural ramifications extended beyond the confines of America. For it is clear from British experience in the early decades of the nineteenth century that the United States was not alone in experiencing a "reformation" in popular religion. Extraordinary as this rolling wave of American revivals was, we necessarily limit our understanding of the phenomenon unless we set it in a much wider cultural context.

Britain, too, had its own Second Great Awakening in the later years of the eighteenth century and the first few decades of the next. Contemporaries did not call it by that name, and neither have later historians, yet these years saw an extraordinary flowering of evangelical religion, most especially in parts of the Celtic fringe and of the industrializing areas of England. Thanks to the labors of Robert Currie, Alan Gilbert, and Lee Horsley we have a good idea of the statistical dimensions of this Awakening. Methodism, in its various manifestations, enjoyed a sustained and rapid expansion at a rate much greater than that of the adult population as a whole up to the late 1830s; in 1840 "the relative strength of Methodism within English society was greater than at any period before or since." At the same time those traditional dissenting denominaions that had been energized by Methodist example, especially Baptists and Congregationalists, enjoyed a similar buoyancy if not quite such spectacular expansion.[7] In conjunction with the consolidation of an evangelical party in the established church, these developments provide the context in which to understand the emerging sensibilities commonly associated with Victorian Britain.

Both the exogenous and endogenous factors in this remarkable British awakening evince substantial points of similarity with the experience of North America. In the first place, it is evident that industrialization, more advanced of course than in the United States, set in train social and economic changes very similar in their impact on the lives of ordinary men and women to those occasioned by the market revolution in American society. The demand for industrial labor operated, in conjunction with periods of agricultural depression, to pull people from rural society and smaller centers of population into rapidly growing towns and cities. Suffering from social disorientation and rootlessness, many—though by no means all—struggling miners, colliers, laborers, and artisans found in the warmth and community of enthusiastic religion a source of comfort and self-respect.[8] Not all particulars of the pattern of British evangelical growth match the American. Currie and his co-laborers argue that economic depression limited, and political excitement stimulated, the growth of the most revivalist of denominations, the Methodists. If true, this was quite the reverse of the experience of American evangelical groups in the new republic, whose vexed ministers in flush times resorted to jeremiads about the enervating effects of prosperity and luxury, and who regarded most political excitement, especially that surrounding elections, as a spiritual bromide; the coincidence of high points of church growth with the economic downturns after 1819, 1837, and 1857 could not be clearer.[9] In the main, however, it is not these incongruities that should register, but the broad similarities in the external pressures on British and American evangelicals as they tried to come to terms with a new social and economic order.

Similarities in transatlantic experience were equally apparent in the developments within evangelical churches as they sought to respond effectively to external change. The significant shifts in the thinking and practice of American churches, to meet the human needs and deprivations resulting from wider cultural change, were paralleled in Britain as evangelicals Arminianized their theology and devised agencies of evangelism that acknowledged more overtly the role of human instrumentality. As in America, it was Methodism that did so much to undermine established Calvinist thinking on election and the Atonement of Christ, to "democratize" evangelical theology, to throw up both new forms of evangelistic activity and a church organization that blended discipline, urgency, local participation and central direction, and to promote a new approach to religious revival.[10]

The complementary character of the evangelical upsurge on both sides of the Atlantic was at its most evident in reciprocated contributions, as British evangelical emigrants found a welcome in American churches and, more memorably, as exponents of American revivalism sought to evangelize the Old World. Lorenzo Dow was an undoubted eccentric, but by no means so peculiar that his visionary zeal could not generate a powerful sympathy among rural Methodists in Ireland, or the indigenous revivalists of Lancashire, Cheshire, and the Potteries. Calvin Colton, through his *History and Character of American Revivals* (1832), Nathan Beman, William Patton, and Edward N. Kirk all helped popularize protracted meetings and itinerant evangelism in the late 1830s and early 1840s, a time of accelerating revivalism on both sides of the Atlantic. No one did more to advance the "new measures" revivalism among Calvinist evangelicals, especially in Wales and Scotland, than Charles Finney himself; his ubiqitous *Lectures on Revivals of Religion* ensured that the revival of 1839–43 in Wales, for instance, would be known popularly as "Finney's Revival." As harvesters of converts in special meetings, however, none enjoyed the formidable success of James Caughey, a Methodist itinerant of little status among historians, but known within the overlapping subcultures of mid-Victorian British dissent as "the king of the revivalist preachers." In this context of transatlantic awareness, it came as little surprise to contemporaries that the revival of 1857–58 in the United States should soon be followed by spectacular revivals in Ulster, Wales, and many parts of Britain.[11]

We should not, of course, attempt blandly to homogenize the experiences of two countries possessing marked cultural dissimilarities as well as congruities. Neither should we seek to avoid the complexities of classification raised by the all-purpose term "revival," which clearly encompassed a number of meanings from one chronological and cultural context to another, ranging from expansive outreach to ritualistic reaffirmation of community values.[12] Nor is it accurate to imply that religious revivals and the subsequent "ism" held as central a place in British society as they did in the United States.[13] Finney's experience indicated that by no means were all evangelical nonconformists receptive to his revivalism; his first visit to England was hindered by the reluctance of many nonconformist ministers to open their pulpits, and for most of his later visit during the revival of 1859–60 his work was peripheral and largely anticlimactic. American Congregationalists and Presbyterians were much readier than their English namesakes to embrace revivals; their gathered churches had generally welcomed and legitimized the "outpourings of the Spirit of God" of the eighteenth-century Awakening. Periodic regeneratory revivals became ingrained in the thinking and practice of the major American Calvinist denominations in a way that was never true of their English namesakes, who quite simply lacked the experience of revivals. As Chauncey Goodrich remarked, "If I were asked why revivals are so frequent in America, and so rare in Europe, my first answer would be, that Christians on one side of the Atlantic expect them, and on the other side they do not expect them."[14]

This contrast was even more significant in the case of the Methodist churches. American Methodism had been at the cutting edge of the Second Great Awakening; such too was its role in Britain. But the commitment of the Wesleyan connection as a whole to revivalism was uncertain at best, and in Buntingite quarters downright hostile. The connectional fissiparousness of revivals, their association in the minds of many with "enthusiastic" disorder, and doubts over the spiritual changes they evoked, made many exceedingly nervous. Wilbur Fisk was not impressed to be asked by a Wesleyan preacher "whether I thought *revivals* were, on the whole advantageous to the church"; he reflected that "what we in America term revivals are comparatively rare" in Britain.[15]

External pressures also kept revivalism at bay, particularly those deriving from the Anglican establishment and its cultural diaspora. When the United States was faced by the challenge of the new revivalism in the early nineteenth century there were no institutions of sufficient ecclesiastical and social authority to repel it; Old School Presbyterians protested, Congregationalists checked the entry of Methodists into New England, but the structure of church authority was too loose and the power of the once-established churches too limited for the new revivalists to be restrained for long. In Britain, by contrast, the Church of England seemed to American and British advocates of aggressive evangelism to be "an incubus resting on the nation to a great extent, so far as revivals and piety are concerned."[16] Calvin Colton was appalled at how Anglican wealth, social status, and patronage, together with its guarantee of state support, dissipated its drive to save souls. The doctrine of conversion had only limited currency in Anglican circles; as the national church, membership was open to all people as a right. But the Anglican liturgy crushed the free spirit of evangelical worship; the Anglican church lacked the sectarian exclusiveness and sense of separation from the world characteristic of the most urgently revivalist churches of the period.

Moreover, the Anglican church was not just one church among others, but the church of the socially powerful, the nobility and gentry, those who shared and helped shape the church's distaste for revivalist excess. The united front of anti-evangelical clergy and the socially influential in some instances had the power to limit evangelical advance. When, for example, nonconformists began to intensify their home missionary efforts, high church clergy and the local gentry threatened to withhold poor relief from those who attended the ministry of itinerating evangelists or to expel them from church schools or tenancies. Just as significant as formal obstruction was the general climate of hostility created by men of "property and rank and influence" in a society marked by the downward percolation of ideas of correct behavior and by an eductaional system dominated by Anglican universities and church schools.

In contrast, America presented a much less deferential social order, while its educational institutions were commonly sustained by evangelical denominations for whom college revivals were a matter of custom and celebration. It is hardly surprising then that the expansion of revivalistic sects tended to occur where the parish system of the established church was failing to meet the needs of remote older settlements and untended new ones.[17] Significantly, in Wales, where the parochial system was most inflexible, where there was a rooted tradition of expansive Calvinism and dissenting itinerancy, clusters of revivals on the American model became a feature of nineteenth-century popular religious life.[18]

Historians of the American Awakening, aware that revivals have to be considered a part of a larger cultural process, have pursued a number of related themes. Did the revivals represent a challenge to the social order, or were they principally instruments of social control? Were they a force for cohesion in political culture, or for divisiveness and instability? Were they an irrational, emotional "enthusiasm" representing resistance to progress and a new capitalist order, or were they one of the means by which American modernity was achieved? It seems reasonable enough that those who have posed the questions should have looked within America itself for the answers. But given that Britain and America shared a common experience of awakening and even certain similarities in the roots of their revivals, we may possibly find in the British Awakening an additional perspective on these questions.

Mercifully, historians of the Second Great Awakening in America have on the whole moved away from the constricting approach that saw the movement essentially as a means by which a historic elite sought to maintain social and political control in a rapidly changing world. It might seem to Paul Johnson that the primary key to understanding the Rochester revival of 1830 was that its leaders were engaged in an effort to sustain their authority in a more market-oriented and democratic society. But it is not just the flowering of studies in black religion in the antebellum period that has encouraged us to view the Awakening as a movement of self-assertion by those men and women, black and white, who lacked social standing and political authority. Gordon Wood, in an interpretation that complements Donald Mathews's analysis of southern religion, approaches surging evangelicalism as an early nineteenth-century counterculture through which ordinary farmers, artisans, laborers, and their families expressed their independence of the world of the gentry and the well-to-do commercial and professional classes.[19] We can recognize that social conservatives in church and state tried to turn revivals into instruments of control, but to see the Awakening as in some sense their creation misconceives both its mainspring and its function as a challenge to the status quo.

Interestingly, much the same interpretative thrust marks recent writing on the popular religious movement in Britain. Few would now choose to cast their lot with E. P. Thompson, at least to the extent of his conclusion that Methodist revivals acted as a means of dampening the aspirations of thwarted radicals, that revivalism was a diversion from the political struggle of class against class into a "chiliasm of despair."[20] Thanks to the scholarship of W. R. Ward, we are in a much better position to recognize the significance of popular revivalism, and to see it as a dimension—not a suppression—of political radicalism.[21] As in the United States, Methodism's democratic, egalitarian theology elicited a powerful response from socially marginal groups. From the 1790s to 1820s and beyond, the ecclesiastical and secular authorities, only too well aware of events in France, regarded revivalistic religion—whether expressed through Wesleyanism, schismatic Methodism, or through the village evangelism of older Dissent[22]—certainly with suspicion, and often with terror. The established church, threatened through the phenomenal expansion of nonconformity with minority status and disestablishment, saw not just the excesses of religious enthusiasm but a dynamic challenge to its ecclesiastical control. This was certainly how Welsh revivalism should be interpreted, though in that case there was the added ingredient of fermenting nationalism. Thomas Laquer's study of the early Sunday school movement, closely related to popular revivalism, makes a similar thrust against Thompson and in favor of the liberating motives and function underpinning popular evangelicalism. David Hempton's fine study of Methodism and politics serves to confirm the verdict. More recently still, Deborah Valenze's imaginative investigation of popular evangelicalism in pre-industrial England has skillfully recreated the world of cottage religion, in which autonomous men and women, including women preachers, resisted the controls of the new entrepreneurial order.[23]

The challenge to the status quo on both sides of the Atlantic, however, remained within limits. In the first place, much of the revivalism of the early stages of the Awakening seems to have been unsympathetic to *direct* political action. The pietism of the revival preachers and those to whom they ministered, as John Walsh suggests, acted to insulate them against French revolutionary doctrine. Baptist and Methodist revivalists in particular, in Britain and America in the early decades of the century, commonly called on their hearers to abjure the excitement of politics and concentrate on their own election, not that of political candidates; when they did offer political judgments their verdicts were often jejune. Though it is clear that the respective political cultures of both countries were powerfully shaped by the revivalist evangelicalism of the Awakening and its legacies (contributing issue and style, and shaping constituencies), in neither case did the surge of revivals take on a single political expression.[24]

Second, whatever the challenge to the status quo, few historians of the British Awakening have argued that revivals aggravated conflict between classes and sexes; the explicit equality of individuals, the melting of differences of age, gender, social station, or even race at the altar or anxious seat may have implicitly questioned social arrangements beyond the house, chapel, and campground; but in practice the revivalist's calling believers into a community of saints was more likely to soften social conflict. In his study of South Lindsey, James Obelkevich concludes: "Farmers and laborers met on equal terms in [Methodist] class meetings and farmers listened to sermons preached by laborers and craftsmen; all of which implied a suspension of class divisions deepening in the wider society." Linking his own work to that of Obelkevich and Robert Moore, David Hempton argues that revival-minded Methodists did not throw up class-warriors as such; stressing that "Methodism both fostered radicalism and opposed it," he finds the roots of the paradox "in the religious mind itself, with its acceptance of authority on the one hand, and its desire to have justice and fair play on the other."[25]

Third, whatever the origins of the Awakenings may suggest about an implicit challenge to the new economic order, the fact is that over time evangelicals were able to integrate themselves comfortably into the new entrepreneurial world, sharing in its philosophy and values. In the United States, by the later years of the Awakening the new revivalism was no longer a movement of the fringes, and had itself become influential, respectable, and middle-class. Nathan Hatch sees in revival theology and the practice of ordinary Methodists and Baptists a religious counterpart to contemporary doctrines of economic laissez-faire and individual self-help. In the blend of temperance and revivalism in antebellum America, Ian Tyrrell discerns both millennialist aspiration and, at a more material level, an avenue for the upwardly mobile, independent-minded artisan. A similar tale of "embourgeoisement" and enterprise marks early and mid-Victorian nonconformity in Britain.[26]

Certainly, revivalistic religion pulled in two directions. Some of the disruptive legacies of the early years of the Awakening remained: revivals could undermine orderly working practices, through the exhaustion of mind and spirit that resulted from high emotion, the multiplication of meetings, and long hours. In Scotland the Kilsyth revival of 1839 seemed to lurch out of control as meetings were held at all hours in church, churchyard, loom shops, factories, and market square. Over time, however, revival meetings were held in the evening and over holidays to mitigate the worst effects of the disruption.[27] More fundamentally, Obelkevich sees Methodism promoting "modern attitudes to life and work" in its emphasis on sobriety, organization, and self-worth. "Methodism acknowledged the infinite worth of the laborer's soul and his practical worth as an active member of his society." He also argues that the voluntaryism of revivalist Methodists fostered "a new outlook, individual as well as collective, towards money" and helped develop their business skills. Just as they did across the Atlantic, revivals and temperance went increasingly hand in hand in Britain (despite the resistance of Wesleyan brewers and innkeepers), suggesting the grip of an ethic of self-help and economic self-improvement.[28]

Revivalism in Britain, then, may have contributed to the emergence of a recognizably modern nineteenth-century economic order. To that extent it has much in common with the progressive, rational evangelicalism that Daniel Howe has persuaded us to contemplate in mid-nineteenth-century America. We may be encouraged to reject the idea of religious enthusiasm as primarily an irrational "movement of counter-enlightenment"[29] and to see the "progressive" elements in revivalism's impact on culture outweighing the regressive. In both societies revivals were often the catalysts of progressive humanitarian and moral reform, drawing on and reinforcing established strains of millennial and perfectionist thought; increasingly, as David Bebbington has noted, evangelicals came to look on the state as an agency by which socially and morally desirable ends might be accomplished. If there was an exception to this predicating of a "modernizing" and "progressive" transatlantic revivalist community, it was to be found within the antimission churches of the western and southern states; and in the defensive resistance of mainstream southern evangelicals to some (though by no means all) calls to use the state for reforming purposes. Certainly it was against the perceived archaism of southern culture, sustained by southern churches (and of course against the essentially "medieval" culture of Roman Catholic societies), that northern and British evangelicals both calibrated and celebrated their own social advance.[30]

These reflections prompt us to consider the role of revivals in creating and sustaining a sense of community, both locally and more widely. For although the conversions that were the primary end of revivals can be seen as the ultimate expression of Protestant individualism (indeed the transatlantic awakenings were but a part of a general burgeoning individualism in both cultures), the revivals themselves were only possible because geographically and psychologically displaced men and women corporately yearned for a shelter in which to "belong," or because, having created such a community, they sought to sustain, reinvigorate, and purify it. The revivals of the early phases of the awakenings in the 1790s and 1800s clearly fulfilled the former role; the camp meetings of the southwestern frontier and the protracted Methodist meetings in growing towns and cities created new social networks in a hostile world. Later on, at mid-century, the urban revivalism surrounding the Young Men's Christian Association may have worked in the same way for rural migrants to the cities. But by that date the adding of the "ism" to revival often meant less the overturning of an established hostile culture (though this was how the revivalists liked to perceive themselves) than the rededicating of essentially sympathetic communities that enjoyed an appetite for the nourishment of evangelical preaching and were attuned theologically to the importance of periodical "refreshing." This is what lay behind the convening of protracted meetings, the late-summer camp meeting in the South, or the "sasiwn," the annual outdoor association meeting in rural Wales, where thousands would turn out at the prospect of hearing one or more of the great folk heroes of Welsh society, the itinerant preachers.[31] On these occasions, the community could share in pleasurable society, engage in social diversion and display, and celebrate and reassert its basic values and beliefs on an occasion whose centerpiece was the preaching of a gospel of repentance.

Thanks to connectionalism, churches that were born of revival and those that were reinvigorated by revival were pulled together into a larger community: through the itinerating ministry, the synodical, associational, or conference structure of denominations, and the power of the religious press, the experiences of revival became events of regional and even national significance. British religious converts could regard themselves as part of a ramifying network of revival churches; by such means were localisms broken down and larger communities established. Obelkevich suggests that Methodism "tended to parochialize villagers . . . every Wesleyan was brought in contact with local preachers from other villages, and from the towns, and with the succession of itinerant ministers. The system promoted circuit mindedness, and beyond that, connection-mindedness."[32] The effect was not limited to connectional churches but extended to those enjoying congregational autonomy and a stationed permanent pastorate; here too the experience of revival could and did act as a bonding agent.[33] A corresponding thrust toward national integration is evident in the United States. The role of revivals and itinerancy in giving birth to a continental vision during the eighteenth-century colonial Awakening was as nothing compared to the capacity for national integration that Donald Mathews plausibly argues was a feature of the Second Great Awakening.[34]

No discussion of the common elements of British and American experience should properly conclude, however, without pointing to legacies that were starkly conflicting. In Britain, the religious revivalism that reinforced the bonds of congregation and class meeting, and worked outward to cement larger communities, operated to mitigate intensities of social class, helping to neutralize one of the most potentially disruptive of social and political forces in an industrializing society, and contributed "cross-pressures" that helped sustain Brian Harrison's "Peaceable Kingdom."[35] Moreover, the converts of revivals, when they were able to vote, were drawn not only into the Whig/Liberal party that enjoyed a natural link with evangelical dissent, but also into "Protestant," anti-Catholic Toryism. Revivalsharpened anti-popery, particularly among Wesleyans, helped set up political cross-pressures that ensured that revival culture did not mesh straightforwardly with a single political party culture.[36] Revivals came closest to acting as a centrifugal force where the cultural and political cohesiveness they helped create locally or regionally was not fully offset by balancing cross-pressures in the wider culture. Most obviously this was the situation in Wales, where revivals worked against a wider integration into British culture and helped cement the potent amalgam of dissent, economic disability, and incipient nationalism in the principality itself.

One may then assert that, given Britain's social configurations, revivals there made for some degree of cultural integration, but it is less plausible to argue that they acted similarly to sustain national consensus in the United States. American revivals in the early decades of the century certainly confirmed a sense of national mission; surely, it seemed, they represented divine approval of the Union and the country's republican arrangements. But after the major denominational schisms of the 1830s and 1840s (themselves both symptom and cause of mounting sectional polarization), revivals as affirmations of the community's basic values worked not toward national harmony but toward convincing each section that God was blessing its distinctive social arrangements. The experience of Methodist and Baptist revivals in the South in the later 1840s and 1850s suggested that the Almighty was smiling on the ecclesiastical and social arrangements of the slave states; a sense of a unique southern destiny paraded hand in hand with an emerging pro-slavery millennialism.[37] And what northerner could doubt the significance of the unequal showering of grace on their churches in 1857 and 1858? The Republican party, as had its forerunner the Freesoilers, drank deeply at the well of evangelical revivalism; indeed, the triumph of the Republicans in 1860 has to be traced back, at one level, to the processes set in train by the Second Great Awakening.

The ensuing violent conflict, as we know only too well, was sustained on both sides by a moral intensity that owed much to a prior—and continuing[38]—millennialist revivalism. British Victorian society did not lack moral crusades sustained by revivalistic fervor, whether against drink, slavery, corn laws, Catholics, or Bulgarian atrocities.[39] But Britain's Peaceable Kingdom mercifully experienced nothing to match America's Holy War.

## NOTES

1. For the context of the Second Great Awakening, see in particular two works by William G. McLoughlin, Jr.: *Modern Revivalism: Charles Grandison Finney to Billy Graham* (New York: Ronald Press, 1959) and *Revivals, Awakenings, and Reform: An Essay on Religion and Social Change in America, 1607–1977* (Chicago: University of Chicago Press, 1978), 98–140. An

outline of the particular pulses of revival, based primarily on Methodist membership returns, is found in Richard Carwardine, *Transatlantic Revivalism: Popular Evangelicalism in Britain and America, 1790–1865* (Westport, Conn.: Greenwood Press, 1978), 45–56, 159–62. Timothy L. Smith, *Revivalism and Social Reform: American Protestantism on the Eve of the Civil War* (Baltimore: Johns Hopkins University Press, rev. ed. 1980) describes and interprets the "awakening" of 1857–58.

2. For a helpful discussion of the relationship between exogenous and endogenous factors in the process of church growth, see Robert Currie, Alan Gilbert, and Lee Horsley, *Churches and Churchgoers: Patterns of Church Growth in the British Isles since 1700* (Oxford: Clarendon Press, 1977), 5–9 and passim.

3. Carwardine, *Transatlantic Revivalism*, 10.

4. Gordon S. Wood, "Evangelical America and Early Mormonism," *New York History* 61 (Oct. 1980): 372.

5. John B. Boles, *The Great Revival, 1787–1805: The Origins of the Southern Evangelical Mind* (Lexington: University Press of Kentucky, 1972); Whitney R. Cross, *The Burned-Over District: The Social and Intellectual History of Enthusiastic Religion in Western New York* (Ithaca: Cornell University Press, 1950); Paul E. Johnson, *A Shopkeeper's Millennium: Society and Revivals in Rochester, New York, 1790–1865* (New York: Hill and Wang, 1978); Mary P. Ryan, *Cradle of the Middle Class: The Family in Oneida County, New York, 1790–1865* (Cambridge: Harvard University Press, 1981); Randolph A. Roth, *The Democratic Dilemma: Religion, Reform, and the Social Order in the Connecticut River Valley of Vermont, 1791–1850* (Cambridge: Cambridge University Press, 1987); Richard Shiels, "The Scope of the Second Great Awakening: Andover, Massachusetts, as a Case Study," *Journal of the Early Republic* 5 (Summer 1985): 223–46; Terry D. Bilhartz, *Urban Religion and the Second Great Awakening: Church and Society in Early National Baltimore* (Rutherford, N.J.: Fairleigh Dickinson University Press, 1986). See also Charles R. Keller, *The Second Great Awakening in Connecticut* (New Haven: Yale University Press, 1942); Marion L. Bell, *Crusade in the City: Revivalism in Nineteenth-Century Philadelphia* (Lewisburg, Pa.: Bucknell University Press, 1977).

6. The phrase is drawn from David Hempton, *Methodism and Politics in British Society, 1750–1850* (London: Hutchinson, 1984; rev. ed. 1987), 279. For a sensitive handling of international themes in the First Great Awakening, see Susan O'Brien, "A Transatlantic Community of Saints: The Great Awakening and the First Evangelical Network, 1735–1755," *American Historical Review* 91 (Oct. 1986): 811–32.

7. Currie, Gilbert, and Horsley, *Churches and Churchgoers*, 21–45; Alan D. Gilbert, *Religion and Society in Industrial England: Church, Chapel and Social Change* (London: Longman, 1976), 30–36.

8. E. T. Davies, *Religion in the Industrial Revolution in South Wales* (Cardiff: University of Wales Press, 1965); Currie, Gilbert, and Horsley, *Churches and Churchgoers*, 56, 90.

9. Carwardine, *Transatlantic Revivalism*, 54–56.

10. Hempton, *Methodism and Politics*, 76; Currie, Gilbert, and Horsley, *Churches and Churchgoers*, 56, 90.

11. Carwardine, *Transatlantic Revivalism*, 59–200; John Kent, *Holding the Fort: Studies in Victorian Revivalism* (London: Epworth, 1978).

12. For a suggestive typology of revivals, see Donald G. Mathews, "Religion in the Old South: Speculation on Methodology," *South Atlantic Quarterly* 73 (Winter 1974): 45–47.

13. For an elaboration of this theme, see Carwardine, *Transatlantic Revivalism*, 147–55; and George M. Marsden, *Fundamentalism and American Culture: The Shaping of Twentieth-Century Evangelicalism, 1870–1925* (New York: Oxford University Press, 1980), 221–28.

14. Robert Baird, *Religion in America; or, An Account of the Origin, Relation to the State, and Present Condition of the Evangelical Churches in the United States* (New York, 1856), 207.

15. Wilbur Fisk, *Travels in Europe; viz., in England, Scotland, France, Italy, Switzerland, Germany, and the Netherlands*, 4th ed. (New York, 1838).

16. Tobias Spicer, in *Christian Advocate and Journal* (New York), 4 November 1846.

17. Hempton, *Methodism and Politics*, 77; see also Alan D. Gilbert, *Religion and Industrial Society*, 97–110. The incidence and function of the extensive revivals in American colleges (not just seminaries) is a much neglected subject.

18. Carwardine, *Transatlantic Revivalism*, 85–89; Christopher B. Turner, "Revivalism and Welsh Society in the Nineteenth Century," in *Disciplines of Faith: Studies in Religion, Politics and Patriarchy*, ed. James Obelkevich, Lyndal Roper, and Raphael Samuel (London: Routledge and Kegan Paul, 1987), 311–23.

19. Wood, "Evangelical America and Early Mormonism," 359–86; Donald G. Mathews, *Religion in the Old South* (Chicago: University of Chicago Press, 1977).

20. E. P. Thompson, *The Making of the English Working Class* (London, 1963), 381–82; see also John Baxter, "The Great Yorkshire Revival of 1792: A Study of Mass Revival among the Methodists," in *A Sociological Year Book of Religion in Britain*, ed. M. Hill, vol. 7 (1974), 46–76.

21. W. R. Ward, *Religion and Society in England, 1790–1850* (New York: Schocken Books, 1972).

22. Deryck W. Lovegrove, *Established Church, Sectarian People: Itinerancy and the Transformation of English Dissent, 1780–1830* (Cambridge: Cambridge University Press, 1988).

23. Thomas W. Laqueur, *Religion and Respectability: Sunday Schools and Working-Class Culture, 1780–1850* (New Haven: Yale University Press, 1976); Hempton, *Methodism and Politics*; Deborah M. Valenze, *Prophetic Sons and Daughters: Female Preaching and Popular Religion in Industrial England* (Princeton: Princeton University Press, 1985). See also E. J. Hobsbawn,

*Laboring Men* (New York: Basic Books, 1964), 23–33; J. C. D. Clark, *English Society, 1688–1832: Ideology, Social Structure, and Political Practice during the Ancien Regime* (Cambridge: Cambridge University Press, 1985); Alan D. Gilbert, "Methodism, Dissent and Political Stability in Early Industrial England," *Journal of Religious History* 10 (Dec. 1979): 381–99.

24. John Walsh, "Methodism at the End of the Eighteenth Century," in *A History of the Methodist Church in Great Britain*, ed. Rupert E. Davies and Gordon Rupp, vol. 1 (London: Epworth Press, 1965), 304.

25. Hempton, *Methodism and Politics*, 215–16, drawing on the work of Robert Colls and of Robert S. Moore, *Pitmen, Preachers and Politics: The Effects of Methodism in a Durham Mining Community* (London: Cambridge University Press, 1974).

26. Ian R. Tyrrell, *Sobering Up: From Temperance to Prohibition in Antebellum America, 1800–1860* (Westport, Conn.: Greenwood Press, 1979); W. J. Rorabaugh, "The Sons of Temperance in Antebellum Jasper County," *Georgia Historical Quarterly* 64 (1980): 263–79; John Munsey Turner, "Victorian Values—Or Whatever Happened to John Wesley's Scriptural Holiness?" *Proceedings of the Wesley Historical Society* 46 (Oct. 1988): 165–84; Nathan O. Hatch, "The Democratization of Christianity and the Character of American Politics" in *Religion and Politics in America: From the Colonial Period to the 1980s*, ed. Mark A. Noll (New York: Oxford University Press, 1988), 92–120.

27. For examples, see Carwardine, *Transatlantic Revivalism*, 78.

28. Obelkevich notes the growing appeal of temperance within Lincolnshire Methodism from the 1830s to the 1870s. James Obelkevich, *Religion and Rural Society: South Lindsey, 1825–1875* (Oxford: Clarendon Press, 1976), 203–8. See also Thompson, *Making of the English Working Class*, 394; Harold Perkin, *The Origins of Modern English Society, 1780–1830* (London: Routledge and Kegan Paul, 1969), 354; Brian H. Harrison, *Drink and the Victorians: The Temperance Question in England, 1815–1872* (London: Faber and Faber, 1971); Louis Bilington, "Popular Religion and Social Reform: A Study of Revivalism and Teetotalism, 1830–1850," *Journal of Religious History* 10 (June 1979): 266–93.

29. Daniel Walker Howe, *The Political Culture of the American Whigs* (Chicago: University of Chicago Press, 1979); D. W. Howe, "Religion and Politics in the Antebellum North" in Noll, ed., *Religion and Politics*, 121–45; Hempton, *Methodism and Politics*, 26–27.

30. The "antimission" elements in evangelicalism, according to Bertram Wyatt-Brown's plausible interpretation, were from the most marginal, least modern areas of the South. Bertram Wyatt-Brown, "The Antimission Movement in the Jacksonian South: A Study in Regional Folk Culture," *Journal of Southern History* 36 (Nov. 1970): 501–29.

31. Richard Carwardine, "Finney's Revival and the Welsh Evangelical Community," *Journal of Ecclesiastical History* 29 (Oct. 1978): 463–80. For revivals and southern community building, see Orville V. Burton, *In My*

*Father's House are Many Mansions: Family and Community in Edgefield, South Carolina* (Chapel Hill: University of North Carolina Press, 1985), 22; Anne C. Loveland, *Southern Evangelicals and the Social Order, 1800–1860* (Baton Rouge: Louisiana State University Press, 1980), 65–90; Theodore Rosengarten, *Tombee: Portrait of a Cotton Planter, with the Journal of Thomas B. Chaplin (1822–1890)* (New York: William Morrow and Co., 1986), 144.

32. Obelkevich, *Religion and Rural Society*, 203. See also Alan Rogers, "When City Speaks for Country: The Emergence of the Town as a Focus for Religious Activity in the Nineteenth Century," in *Studies in Church History 16: The Church in Town and Countryside: Papers Read at the Seventeenth Summer Meeting and the Eighteenth Winter Meeting of the Ecclesiastical History Society*, ed. Derek Baker (Oxford: Basil Blackwell, 1980), 335–59; David M. Thompson, "Church Extension in Town and Countryside in Later Nineteenth-Century Leicestershire," in Baker, ed., *Studies in Church History 16*, 427–40.

33. Lovegrove, *Established Church, Sectarian People.*

34. Donald G. Mathews, "The Second Great Awakening as an Organizing Process," *American Quarterly* 21 (Spring 1969): 23–43.

35. Harrison shows that though the two worlds of pub and chapel came into conflict in Victorian England, these worlds fashioned alliances across classes and served to help the process of national integration. Brian Harrison, *Peaceable Kingdom: Stability and Change in Modern Britain* (Oxford: Clarendon Press, 1982), 4–5, 123–56. Harold Perkin, *Origins of Modern English Society*, 196–208, 347–64, discusses the role of evangelical religion in the creation of a "viable class society."

36. David W. Bebbington, *The Nonconformist Conscience: Chapel and Politics, 1870–1914* (London: George Allen and Unwin, 1982); Robert L. Kelley, *The Transatlantic Persuasion: The Liberal-Democratic Mind in the Age of Gladstone* (New York: Alfred A. Knopf, 1969).

37. Mathews, *Religion in the Old South*; Jack P. Maddex, Jr., "Proslavery Millennialism: Social Eschatology in Antebellum Southern Calvinism," *American Quarterly* 31 (Spring 1979): 46–62.

38. James H. Moorhead, *American Apocalypse: Yankee Protestants and the Civil War* (New Haven: Yale University Press, 1978); Drew Gilpin Faust, "Christian Soldiers: The Meaning of Revivalism in the Confederate Army," *Journal of Southern History* 53 (Feb. 1987): 63–90.

39. Patricia Hollis, *Pressure from Without in Early Victorian England* (London: Edward Arnold, 1974); Howard Temperley, *British Antislavery, 1833–1870* (Columbia: University of South Carolina Press, 1972); Betty Fladeland, *Men and Brothers: Anglo-American Antislavery* (Urbana: University of Illinois Press, 1972); Harrison, *Drink and the Victorians*; D. A. Hamer, *The Politics of Electoral Pressure: A Study of the History of Victorian Reform Agitations* (Hassocks, England: Harvester Press, 1977); Richard Shannon, *Gladstone and the Bulgarian Agitation, 1876* (London: Nelson, 1963).

# 6

# Insights from Norwegian "Revivalism," 1875–1914

✦

FREDERICK HALE

NORWAY OFFERS A USEFUL setting for an examination of revivals in a religious culture dominated by a state church. Since the sixteenth century, its Lutheran establishment has had deeply entrenched evangelical theology and well-developed liturgical traditions. On the surface, this heritage may seem inhospitable toward revivalism. The prevailing stereotype of European Protestant state churches, after all, highlights little more than "maintenance ministry," arcane academic theology, moribund confessionalism, tradition-bound liturgies, and clerical domination of religious life. On closer examination, however, this stereotype becomes an oversimplified caricature.

Despite dissension within official Lutheranism, perceptions of Norwegian religious homogeneity did not break down appreciably until after 1850. Until well after 1900, the overwhelming majority of the people—more than 95 percent—remained at least nominal members of the Lutheran establishment. Nonetheless, the nineteenth century was a period of significant change within the state churches. Moreover, because of a general relaxation of restrictions on religious toleration and increasing contacts with British and American denominations and religious currents, denominational pluralism blossomed.

Some Scandinavian theologians, especially those defensively wary of both lay-led movements within the Lutheran establishment and denominational challenges to the monopoly that the state church long held on organized religious life, have used the term "revival" polemically. Yet both contemporary observers and historians looking back at this period have also pinned the label "revival" on many of the phenomena related to—and ostensibly underlying—these develop-

ments. Church historians representing a fairly broad spectrum of
Scandinavian liturgical traditions and theological emphases—such as
Berndt Gustafsson, Hjalmar Holmquist, P. G. Lindhardt, Anders
Pontoppidan Thyssen, Andreas Aarflot, Einar Molland, and Carl
Fredrik Wisløff[1]—have employed the word "revival" and related
terms, though they have seldom attempted a definition.

In Norway, as in many other countries on both sides of the
Atlantic, use of the nomenclature of revival has run far ahead of its
definition. In the English-speaking world, the indiscriminate use of
the word "revival" has probably contributed to historical misunderstanding. When applied to the Nordic countries, the word immediately raises questions. In a literal sense, for example, what was being
revived (brought from death to life)? By any account, the vigor of
the Norwegian church has fluctuated through the centuries, but it
can hardly be said to have been "dead." Even during the Enlightenment, which is often viewed as a low point in church life in northern
Europe—an era when many pastors propounded rationalist views
and used their pulpits to promote agrarian reforms—the churches
survived, perhaps as much because of waves of pietism as because
of persistent sacramental emphases. In the nineteenth century, Søren
Kierkegaard (1813–55) and other internal critics of the Scandinavian
Lutheran establishment decried both a perceived lack of spiritual zeal
among the clergy and the lassitude that inclusive ecclesiology nurtured, but none seriously charged that the churches had died. Their
pastors continued to preach the gospel and administer the sacraments,
and both pietists and defenders of orthodoxy participated in movements of unprecedented magnitude to promote the propagation of
Christianity abroad. Lay people played instrumental roles in this
foreign outreach as well as in endeavors to evangelize the Scandinavian people more effectively in both industrial and rural areas.
Theologically, in all the Scandinavian countries in the mid-nineteenth
century, confessional reactions against the rationalism of the Enlightenment enhanced the degree of Lutheran orthodoxy.

The most common Scandinavian term for "revival" (*vekkelse* in
Norwegian) literally means "awakening." It is thus less severe than
the Latin-rooted English word, but it nevertheless poses a similar
semantic problem. Instead of asking what or who was dead, one
must query whether either the people or their churches were asleep.
If many of the nominal members of the established churches were
spiritually dozing, their state merely reproduced a pattern that has
probably obtained throughout the history of Christianity. Their religious institutions, nonetheless, could hardly be characterized as asleep
for the same reasons that they were not "dead." Despite these obvious

problems, Scandinavian church historians, including Lutherans of both pietistic and orthodox-formalistic bent, have frequently resorted to this term, almost invariably without defining it. Its usage in northern Europe has generally been as broad and inclusive as in North America. One thus searches the historiography of Scandinavian Christianity in vain for noteworthy semantic aid in establishing a conceptual framework for the developments in question.

For that matter, the assistance one can garner from the English-speaking world in this respect is also limited. In the United States, as in Scandinavia, the term "revivalism" has often been used casually and imprecisely. To be sure, there are exceptions, although they appear to raise as many problems as they solve. But there is no consensus about the meaning of the word, which has been stretched to cover many different and occasionally unrelated phenomena. For example, in his classic history of "great revivalists" in American religious history, Bernard A. Weisberger insisted that the words "revivals" and "revivalism" had taken on specific meanings in the United States. However questionable that generalization may be, at least in Weisberger's vocabulary these terms have definite denotations. Weisberger declared that "revival" was essentially a moral word that clergymen around 1800 deliberately selected "to scold a naughty world by the suggestion that it was necessary to 'revive' the piety of an earlier day, when Americans supposedly had more respect for God and His anointed."[2] Richard Carwardine, by contrast, has defined "revival" in a more specifically religious sense, declaring that it actually referred to two related phenomena; it could designate either a "period of unusually intense religious interest in a single church, a time when penitents sought counsel and salvation in above-average numbers," or "the multiplication of local revivals over a broad geographical area for a prolonged period of perhaps several years."[3] Looking beyond specifically religious movements to some of their cultural effects, William G. McLoughlin distinguished "revivals" from "awakenings." The former, he argued, is the "Protestant ritual . . . in which charismatic evangelists convey 'the Word' of God to large masses of people who, under this influence, experience what Protestants call conversion, salvation, regeneration, or spiritual rebirth." Awakenings, on the other hand, "are periods of cultural revitalization that begin in a general crisis of beliefs and values and extend over a period of a generation or so, during which time a profound reorientation in beliefs and values take place."[4]

When these definitions are transferred to Europe, they suggest as many difficulties as they solve. The Scandinavian context amply illustrates this. McLoughlin's definition of "revivalism" virtually identifies it with much of conventional week-by-week preaching and other work of the churches. Distinguishing "evangelists" from parish pastors is a related difficulty, as is his undefined use of "charismatic." The latter problem is especially vexing to scholars with an awareness of the meaning of *charismata* in 1 Corinthians 12 and the responsible use of this term in Christian theology. The same can be said of "the Word" and the many uses of this expression in both the Old Testament and the New. There is nothing unusual about conveying "the Word" to the masses in the normative ecclesiastical traditions of Scandinavia or, for that matter, most other corners of Christendom. Carwardine's more conventional definition, emphasizing a time of "unusually intense 'religious interest'" and, consequently, an increase in the number of people seeking "counsel and salvation" is perhaps more applicable, but it immediately raises a problem of quantification where corroborative data are unavailable, thus compelling the historian to rely on impressions by contemporary observers. Weisberger's emphasis on reasserting "the piety of an earlier day" seems to have little relevance to religious movements in Scandinavia, whose leaders rarely appealed to an idealized past as a rhetorical device in their proclamation of the gospel.

Despite these reservations, however, I make qualified use of the terms "revival" and "revivalism" as common usage for various phenomena that lent additional vitality to public religious life and that appear to have contributed to the spirituality of individual Norwegians in ways that conventional religious practices did not. My focus, then, is on personal spirituality rather than the revival of churches.

By 1875, revivals of various sorts in all Nordic countries had transformed the Lutheran establishments to varying degrees. Within the state churches, many revivals stemmed from pietistic movements. In Norway, the most influential of these was launched by the renowned lay preacher, Hans Nielsen Hauge (1771–1824). The impact of Hauge and his followers, especially in southern Norway, is difficult to exaggerate. Most Haugeans remained in the Church of Norway, thereby imbuing it with a deeply seated tradition of inter alia conventicles, lay initiative in a broadening range of parachurch organizations, and, at times, anticlericalism. Their place in the religious life of the country was assured in 1842 when parliament abrogated legal restrictions on conventicles and lay preaching (thus arguably violating Article XIV of the Augsburg Confession), although in some cases lay pietists had long ignored these laws. Chiefly in response to Haugean influence, Norway became (on a per capita basis) a leading nation in foreign missionary work. The Haugean tradition, which also left a deep imprint on Norwegian-American Lutheranism, probably changed nineteenth-century religious life in Norway more than any other movement. Largely because of it, Norway today is markedly less secularized than either Denmark or Sweden, where comparable movements were less influential and in some cases limited to small segments of the population because they resulted in separatism. Revivalism after 1875 must be seen against the backdrop of this far-reaching legacy. Without Hauge early in the nineteenth century, it is uncertain that subsequent revivals would have enjoyed the success they achieved.

By 1875, the principal hallmarks of Norwegian Lutheranism were a firmly entrenched state church system in which members of the Church of Norway were legally required to submit their children for baptism and confirmation; moderate orthodoxy; deeply rooted pietism; lay initiative in parachurch bodies; and a general aversion to separatism. The ratio of lay people to clergy was approximately 3,000 to 1. Attendance at weekly services varied greatly from region to region but was greatest along the southern and southwestern coasts. The liturgy was essentially that which had been prescribed in 1685, although, owing primarily to the creative genius of the prominent psalmist Magnus Brostrup Landstad (1802–80) and the efforts of various other compilers of ecclesiastical music, the hymnody underwent a partial renewal during the middle third of the nineteenth century. Increasing literacy had also influenced the distribution of Bibles and other devotional literature.

The Norwegian constitution, promulgated in 1814, preserved Lutheranism as "the official religion of the state." Its established status was never seriously threatened, but in 1845 the Norwegian parliament bestowed on the country a measure of religious toleration by enacting what was called the "Dissenter Law." This groundbreaking statute made it possible for Norwegians, for the first time in their history, to withdraw legally from the state church. It also permitted non-Lutheran denominations to function in Norway as long as the supreme court did not rule them non-Christian. This qualification soon proved significant. In the early 1850s, Latter-day Saints sought protection under the new law but were found to be outside its purview, a status that was eventually changed. But several other denominations, some of them resulting from indigenous separatism, and others imported from the United Kingdom or North America (in some cases brought by returned Scandinavian immigrants who had tasted religious pluralism in the New World) gained footholds in dozens of coastal towns during the third quarter of the century. Their numbers grew slowly, but by 1876 there were 7,180 people in nonconformist congregations; 2,775 of them were Methodists. The Baptist, Mormon, Roman Catholic, Quaker, and a few other denominations each boasted several hundred members in Norway at that time. During the last quarter of the nineteenth century, the Evangelical Lutheran Free Church (modeled partly on the Scottish Free Church), the Seventh-day Adventists, the Salvation Army, and other denominations either arose within the country or were organized by foreigners. By 1891 there were more than 30,000 legally registered dissenters in Norway.[5] Approximately 98 percent of the Norwegian population was still nominally in the established church. Yet nonconformist bodies showed considerable vitality and, as we shall see, they were bridges over which various new evangelistic techniques entered the country.[6]

Because the Lutheran establishment claimed the nominal loyalty of most Norwegians and encompassed several revival movements of various kinds after 1875, it seems most appropriate to begin with it. We shall consider Lutheran revivalism as manifested in interrelated movements before turning to their historical interplay with evangelists from abroad.

The first of these was the continuation of widespread rural lay preaching in the Church of Norway. Unordained men had gained some prominence in proclaiming the gospel at least as early as the time of Hans Nielsen Hauge, although their preaching activities were not legalized until 1842. The last quarter of the century witnessed a powerful resurgence of this phenomenon, one to which many local and regional revivals are credited. In contrast to the university-educated clergymen, the majority of whom came from the relatively privileged strata of Norwegian society and spoke a Danish-influenced, literary form of Norwegian, nineteenth-century lay preachers tended to emerge from the peasantry and to proclaim the gospel in speech more closely related to the rural dialects of their audiences. It is likely that these factors contributed to lay preachers' effectiveness. Strong anticlericalism in many pietist circles may also have given lay evangelists an advantage.[7] Indeed, it is hardly coincidental that the majority of the lay-led rural revivals that gained appreciable attention took place in southern Norway, where pietism was still a powerful factor in ecclesiastical and popular religious life. Men like Nils Belland (1878–1966), Johan Gjærdal (1871–1929), Gabriel Homme (1868–1939), and Sven Foldøen (1878–1966) traveled widely in that part of the country, preaching mainly in the "prayer chapels" that parachurch organizations, most of them nominally Lutheran but strongly pietist, maintained for the nurturing of spiritual life. Before the end of the century, lay preaching in the sanctuaries of the Church of Norway was legalized, a change that gave these evangelists more convenient venues but also engendered conservative ecclesiastical reactions.

No Lutheran lay preacher gained as much national attention as Ludvig Hope (1871–1954), an erstwhile construction worker who received his formal training in Bergen at a school which that city's domestic missionary society conducted for training evangelists. The fact that Hope, almost certainly unlike most other lay preachers, carefully drafted and read his sermons did not seem to reduce his effectiveness. Like many other unordained evangelists in the Church of Norway, his attitude toward the church was at best lukewarm. Some of his opponents considered his distinguishing the state church from the genuine communion of the saints a departure from Article VII of the Augsburg Confession, which defined the church as "the assembly of all believers among whom the Gospel is preached in its purity and the holy sacraments are administered according to the Gospel." Hope was frequently alleged to regard the state church as "a scaffold on which we stand while building the Church of Christ," a folk-pedagogical institution whose task was to prepare people for revivals. This position, of course, hardly ingratiated Hope and likeminded evangelists with the clergy, but his attitude was nevertheless popular. Like many other Norwegian and Scandinavian Lutheran revivalists, Hope cared little for what he regarded as confessional minutiae, preferring instead to find his theological guidelines in the Scriptures.

Revivalism did not remain a characteristically rural activity. Like most other European countries, Norway underwent rapid urbanization in the nineteenth century. The capital, Kristiania (since 1925 called Oslo), which in 1800 was a quiet harbor town with fewer than 10,000 inhabitants, boasted approximately 135,000 in 1885 and in 1910 had a population of nearly 250,000. During the second half of the century it also became the focal point of many new departures in religious life, including lay preaching and other forms of revivalism. The rural emphasis of Lutheran evangelism remained strong, but Kristiania increasingly became the center of new initiatives. Some of these were evangelistic endeavors aimed specifically at the uprooted masses who were perceived, largely correctly, as disaffected from the conventional life of the state church. The "Treider Circle" stood at the center of these efforts. Led by Otto Treider (1856–1928), the founder of a commercial college in the capital, Captain Hans Guldberg (1843–96), an officer in the Norwegian cavalry, and Johannes Jørgensen (1850–92), a teacher and sexton, this group of concerned members of the Church of Norway engaged in various ventures to reach people who otherwise had little or no meaningful contact with formal religious life. A principal focus of their activities was the Mission House in Calmeyergate (*Calmeyergatens Misjonshus*), a gospel hall with a seating capacity of 3,800 that was dedicated in 1890 as the largest of its type in Scandinavia. Both laymen and ordained pastors representing the Church of Norway and various nonconformist denominations preached there, as did a small number of men without formal religious affiliation. The Mission House did not accommodate a church in a sacramental sense; the Lord's Supper was not celebrated in it. Some of the Lutheran laymen who preached there, however, were advocates of the movement to allow unordained men to administer the Eucharist, a position that brought the Mission House under fire from conservative ecclesiastical circles. The fact that some of the leaders, most notably Jorgensen, espoused neo-evangelism also prompted a reaction from theologically conservative churchmen. Neo-evangelism was a theological current that had come to Norway from Sweden and deviated from both the main thrust of pietism and what was regarded as Lutheran orthodoxy. It rejected subjective conditions for salvation and emphasized the death of Jesus as sufficient not only for Atonement but also for justification, asserting that God had forgiven the sins of everyone, regardless of the presence of faith in individuals. Despite these and other challenges, the Mission House remained the most prominent focus of urban revivalism in Norwegian Lutheranism until well into the twentieth century. It thus paralleled the Anglo-American tradition of using such settings as extra-ecclesiastical forums for the proclamation of the gospel. Even before its dedication, however, in 1888 lay preaching had been legalized in the state church.

Intimately related to lay preaching as a revival technique within the Church of Norway was the development of parachurch organizations. The most influential of these, the Norwegian Luther Foundation (*Den norske Lutherstiftelse*), was founded in 1868 as an outgrowth of the revival movement led by Gisle Johnson and others in Kristiania. Its principal purpose was to promote Christian enlightenment and morality by distributing devotional literature. It employed dozens of colporteurs who were also free to preach at their discretion, a practice Johnson defended on the basis of what he termed the "principle of necessity" (*nødsprinsippet*). He and like-minded allies, most of them laymen, thereby circumvented the prohibition of lay preaching in Article XIV of the Augsburg Confession, arguing that in some situations factors like rapid population growth outstripped the ability of the clergy to meet demands and thus necessitated lay proclamation of the gospel. This practice consistently encountered stiff ecclesiastical resistance. In western Norway lay preaching was even more common, and in the early 1880s a national merger of various domestic missionary societies led to the formation of the "Norwegian Lutheran Home Missionary Society" (*Det norske lutherske Indremissionsselskab*) and entailed the abandonment of the "principle of necessity" in favor of virtually unrestricted lay preaching. The new organization, however, also pledged to cooperate with the clergy of the Church of Norway. This compromise assured continued prominence of lay preachers—especially in pietist circles—and also helped preserve firm (though occasionally strained) ties between revival movements and the Lutheran establishment.

Voluntary Christian organizations from abroad strengthened religious life outside the normal parameters of the state church but also fell under the de facto aegis of Norwegian Lutheranism. The Young Men's Christian Association offers a typical example. The first local unit in Norway was founded in 1869, and a national association was created in 1880. From the outset the constitution of the national association contained a reference to its confessional Lutheran character. When the Norwegian YMCA eventually merged with the Young Women's Christian Association (which was established in Norway in 1887) the resulting body was among the largest voluntary religious organizations in Norway. It played a key role in retaining the loyalty of large numbers of spiritually awakened Norwegian youth for the state church at a time when many nonconformist denominations were rapidly growing.

Revivalism followed a similar course in Swedish and Danish Lutheranism. In Sweden, the Evangelical Homeland Society (*Evangelisk fosterlandsstiftelsen*) was founded in 1856 partly to lend structure and direction to the revivals occurring in Sweden. From the outset its leadership included both Lutheran clergy and laymen, and lay preachers and colporteurs were responsible for most of the distribution of Christian literature and the proclamation of the gospel under its auspices. Eventually the Society founded a Bible school in Stockholm for training such workers.

Perhaps more meaningful for comparisons with developments in the English-speaking world was the revivalistic Inner Mission (*Indre Mission*) in Denmark. Established in 1853 but refounded in 1861, it included both pastors and laymen. Vilhelm Beck (1829–1901), ordained in the Church of Denmark, headed the Inner Mission for decades. Like the Evangelical Homeland Society, it emphasized the role of the laity in proclaiming Christianity in a rapidly secularizing society. Indeed, in defending its use of lay preachers, Beck cited the prophets of the Old Testament and the evangelists of the New. Of particular interest was the work of the Copenhagen Inner Mission, which dates from 1865. At that time, the population of the Danish capital was growing rapidly: some parishes had tens of thousands of nominal members. To supplement the limited personal involvement of pastors with such extensive flocks, Beck and some colleagues constructed Bethesda Mission House in 1882. Efforts at the gospel hall paralleled those at the Calmeyergaten Mission House in Kristiania and at countless other missions elsewhere. They also evoked severe criticism from the secular press and radical intellectuals. But, like the corresponding ministry in Kristiania, they helped to contain most of a significant revival movement within the Church of Denmark.

Several reforms in the Scandinavian state churches probably fostered revivalism; again, Norway offers a test case. First, a moderate restructuring of corporate worship including an alternative liturgy was adopted in 1887, as were additional lectionaries. Already in 1886, the Church of Norway had dropped the requirement that prospective communicants first participate in individual confession of their sins.

In a related development, in 1889 the New Testament was translated into *nynorsk,* the new vernacular form of Norwegian that drew on various regional dialects and was favored by many rural Norwegians over the Danish-influenced literary language used in previous Norwegian translations of the Scriptures. The amount of devotional literature in both forms of the national language grew rapidly as literacy became universal in Norway.

Reference has already been made to the birth of denominational pluralism in Norway shortly after 1850, a development that occurred throughout Scandinavia. During the last quarter of the century, the nonconformist kaleidoscope became increasingly complex. To some extent growing diversity was linked to the arrival of British and American forms of millenarianism.[8] Expectation of the imminent return of Christ triggered new waves of revival that not only attracted thousands of Norwegians to some of the newer denominations but also left an imprint on the Church of Norway.

The first intensely millenarian communion to reach Norway during this period was Seventh-day Adventism. The Danish-American apostle to the Nordic countries was John G. Matteson (1835–97), who landed in Norway in 1878. He arranged meetings in Kristiania, where his audiences frequently exceeded the 1,000-person seating capacity of the theater he rented. Matteson gathered an Adventist congregation in the Norwegian capital in 1879 and several others elsewhere in the country during the 1880s. Most of these were either in pietistic strongholds along the southern coast or in rapidly growing industrial and shipping towns on the Kristiania Fjord (now the Oslo Fjord). Despite enthusiastic reports that Adventist colporteurs sent from various parts of Norway, however, the new denomination remained small, and for decades its official membership lagged far behind the numbers of people who thronged their public meetings.[9]

The fear of social ostracism may have played a role in this. The Norwegians who had experienced spiritual renewal in Adventist revivals and who affiliated themselves with that denomination remained far outside the mainstream of religious life in their own country. The revival that Matteson inspired cannot be said to have made an impact on Norway that extended beyond narrow sectarian bounds.

The same is not true of the country's second avowedly millenarian denomination, the Norwegian Mission Covenant (*Det norske Misjonsforbund*). This communion traced its roots indirectly to the eschatological emphasis of American revivalism in the tradition of Dwight L. Moody (1837–99). Fredrik Franson (1852–1908), an immigrant from Sweden who underwent a conversion experience while a youth in Nebraska and later assisted Moody's ministry in Chicago by preaching to his fellow Scandinavians during the late 1870s, became an influential advocate of the futurist millenarianism shaped by Irish evangelist John Nelson Darby.[10] Franson adopted not only Darbyite doctrines of the "Secret Rapture" and the "any-moment coming" of Christ, but also such proven Moody techniques as the use of a gospel singer and "after-meetings." After revival tours among Scandinavians in the United States, Franson returned to Sweden in 1881 and launched a global evangelistic ministry that persisted for over twenty-five years and brought him to every continent.[11] Franson reached Norway in 1883 and spent approximately a year and a half traversing the country, preaching at revival meetings held in nonconformist chapels, the prayer chapels of predominantly Lutheran voluntary organizations, and, on a few occasions, illegally in state church sanctuaries. Even though Moody never preached in Scandinavia, many of the songs of his gospel singer, Ira Sankey (1840–1908), had been translated into all the Scandinavian languages and published in popular editions. Franson both gained attention and encountered stiff resistance, especially from Lutheran pastors who resented nonconformist competition. Unlike many other non-Lutheran evangelists, Franson encouraged members of the state church to remain in it; apparently most of his Lutheran followers did. In Norway, unlike Sweden and

Denmark, his revival methods rarely came under criticism. When the Norwegian Mission Covenant was constituted in 1884 as a loosely organized, nonconfessional association of the congregations that Franson and others gathered in the wake of his revivals, it encountered far less hostility than had the Adventists only a few years earlier. The majority of the members of these local bodies retained at least nominal membership in the Church of Norway, thus forging a weak link between the new revivalistic movement and the established religion of the state.

Owing partly to the influence of Franson's millenarian revivalism, but also to the popularity of several British books about the second advent, during the 1880s and 1890s several books on the subject were published in Scandinavia. Most of these were either translated from English or modeled on the work of foreign scholars. Occasionally professional theologians reacted strongly against what they perceived as irresponsible excesses and spoke and wrote against them. Lars Dahle (1843–1925) of the Norwegian Missionary Society, for example, was infuriated at the popularity of Jabez Bunting Dimbleby's book of 1896, *The Appointed Time*, which predicted that Christ would return in April 1898. Dahle countered with a series of public lectures in Stavanger and a book in which he attacked many of the presuppositions of popular eschatological speculation. Despite such resistance, millenarianism in various forms survived as an integral part of Scandinavian revivalistic preaching.

Another imported catalyst for this interest was the arranging of nondenominational prophetic conferences that attracted large audiences and offered forums for the presentation of diverse views. Franson helped establish this tradition in Scandinavia. The conferences drew members of both the state churches and many nonconformist denominations.

Revivalism in the Moody tradition flowed from North America to Scandinavia through personal channels. In Norway, shortly after the turn of the century, it provided the impetus for the formation of another small denomination linked to its leader, Albert Lunde (1877–1939). Born in an intensely pietist area of southern Norway, this Lutheran layman migrated to the United States in 1895 and soon came under the influence of Moody. Lunde accepted rebaptism and served briefly as a nondenominational evangelist in North Dakota before returning to his native land in 1900. In Norway he became a full-time lay preacher and gained a reputation in the western and southern regions of the country as a gifted orator who consistently attracted large numbers of hearers. Lunde met firm resistance in the

Lutheran-dominated Bergen Inner Mission Society, however, where O. K. Grimnes (1849–1932), one of the few pastors in the Church of Norway who played a highly visible role in largely lay-led voluntary organizations, took exception to Lunde's baptistic preaching and his use of after-meetings. Lunde consequently moved to Kristiania in 1905 and entered the most effective stage of his career. He gained use of the Calmeyergaten Mission House only after promising its Lutheran leaders that he would neither criticize their confessional tradition nor ask his audiences to "lift up holy hands" in praise. Lunde drew as many as 5,000 people to nightly meetings in the Norwegian capital, at which he preached the need for immediate conversion and emphasized Christian personal ethics. His homiletics and the willingness of large numbers of Norwegians to attend his after-meetings prompted qualified commendations from the Bishop of Kristiania, Anton Christian Bang (1840–1913), and other prominent Lutheran clergy in the city. Their explicit appreciation of Lunde's ministry was a relatively new development and did not herald generally favorable clerical attitudes toward revivalism outside the formal structure of the state church. In 1910 Lunde and some of his colleagues founded their own proto-denomination, The Evangelical Association (*Den evangeliske forening*), which admitted people to its membership without regard to their stance on infant baptism. This and other factors cost Lunde use of the Calmeyergaten Mission House, thus compelling him to develop another agency for his ministry in Kristiania. By doing so he added another permanent segment to the kaleidoscope of revivalistic denominations in Norway, one which had much in common with the Norwegian Mission Covenant. It eventually developed into a small denomination and, like many of the others that stemmed from revival movements, launched a program of foreign missionary work.

The last major revival in Norway prior to the outbreak of the First World War was the coming of Pentecostalism to the country. Its principal bearer was Thomas Ball Barratt (1862–1940), an English Methodist who had devoted much of his career to ministering in the Norwegian capital. He experienced the baptism of the Holy Spirit while in the United States in 1906 and also received the gift of glossolalia at that time. When he returned to Kristiania late that year, he began to lead a revival that gained unprecedented attention in the Norwegian press. Journalistic and clerical opposition was especially strong, in part because very few Norwegians had previously experienced glossolalia, which became a frequent and suspected phenomenon. Barratt nevertheless took his revival beyond the capital and gained followers in several parts of Norway. For several years he sought not to disturb the existing denominational order, a desire thwarted by the subjectivity characteristic of his perfectionist message. His rebaptism in 1913 also kept critics hostile. Not until 1916 did Barratt and his allies begin to form independent congregations. This move transformed his revival movement into a loosely organized denomination without, however, isolating it from other ecclesiastical circles and voluntary Christian organizations. But it did signal an eventual bureaucratization and, according to some critics of this development, a related decline in vigor. Norwegian Pentecostals undertook foreign missionary work during the First World War and eventually became, on a per capita basis as well as in absolute terms, a major force in Norwegian efforts to propagate the gospel overseas. During the years between the world wars the Pentecostals surpassed the Evangelical Lutheran Free Church, which dated from the 1870s, as the largest nonconformist denomination in Norway.[12] Pentecostalism remains an important factor in Norwegian religious life; its influence there and in Sweden and Denmark extends well beyond its membership.

This brief examination of forms of revivalism in Scandinavia during the late nineteenth and early twentieth centuries yields several tentative conclusions relevant to the study of revivals in English-speaking countries. First, it should be noted again that one cannot legitimately refer to revival of the churches in nineteenth-century Scandinavia; they were alive and functioning without interruption throughout the period. To be sure, the vitality of the Norwegian Lutheran establishment during the last quarter of the century reflected the influence of earlier "revivals," especially those connected with Hans Nielsen Hauge, but even without Haugeanism the Church of Norway would have been a functioning vehicle of the Word and sacraments. To the extent that analogous situations obtained in other countries, regardless of the nature of Church-state relations, this serves as a warning against indiscriminate use of the terms "revival" and "revivalism." This may be the most widely applicable lesson to be learned from a consideration of these phenomena in countries with deeply entrenched state churches.

Nevertheless, revivals left their marks on the Lutheran establishments. Perhaps most importantly, they enhanced the role of the laity, who in many cases led these movements. In Norway this represented not a new departure but rather a continuation of the Haugean tradition. Similar movements elsewhere in Scandinavia provided fertile ground for lay initiative during the last few decades of the century.

Probably owing largely to the loyalty of the Haugeans to the Norwegian state church, subsequent revivalism did not lead to nearly as much separatism as might otherwise have been the case.

The factors that nurtured revivals are not always easily identified, but at least in Norway it is striking that they progressed most rapidly in two different geographical settings. Most of the revivalism that yielded observable institutional results occurred either in rural areas with distinct pietistic traditions (especially in southern and southwestern Norway), or in rapidly changing coastal towns with growing migrant populations. Receptivity toward Anglo-American eschatological currents also prompted religious interest in various places, especially in coastal towns and cities. These millenarian ideologies brought Lutherans and members of various nonconformist denominations into transatlantic communities, giving them greater exposure to impulses that would come from abroad during the twentieth century. Much research remains to be done to determine the kinds of people who were most likely to respond to such impulses.

Some results of Scandinavian revivals are readily observable, while others are difficult to assess. Most obviously, it is difficult to gauge the extent to which they nurtured individual faith. The annals of Scandinavian church history are replete with individual Christians who have attributed their spiritual transformations to experiences at revival meetings. What remains uncertain is how many of them already had strong Christian faith or would have achieved it at some point through the normal ministry of the churches. The growth of nonconformist denominations fails to illumine this. Almost all non-Lutheran evangelists reported greater popular interest in their preaching than do official statistics of religious dissent. This is attributable in part to the loyalty of most Scandinavians to their established religious traditions as well as to their fear of risking ostracism by affiliating with nonconformist denominations.

Certain conclusions, on the other hand, seem beyond dispute. One is that revivals strengthened existing traditions of lay initiative stemming from pietism. This, in turn, resulted in more religious voluntary organizations, including several that were manifestations of broadening popular interest in foreign missions. At least in Norway (and to a lesser extent in Sweden and Denmark), the presence of relatively large numbers of people influenced by revivals who remained in the state church assured a continuation of liturgical traditions along so-called low church lines, albeit with continuing emphasis on the sacraments. This in itself may have served to keep many revived Christians in the established church. The links to earlier pietist emphases are readily apparent. Outside the state church, one can see a related development in the institutionalization of new movements. Franson's itinerant evangelism and the genesis of the Norwegian Mission Covenant, Lunde's preaching in Kristiania, or the coming of Pentecostalism eventually gave rise to denominations that had much in common with many of the religious organizations already on the Norwegian scene. Despite some contemporary uneasiness about such movements, they did not seriously erode the revivalistic character of those groups rooted in the pietist past.

## NOTES

1. Berndt Gustafsson, *Svensk kyrkohistoria* (Stockholm: Svenska Kyrkans Diakonistyrelses Bokförlag, 1957); Hjalmar Holmquist, *Handbok i svensk kyrkohistoria*, 3 vols. (Stockholm: Svenska Kyrkans Diakonistyrelses Bokförlag, 1962); P. G. Lindhardt, *Vækkelser og kirkelige Retninger i Danmark* (Copenhagen: Det danske Forlag, 1951); Anders Pontoppidan Thyssen, ed., *Vækkelsernes Frembrud i Danmark i første Halvdel af det 19. Århundrede*, 6 vols. (Copenhagen: G. E. C. Gads Forlag, 1960–62); Andreas Aarflot, *Norsk kirke i tusen år* (Oslo, Bergen, and Tromsø: Universitetsforlaget, 1978); Einar Molland, *Fra Hans Nielsen Hauge til Eivind Berggrav* (Oslo: Gyldendal Norsk Forlag, 1951); Carl Fredrik Wisløff, *Norsk kirkehistorie*, vol. 3 (Oslo: Lutherstiftelsen, 1971).

2. Bernard A. Weisberger, *They Gathered at the River: The Story of the Great Revivalists and Their Impact upon Religion in America* (Chicago: Quadrangle Books, 1966), vii.

3. Richard Carwardine, *Transatlantic Revivalism: Popular Evangelicalism in Britain and America, 1790–1865* (Westport, Conn.: Greenwood Press, 1978), xv.

4. William G. McLoughlin, *Revivals, Awakenings, and Reform* (Chicago: University of Chicago Press, 1978), xiii.

5. Norges officielle Statistik. Tredie Række No. 284. *Oversigt over de vigtigste Resultater af de statistiske Tabeller vedkommende Folketællingen i Kongeriget Norge i Januar 1891* (Kristiania: Det statistiske Centralbureau, 1898), 112–13.

6. For a detailed analysis of the historical unfolding of denominationalism in Norway, see Frederick Hale, "The Development of Religious Pluralism among Norwegians in Norway, the United States of America, and Southern America" (Master of Theology thesis, University of South Africa, 1987), chapters 1–4.

7. For analyses of Norwegian anticlericalism before 1875, see Frederick Hale, "The Impact of Kierkegaard's Anticlericalism in Norway," *Studia Theologica* 34, no. 2 (1980): 153–71; and Frederick Hale, "Anticlericalism and Norwegian Society before the Breakthrough of Modernity," *Scandinavian Studies* 52, no. 3 (Summer 1980): 245–63.

8. For an analysis of the subject in general, see Frederick Hale, "British and American Millenarianism in Norway during the Breakthrough of Modernity," *Fides et Historia* 19, no. 1 (Feb. 1987): 35–50.

9. Øivind Gjertsen, "The Seventh-day Adventist Church in Norway: A Factual Account," in Sigmund Skard, ed., *Americana Norvegica: Norwegian Contributions to American Studies*, vol. 2 (Philadelphia: University of Pennsylvania Press, 1968), 74–93, is a convenient synopsis of the early years of the denomination in Norway.

10. For the general context of this millenarian movement and its relationship to Anglo-American revivalism, see Ernest R. Sandeen, *The Roots of Fundamentalism: British and American Millenarianism, 1800–1930* (Chicago: University of Chicago Press, 1970).

11. The most detailed compilation of material about Franson's ministry and theology is Edvard Paul Torjesen, "A Study of Fredrik Franson: The Development and Impact of His Ecclesiology, Missiology, and Worldwide Evangelism" (Ph.D. diss., International College, 1984).

12. The classic study of the coming of the Pentecostal movement to Norway and its development there is Nils Bloch-Hoell, *Pinsebevegelsen* (Oslo: Universitetsforlaget, 1956).

# 7

# Keswick and the Experience of Evangelical Piety

## DAVID BUNDY

KESWICK IS A SMALL town in the scenic Lake Country of northwest England. Through the religious conference that has been held there annually since 1875, the town has had its name attached both to a number of similar conferences throughout the world and to a theological perspective. This perspective is not formally attached to any denomination, and the parameters of definition for the conferences and participants have always been ambiguous. The convention draws people from a variety of backgrounds who are in general sympathy with the teachings presented at the conferences and in the related publications. Central to these teachings is a concern for a "higher Christian life," which includes the classical pietist foci, and a carefully nuanced middle-class asceticism. Keswick's theological perspective has been remarkably successful in defining what it means to be "evangelical" in North America and in England. It is impossible to study American Evangelicalism/Fundamentalism, Pentecostalism, or the Wesleyan/Holiness traditions without interacting with Keswick.

The historiography of Keswick has been in remarkable agreement. For more than a century, there has been consensus about the Convention's origin and purpose. Early histories from within the Keswick mainstream were unashamedly apologetic.[1] For their writers, Keswick was American Wesleyan/Holiness spirituality shorn of the troublesome feature of perfectionism. This interpretation was accepted by critics and early analysts of the movement[2] as well as by scholars of transatlantic Christianity.[3]

Either implicit or explicit in the historiography was the assumption that the Keswick tradition arose in Britain *ex nihilo* under the influence of the American revivalists. Keswick was an American Wesleyan/Holiness export to England that broke with its past to form a competing voluntary organization.[4] Recent scholarship on evangelicalism suggests the need to reassess this view, which fails adequately to explain Keswick's structures. For all their efforts through two centuries, American evangelists have found it virtually impossible to impact Europe significantly without joining forces with a European network.

Any comprehensve look at Keswick must begin with its European antecedents, account for the American influence, and trace the evolution of the convention's relationship with the American Wesleyan/ Holiness movement. The broader contexts in which American perfectionist spirituality was interpreted in Britain, France, the Netherlands, Germany, and Switzerland between 1873 and 1875 also form an integral part of the story.

## Before Keswick: A Common Vision

Memories of the 1858 revival still warmed many hearts in the 1870s, and both formal and informal networks of individuals and organizations nurtured vital spirituality. In the English context, perhaps the most important such networks were those emanating from the Mildmay Conference and the Evangelical Alliance. On the Continent, the Evangelical Alliance had intersecting sets of participants and interests with the French revival movement known as *Réveil*.

The ministry at Mildmay was the creation of William Pennefather (1816–73).[5] It began as a parish, with a mission to the poor, at the edge of London's industrial section. It developed into a renowned deaconess center, an effective social ministry and conference center. By 1870, the annual Mildmay Conference brought together 2,500 persons to reflect on personal holiness, mission, Christian unity, and social issues with the "soon return of Christ" as a unifying theme.

Pennefather was born in Ireland and at age 13 was sent to England for an education. Ordained an Anglican priest, he ministered first in Ireland and then in England. He was assigned to Barnet (near London) in 1852. As he reflected on his experience of ministry, informed by the work of the Evangelical Alliance and the Darbyists (Pennefather was a nephew of J. N. Darby),[6] he longed to make a contribution to the realization of "the essential unity of all who 'name the name of Christ and depart from iniquity,'" desiring "to bring into closer *social communion* the members of various churches."[7] In June 1856, he circulated the following announcement:[8]

> It is in contemplation to hold (God willing) a Conference of the Lord's people in this town on Tuesday, Wednesday, Thursday and Friday, the 26th, 27th, 28th, and 29th of August

next. The object of the proposed conference is to promote personal holiness, brotherly love, and increased interest in the work of the Lord. The persons attending the Conference will meet (God willing) every morning, from 11 to 1 o'clock for prayer and intercession and the reading of God's Word.

There will be evening meetings from 7 to 9 o'clock, when addresses will be given on 'Foreign Missions,' 'Home Missions,' 'Personal Holiness,' and the 'Lord's Coming, the hope of the Church.' Afterwards the subject for the evening will form the topic of conversation (Mal. iii. 16; Acts xiv. 27).

One hundred twenty attended that first meeting. At the second conference, in 1857, the Association of Female Workers was formed with Mrs. Pennefather as president. Three years later, a home was organized to house women in ministry.[9] The conference, women's organization, deaconess house, and a variety of other social-evangelistic agencies were transferred to Mildmay with Pennefather in 1864. Eventually soup kitchens, a hospital, flower gardens (a period version of "green space"), a circulating library, classes on theology and manual arts, a deaconess home, a training school for deaconesses, home nursing services, a home for converted prostitutes, a missionary training school and missions to Malta, Jamaica, and Palestine were added. There were also extensive evangelistic efforts in the Jewish community.

Pennefather's theological interests and ministry concerns made him a focal point of a number of networks. Although an Anglican priest, he was interested in the Darbyist understanding of eschatology, influenced by the Powerscourt meetings. He was for many years a member of the Bloomsbury "Prophetical Society."[10] His interest in personal holiness made him sympathetic toward Wesleyan tractarian traditions, and he cultivated contacts such as William Arthur and William Haslam. Quaker holiness teachers provided theological language and influenced behavioral expectations. The deaconess project was begun after Pennefather had visited major centers for deaconess training on the continent.[11] In turn, Mildmay became a model for a deaconess movement in the Methodist-Episcopal Church.[12] Mildmay was a significant force in the international and interchurch effort to develop structures for lay ministry, a vision that made the churches receptive to lay evangelists from North America.[13] Ecumenical involvement brought Pennefather into the Evangelical Alliance[14] and other nonconformist networks. Speakers at the Mildmay Conferences included persons from the various Christian traditions of England, continental Europe, and North America.

An important relationship between William Pennefather and Richard Cope Morgan developed from 1859 onward. Following the 1858 revival, Morgan oversaw an expanding religious publishing business. In July 1859 he launched *The Revival*, "an eight page sheet, containing accounts from eye-witnesses of some of the most wonderful manifestations of God's convicting and converting power that were ever told."[15] Demand apparently peaked at about 8,000 copies. However, an invitation from Pennefather to the Mildmay Conference pushed circulation to 80,000 copies in the space of a single week.[16] *The Revival* and Mildmay continued to promote each other and each other's friends. Both contributed to the success of the Salvation Army, as well as that of American revivalists in Britain.

## The Evangelical Alliance

During the 1840s the need for an international transconfessional structure to facilitate communication and cooperation among evangelicals seemed compelling. The result was the Evangelical Alliance, formed in London in 1846. The founders were predominantly British, but significant contingents from the United States, France, Germany, and Switzerland participated. William Arthur, British Wesleyan Methodist, future author of *Tongue of Fire*, and advocate of American Wesleyan/Holiness causes, was present at the 1846 organizational meeting and became a regular speaker at the British and international conventions.[17]

By the end of 1847, the Evangelical Alliance was organized in France (and French-speaking Belgium and Switzerland), Germany (Northern, Southern, and Western branches), Canada, Sweden, and the United States. Supporters tended to be upper and upper-middle class. International conferences were sponsored by royalty and the aristocracy. For example, at the Berlin Conference in 1857, Kaiser Frederick William IV transported the entire conference to Potsdam on special trains and addressed the assembly in his gardens.[18] During the New York conference in 1873, President Grant invited the organization to the White House for a day. The excursion was paid for by wealthy businessmen.[19]

The Evangelical Alliance was united by an ecumenical agenda, an aversion to developing rationalism, a commitment to traditional articulations of pietistic orthodoxy, evangelism and mission, pietistic spirituality, and fear of a revitalized Roman Catholic Church. Members were persuaded by the American churches not to address social issues, including slavery.[20] Most of the foreign participants at a major

higher life conference at Oxford in 1874 were active participants in
the Evangelical Alliance.[21] Many more were present at the Brighton
meeting of August 1875.[22]

The *Réveil* began in Switzerland about 1810 and spread through
France, Belgium, and the Netherlands.[23] It had its roots in pietism
and the Swiss Reformations but was also influenced by Methodists
and Darbyists. The foci of concern varied from country to country
and from decade to decade, but the basic issues were the nature of
the Church, the spirituality of the Church, and its social witness.
Participants in this renewal insisted on personal conversion and a
Christian life congruent with the leading of the Holy Spirit. The
*réveil* also took a stand against modernism, established Sunday
schools and missions to the Jews, fought alcoholism, produced and
distributed literature, and organized social-evangelistic ministry
among the urban underclasses. The Social Democratic tradition and
a number of institutions, including the Free University of Amsterdam,
have roots in the *réveil*.[24] However, it did not organize (except into
occasional local or regional parachurch structures) and remained quite
amorphous. Participants in the *réveil* often actively supported the
Evangelical Alliance, Student Volunteer Movement, and other "pietistic" ecumenical voluntary organizations. The Dutch, French, Belgian, and Swiss participants at Oxford and Brighton were mostly
from the *réveil* tradition.[25]

Mildmay, the Evangelical Alliance, and the *réveil* were intersecting networks with common concerns and goals. The nature of
the Church was central to each, as was the quality of the Christian
life. The *réveil* and Mildmay were more committed to social change
as obedience to the Christian message. Mildmay, the European
branches of the Evangelical Alliance, and the *réveil* were committed
to a developmental model of spiritual life, derived from the pietist
tradition, with its historic emphases on personal conversion, spiritual
growth, and entire consecration.

From the early 1860s, Europeans interacted with the American
Wesleyan/Holiness understanding of the Wesleyan tradition. One
after another, East Coast Holiness leaders like Charles Cullis, William
Taylor, James Caughey, and Phoebe Palmer traveled to England. In
1870, Richard C. Morgan changed the name of his periodical from
*The Revival* to *The Christian* to provide a more widely acceptable
forum for promoting American-style perfectionist revivalism. The
relationship between Morgan and American Wesleyan/Holiness revivalism dates back at least to 1867, when he published a series of essays

by Hannah Whitall Smith in *The Revival*. These were gathered and reprinted as *The Way to be Holy*.[26] By June 1869, Morgan was in America as a guest of the Smiths "on purpose to seek the blessing of holiness, & to attend the Camp Meeting"[27] at Round Lake. Significantly, Hannah Whitall Smith noted that although "he consecrated himself wholly, . . . he has not yet realized the Kingdom of God set up within."[28] Morgan became the primary publicist for Moody and for the Smiths at Oxford and Brighton and interpreter of their strengths (and weaknesses) to the British evangelical community.

Another Mildmay connection contributed to the penetration of American Wesleyan/Holiness views into the British Methodist tradition. Cuthbert Bainbridge, a wealthy layman of Newcastle and major contributor to Mildmay ministries, funded the publication of the Wesleyan/Holiness "higher life" periodical, the *King's Highway*. From its inaugural issue in January 1872, its influence extended far beyond Methodism, and it extended the British influence of American revivalists by publishing articles and "news" of American Wesleyan/ Holiness activities.[29]

The influence was not entirely one sided, however. Interaction with Mildmay facilitated the spread of Darbyist eschatology and ecclesiology in related networks, and among Moody's supporters.

### American Wesleyan/Holiness Evangelists in Europe, 1873–75

During the brief period 1873–75, several American Wesleyan/ Holiness evangelists significantly impacted the European evangelicalism. The first of these was William Boardman. Boardman's book, *The Higher Christian Life* (1858) was widely circulated in Britain: for at least fifty years extracts were reprinted in British religious periodicals. He undertook as his mission the transmission of the Wesleyan/Holiness understanding of sanctification to those in other traditions.[30] During his second visit to England in 1869, he spoke at Mildmay.[31] He returned to the United States, where he attempted, with minimal success, to duplicate Mildmay in his "Association for Holding Union, Holiness Conventions."[32] Spring 1873 found him back in England, where, through the Mildmay network, he gained introductions to clergy and invitations to breakfasts with influential persons.[33] His essays were published and his books reviewed in such popular evangelical magazines as *The Revival*, *The Christian*, the *King's Highway*, and the *Christian's Pathway to Power*.

I include D. L. Moody as a Wesleyan/Holiness evangelist with full awareness of his complex and eclectic roots in mid-American pietism. Despite his well-documented connections with the American Wesleyan/Holiness tradition, he never identified with the holiness perspective. However, in an effort to make an impact in Britain, he attempted to look like a Wesleyan/Holiness revivalist and was marketed by Morgan as such. He was also presented as a holiness figure in reports in M. Baxter's *Signs of Our Times*.[34] When R. Pearsall Smith's perfectionist concept of "eradication" of sin in this life stirred considerable controversy in 1874, some British evangelicals attempted to preserve the more influential Moody for their cause by distancing him from Smith. These efforts were generally ineffective in Britain. Moody's book *Life Words from Gospel Addresses* sounded remarkably like Hannah Whitall Smith, and his *Power from on High* was designed to parallel Boardman's *The Higher Christian Life*.[35]

Moody hagiography has tended to mislead historians. Early biographers, notably Goodspeed, Clark and Hall, and Stuart intimated that Moody arrived in England in June 1873 knowing no one, a myth that William Moody's abbreviated narrative of his father's early trips to England did little to dispel.[36] James Findlay was the first to consider the trips important for Moody's eventual success in England. Moody had been in England twice previously. During a three-month visit in the spring of 1867, he visited evangelical leaders throughout England, making the acquaintance of men like George Muller, Henry Varley, J. N. Darby, William Pennefather, F. B. Meyer, and especially Richard C. Morgan.[37] As a result, Darby and others were invited to speak at Moody's church in Chicago.[38]

In the summer of 1872, Moody went back to England and worked with the London YMCA (directed by Morgan). Significantly, he also gave a major address at the Mildmay Conference.[39] The sermon evoked spontaneous applause and was later published in its entirety in *The Christian*, where it reached most English evangelical homes.[40] As a result, William Pennefather and Cuthbert Bainbridge invited Moody to return to England for a campaign under their sponsorship.[41] However, both died in 1873 before Moody arrived. Pennefather's funeral was preached by the Holiness leader and future Keswick regular, his former curate, W. H. Aitken.[42] Moody arrived in England a few months later. The story of his campaigns in England has been analyzed by Findlay[43] and does not concern us here except at the point of his support of William Boardman and Robert Pearsall Smith.[44]

Smith had arrived in England early in 1873, encouraged by his friends, William Boardman and Richard Cope Morgan. Little is known of his early activities, but he did speak at the Mildmay Conference in July 1873 and was hosted by the former Tractarian and Mildmay regular William Haslam.[45] Both Robert and Hannah Smith made numerous contributions to *The Christian*. Smith and Boardman organized a Holiness conference at Mildmay in January 1874. After Hannah Whitall Smith arrived in England in January of 1874, she also became involved with Mildmay.[46] Pennefather's trusted advisor, Admiral E. G. Fishbourne became Smith's advisor during the period 1874–75.[47] However, there were strains in the relationship between the Americans and the Mildmay network. By July 1874, Robert had alienated Mrs. Pennefather and/or certain of her advisors and was not allowed to speak at the large 1874 Mildmay Conference. Hannah, however, was invited to speak at the Women's Conference.[48] She did advise a friend that "our conference on the subject of the Higher Life to be held at 'Broadlands' . . . will be of more value to thee I think than the Mildmay Conference."[49]

In February 1874, Robert Pearsall Smith and William Boardman started a "higher life" periodical, the *Christian's Pathway to Power*. Its single goal was the promotion of the perfectionist understanding of Wesleyan/Holiness spirituality. The first issue contained articles by Evan Hopkins, S. A. Blackwood, Henry Varley, Robert Pearsall Smith, William Boardman, E. W. Moore, P. C. Headley, and Hannah Whitall Smith. The second reported on meetings in January at Mildmay "For the Promotion of Spiritual Life."[50] March brought the first contribution from William Arthur. There were reports of "higher life" meetings conducted by Robert Pearsall Smith, Boardman, and others throughout London.[51] The May 1874 issue contained a report on the 1873 New York meeting of the Evangelical Alliance.[52]

The August 1874 fascicle augured change. It included a brief note about the recent Broadlands Conference, an article by Mrs. Pennefather,[53] and a brief account of the Mildmay Conference at which Robert Pearsall Smith was not allowed to speak.[54] These were followed directly by an invitation to the Oxford Conference. Mildmay and Mrs. Pennefather would not be mentioned again.

The Broadlands "Meeting for Consecration" (17–23 July 1873) brought together persons from both the Evangelical Alliance and the Mildmay network. It adapted the Mildmay conference format and had similar ecumenical inclusiveness, but as might be expected from its location on the Cowper-Temple estate, it included more titled and wealthy persons. These conferences would continue through 1888. The American Wesleyan/Holiness evangelists Hannah Whitall Smith and Amanda Berry Smith participated even after allegations of moral improprieties ended Robert Pearsall Smith's public involvement in mid–1875. However, it appears that the meetings dropped perfectionism despite the continued involvement of the American female revivalists.[55]

At the first Broadlands Conference, an Oxford "Union Meeting for the Promotion of Scriptural Holiness" was announced and promoted in both the *Christian's Pathway to Power* and *The Christian*.[56] The same journals published extensive descriptions of the meeting followed by the authorized report.[57]

Participants at Oxford included many of the Mildmay and Evangelical Alliance leaders, for example, Lord Radstock, W. H. Aitken, A. M. W. Christopher, Samuel Morley, C. L. Braithwaite, J. Fleming, E. W. Moore, E. P. Hathaway, S. A. Blackwood, H. Varley, and William Arthur from England. From the Continent came G. Monod, Theodore Monod, Adolphe Monod, Theodor Jellinghaus, Paul Kober, J. C. van Loon, V. von Niebuhr, Otto Stockmeyer, and Samuel Zeller. The American speakers included the Smiths, Boardman, and Asa Mahan. Future Keswick founders T. D. Harford-Battersby and Evan Hopkins were also involved. Some 1,500 persons attended.[58] Accounts of the meeting indicate that its perspective was that of the American perfectionist tradition. A number of other meetings "for the promotion of scriptural holiness" were held throughout England, but their appeal seems to have been limited and their influence at best regional.[59]

Robert Pearsall Smith began planning a trip to the Continent immediately after Oxford, although it appears that he did not actually have invitations in hand by the end of the meeting.[60] However, reports of "higher life meetings" in France conducted by Adolphe Monod were published in the *Christian's Pathway to Power*.[61] Portions were translated from *Des Christen Glaubensweg*, published by none other than C. F. Spittler at Basel.[62] A correspondent to the *Christian's Pathway to Power* reported that Monod and C. H. Rappard held meetings in Geneva attended by between 2,000 and 3,000 persons.[63] Similar meetings were held in Neufchatel, Nimes, Strasbourg, and Stuttgart. Two books by Robert Pearsall Smith (*Holiness through Faith* and *Walk in the Light*) were translated into German and widely circulated. The message was "the good news of entire liberty and peace by faith in Christ."[64] It should be noted that Monod and Rappard were leaders in the Evangelical Alliance.

On 1 March 1875, Smith reported that he had "accepted a call to Berlin for the latter part of March."[65] In Berlin, the first morning meeting of "first families of the country" was held at the estate of Count Egloffstein, president of the German Evangelical Alliance.[66] Others influential in the Smith meetings were also members of the Evangelical Alliance. In Barmen, he was hosted by Evangelical Alliance activists Theodor Christlieb and D. Fabri. The Evangelical Alliance also made arrangements for the Smith meetings in Basel and Stuttgart. They perceived that Smith was addressing their concerns. Smith was convinced that they were responding to something new. The lead article in the June issue of the *Christian's Pathway to Power* dealt with the issues raised by the Evangelical Alliance. It stated that the Alliance "has been of untold blessing to Christendom" but the unity was based on keeping differences hidden. Smith argued that his meetings went one step further by forgetting all denominational distinctions and avoiding theological issues. It was this "fusion of hearts" that he expected to occur at Brighton. Only thus did he believe the ultimate Alliance of Christians could be accomplished.[67]

The "Convention for the Promotion of Scriptural Holiness" at Brighton was announced in the *Christian's Pathway to Power* and advertised faithfully in *The Christian*.[68] The invitation was well received in the Evangelical Alliance on the Continent. Most of the foreign participants who came were active in the Evangelical Alliance.[69] Those from France, Switzerland, Belgium, and the Netherlands were also committed to the perspective of the *Réveil*. The English participants were from the Mildmay and/or Evangelical Alliance groups. The activities of the Convention were widely reported in *The Christian*, the *King's Highway*, *Signs of Our Times*, and *The Record*. A report of the Brighton Convention was published and its complexion and initial impact has been admirably described by Dieter.[70] The message, that by faith one can be sanctified *now*, was articulated in Wesleyan/Holiness perfectionist categories. It was not the message, but rather the categories for stating it, that would be changed after the "fall" of Robert Pearsall Smith. Smith's perfectionism, with the attendant expectations of an American-style religious experience, had been troublesome even to some of Smith's supporters. It would appear that an indiscretion on Smith's part gave them a basis for eradicating him. Interestingly enough, Hannah Whitall Smith continued to minister in the Evangelical circles, and her book, *The Christian's Secret of a Happy Life*, devoid of the chapter on "Baptism in the Holy Spirit" and understood in terms of developmental spirituality, remained influential.[71] Robert Pearsall Smith withdrew from active ministry, and only once was Charles Cullis able to convince him to take part in a conference.

It would appear that the American contributions to the events of 1873–75 were different than have usually been suggested. The issue of Christian holiness was not new. The perfectionist interpretation was not new. Numerous American Wesleyan/Holiness advocates and some British Methodists had articulated that perspective for years. And yet, the testimonies are remarkably uniform. People experienced a paradigm shift at Oxford and Brighton as well as on the Continent under the ministries of A. Monod, C. H. Rappard, R. P. Smith, and others. The sociopolitical stress of the Franco-Prussian war has to be considered a factor in the response. The Christian community was ready for the vision of a Christian perfection that is internal, achieved by faith, and has no other requirement than to lead a quiet, devout, personal Christian life. It is interesting to note that after the 1873–75 Holiness revivals, there was a break in the link between the Christian social responsibility and the personal holiness that had been the genius of Mildmay and many other centers. The new ministries adapted only the "Conference" format. They did not look for other avenues of ministry, despite the support offered to related *foreign* mission groups.

## Keswick and Related Phenomena

After July 1875, when Smith withdrew from ministry in disgrace, Smith's perfectionist understanding of Christian holiness fell on hard times. The concept of "sanctification through faith" as a result of entire consecration remained, but it was reinterpreted into the sociotheological framework of the audience. In England this took place primarily through the means of a series of conferences now entitled "Devotional Meetings for the Promotion of Spiritual Life."[72] These were held throughout England. It was however, the conference at Keswick that became the most regular and lasting.

The longevity and success of this annual conference was due to the prodigious efforts of T. D. Harford-Battersby. Harford-Battersby had been active in the Evangelical Alliance both in England and internationally.[73] He also had connections with Mildmay and William Pennefather.[74]

In the early 1870s, Harford-Battersby began to long for the "higher Christian life" as described by W. E. Boardman's book and R. P. Smith's articles in *The Christian*. He expressed concern over the "dangerously unguarded language" that seemed to hint at "sinless perfection," but felt that these writings "brought forward a very high ideal of the duties and responsibilities of Christian holiness of life."[75] He attended the conferences at Oxford and had a significant religious experience.[76] The "Keswick Union Meetings for the Promotion of Practical Holiness" were held from 29 June to 2 July 1875. Harford-Battersby reported in the *Christian's Pathway to Power* that the testimonies to "full surrender to the Lord, and the subsequent experience of an abiding peace" were many.[77] During the first few years of the Keswick Convention, it is clear that there was an evolution in the language used to express "Keswick" spirituality away from the perfectionist tradition and back toward the synthesis of Mildmay that incorporated low church Anglican, Darbyist, Quaker and Baptist theological language. This coincided with the establishment of a close relationship between the two conferences and reflected the hesitancy of the Keswick founders to be identified with American perfectionist thought. Often the same speakers were at both annual conferences. For example, in 1892, S. A. Blackwood, H. C. G. Moule, J. B. Figgis,[78] A. T. Pierson, F. B. Meyer, Evan Hopkins, H. E. Brooke, and George Wilson, traditional Keswick speakers, were on the platform at Mildmay.[79] This continued into the early 1900s. A key bridge figure between the two conferences and in the evolution of a Keswick point of view was Baptist pastor-folk theologian Frederick Brotherton Meyer.[80] *The Christian*, the *Christian's Pathway to Power*, which became the *Life of Faith*, and after 1909, Jessie Penn Lewis's *The Overcomer* (heavily influenced by Meyer) served as media for communication within the networks and to the larger evangelical movement.

In Germany, the "higher life" wing of the Evangelical Alliance sponsored a number of conferences out of which flowed the *Gemeinschaftsbewegung*. Detailed descriptions of this development have been published by Fleisch and Lange.[81] The German "higher life" evangelicals retained the concept of "holiness through faith" that is "available now," but as Dieter has indicated, it was interpreted using the conservative pietist theological categories.[82] For example, Theodor Jellinghaus interpreted the insights gained at the Oxford meeting in light of pietistic Lutheran theology.[83] He also published regularly in *Des Christen Glaubensweg* and conducted Bible schools in which, between 1885 and 1910, over 10,000 laity and young clergy were introduced to the theoretical structures of "higher Christian life."[84]

Theodor Monod organized "higher life" conferences throughout French speaking Europe. He hosted Smith during his visit to the Continent and recruited French, Swiss, and Belgian pastors to attend Brighton (including Adolphe Monod, William Monod, Frederic Dumas, and Elie Vernier). After Brighton, he continued his conference schedule. French Protestant periodicals frequently included translations of perfectionist devotional material. However the language and the experience became that of the *réveil* and was shorn of its perfectionist elements.[85]

Monod remained a churchman and the results of his activities were confined primarily within the Protestant churches in France, although many individuals found expression for their spirituality through parachurch organizations such as the Student Volunteer Movement and other ecumenical organizations. Monod continued to be active in the international leadership of the Evangelical Alliance. Eventually the spirituality moved in three directions: Christian Socialism; the fundamentalism represented by Brigade de la Drome; and, pentecostalism.[86] Significantly, Wilfrid Monod, theologian of Christian Socialism, wrote the two-volume work *"La nuée des témoins,"* which traced the founding, deformation, reformation, and transformation of the church. In the panoply of saints he included Wesley, Frederic Oberlin, Adolphe Monod, William Booth, Francois Coillard, and Tommy Fallot. Theirs was a tradition of social responsibility based on a realization of the "higher Christian life."[87]

The Evangelical Alliance *(Nederlandsche Evangelische Protestantsche Vereenigin)* was founded in 1853 by P. J. E. van Soeterwoude, who had been active in *Het Réveil*. Baron J. W. van Loon was part of the steering committee for the Dutch Evangelical Alliance.[88] The English campaigns of Moody were reported in the Dutch press, and attracted attention as well.[89] Both van Soeterwoude and van Loon attended the Oxford meeting. When Smith visited the Netherlands, he spoke in the home of van Soeterwoude to many upper-class Dutch, including Queen Sophie, Prince Frederick, and Princess Marie.[90] Van Soeterwoude recruited pastors to attend Brighton, and personally paid the way of many. Among those who attended were Frans Lion Cachet,[91] Abraham Kuyper, Gerth van Wijk, Adama van Scheltema, and Baron von Boetzelaar.[92]

Kuyper hosted the Dutch contingent at his home in August 1875 and they began to publish a periodical, *De weg ter Godzaligheid*, to spread the Wesleyan/Holiness ideal of "sanctification by faith through entire consecration."[93] A series of meetings were held throughout the country and there were numerous publications both for and against the concept. Soon, again, the Methodistic Wesleyan/Holiness perfectionism of Smith was replaced with the language of the *réveil*, influenced as it was by the Darbyist eschatology and ecclesiology.[94]

The pattern for the Moody and Smith campaigns was the same in each country. In each there was a network provided by the Evangelical Alliance and either pietism or the *réveil*. The access of Smith to the upper classes on the Continent was made possible by this network. In each situation there was initial acceptance of Smith's perfectionistic expression of Wesleyan/Holiness spirituality. The frequent comments about his "unguarded language" suggest, however, that his audiences did not understand the perfectionist (especially eradicationist) language as serious or as reflecting a novel spirituality. They heard the descriptions of the "higher Christian life" in terms of their own spiritual heritages. After Brighton, "higher life" revivalists rejected any hint of perfectionism. They increasingly moved toward a more developmental model of spirituality congruent with the pietist and *réveil* traditions of spirituality. In each country the revivalists adapted the language and accommodated the structures in their efforts to make them more comprehensible to the local religious scene.[95] I have been unable to document efforts to hold international, ecumenical "holiness-higher life" conferences on the model of Brighton. Even Mildmay became more cautiously British.

## Keswick Comes to America

Accounts of the campaigns of Moody and Smith were carried in both the religious and secular American press. The narratives made Moody an American hero, and people stood ready to accept Smith even after his disgrace.[96] After his return to the United States, Moody began to position himself in contradiction to the perfectionist vision of entire sanctification.[97] Moody self-consciously revised the structures of his ministry. His constituency changed from Chicago lower and middle class (with upper-class and new money patronage) to the upper-middle and upper classes of the North East. He moved away from the model of the National Holiness Association toward the model of Mildmay.[98] The Northfield Conference was modeled after that of Mildmay, focusing on eschatology and holiness within an ecumenical context. It is not surprising that among the foreign visitors was F. B. Meyer, who analyzed the situation in the States: "these . . . have prejudiced the minds of thinking people, especially ministers, against what is known as *the movement for the Deepening of the Spiritual life*. I was told . . . never mention a word about holiness if I desire to make people really holy."[99] Meyer prided himself in being able to articulate a view of sanctification that was not contaminated by perfectionism. He discovered that the Mildmay-Keswick description of sanctification/ baptism in the Holy Spirit brought people into a renewed experience of spirituality. The teaching was accepted at Northfield.[100] Meyer spoke at four successive conferences from 1891 to 1894. He was succeeded by H. Webb-Peploe and Geddes H. C. MacGregor.[101] Sandeen has observed that at Northfield, Keswick spirituality and millenarianism were wed.[102] Northfield was like Mildmay in its results as well as its structure.

Northfield and the millenarian activities of the last two decades of the nineteenth century were in different socioeconomic and religious circles than the Wesleyan/Holiness movement. It would appear that, through 1909, the Wesleyan/Holiness movement considered Keswick an ally defective only at the point of denial of "eradication" of the sinful nature at the moment of sanctification. One of the most extensive early treatments found thus far in the Wesleyan/Holiness periodicals is by J. B. Culpepper:[103]

> Mr. Moody has brought the recipients of this "Keswick experience" to Northfield, and thousands have been instructed of them in the deeper things of God. In but one tenet do their teachers seem to differ from ... more modern advocates of the deeper life ... they ... teach not ... eradication.
>
> After I first read of this movement, two or three years ago, my animadversions led me to ask ... why cross the Atlantic ocean and publish as a great discovery, that which every Methodist held ... it is similar to what Mr. A. B. Simpson teaches ...
>
> [Opposition to the Wesleyan/Holiness teaching comes because] we send out too many young, inexperienced and, often densely ignorant teachers. They offend ... and disgust intelligent natures. The Salvation Army puts each would be leader through a long drill. With us anything can talk endlessly of the deep things of God. We are reaping a just harvest.
>
> We talk much of the blessing—the blessing. The Keswickites talk much of the Blesser–the Blesser. They are seized by a *Him*, we by an *it*. They talk of the great Person who has come into their body and soul and life. We speak more of a thing which we received of Christ. One of the many consequences seems to be an easy drift with many of us into lightness, then vagueness.

The self-criticism reflected in Culpepper's essay was not typical. However, attacks on Keswick came because of the experiences of two Wesleyan/Holiness evangelists in England and India. W. B. Godbey, while in India, found the audience at a Keswick Convention in India unreceptive to his theory of the "eradication." He wrote an acerbic essay entitled *Keswickism* in which he argued that their views were a "deficiency rather than a heresy," and that, "Keswickism . . . breaks down because the Holy Ghost will not abide, while old Adam remains in the heart."[104]

More widely read was A. M. Hills's *Scriptural Holiness and Keswick Teaching Compared*, which grew out of his personal pique at not being accepted at Keswick. His became the standard Wesleyan/Holiness critique of Keswick.[105] These were the first of an extensive apologetic literature that argued against the Keswick tradition, even as Wesleyan/Holiness theologians were themselves adapting a developmental model for spirituality.[106] Wesleyan/Holiness readers happily read the work of A. B. Simpson, F. B. Meyer, W. H. Griffith Thomas, Geddes H. C. MacGregor, and others. Today most Wesleyan/Holiness Christians hold a Keswick theory of sanctification along with a premillennial eschatology.

The rhetoric of Godbey and Hills would probably not have been so influential if Keswick had not surfaced after 1913 among the Presbyterians. Charles G. Trumball, editor of the *Sunday School Times*, converted to millenarianism and a "higher life" spirituality in 1910.[107] The *Sunday School Times* became an important forum for the advocacy of the Keswick "higher Christian life" and was influential in developing a Keswick consensus among evangelicals. With the assistance of his associate editor, Robert C. McQuilkin, Trumball organized "Victorious Life" conferences beginning in Oxford, Pennsylvania, 19–27 July 1913.

The featured speaker in 1913 was none other than W. H. Griffith Thomas. Later conferences were held at Princeton, New Jersey (1914–18), where they attracted the wrath of B. B. Warfield.[108] Although the speakers and literature sought to express the Keswick ideals in terms used at England's Keswick, sociocultural factors made the target audience, which was heavily Presbyterian, reinterpret the message in terms of the Presbyterian heritage. Both Keswick millenarians from the Prophecy Conference network and Presbyterians frustrated with their churches would withdraw to form fundamentalist churches.[109] However, through these two streams, Keswick spirituality became entrenched in Baptist and Presbyterian denominations.

## Conclusion

Keswick cannot be viewed as a solitary unit evolving *ex nihilo* from the efforts of a group of American Wesleyan/Holiness evangelists. The work of these evangelists must be seen in the context of the Mildmay ministries and the Evangelical Alliance. On the Continent, there were also well-established networks into which R. P. Smith was able to inject his message, especially the Evangelical Alliance and the *réveil*. It is certain that the message delivered to the Europeans was that of the American Wesleyan/Holiness tradition. It is much less certain what was heard. It is evident that the message of "sanctification by faith—now" was reinterpreted and promulgated in established theological and experiential categories by the target audiences. The ongoing debates over the nature of the church and of spirituality were addressed, but not resolved.

If this analysis is sustained by further research, it will require some revision of our understanding of the European evangelical tradition, American Evangelicalism/Fundamentalism, and of the relation of the American Wesleyan/Holiness tradition to both.

## NOTES

1. T. D. Harford-Battersby, founder of Keswick, *Reminiscences of the Keswick Convention, 1879, with Addresses by Pastor Otto Stockmayer* (London: S. W. Partridge, 1879), provided an early account, indicating its dependency on the conferences of Broadlands (1874), Oxford (1874), and Brighton (1875). He acknowledged the role of the American revivalists William Boardman, Robert Pearsall Smith, and Hannah Smith. His perspective was reiterated in a biography by his sons, *Memoir of T. D. Harford-Battersby together with some accounts of the Keswick Convention*, with a preface by H. C. G. Moule (London: Seeley, 1890). Evan Hopkins, "Preliminary Stages," *The Keswick Convention, Its Message, Its Method and Its Men*, ed. Charles F. Harford (London: Marshall Brothers, [1907]), 1–21, H. W. Webb-Peploe and E. W. Moore, "Early Keswick Conventions," ibid., 35–47, and Evan Hopkins, *A Standard Bearer of Faith and Holiness; Reminiscences with a Memoir by the Author* (London: Morgan and Scott, 1919), all early participants, continued the argument of the American origins of Keswick, as did J. B. Figgis, *Keswick from Within* (London: Marshall Brothers, 1914) [note: this volume was written at the request of Hannah Whitall Smith. See J. Westbury-Jones, *"Figgis of Brighton," Memoir of a Modern Saint* (London: Marshall Brothers, 1917), 192–93.], Walter B. Sloan, *These Sixty Years, The Story of the Keswick Convention* (London: Pickering and Inglis, [ca. 1935]), and J. C. Pollock, *The Keswick Story, The Authorized History of the Keswick Convention* (London: Hodder and Stoughton, 1964).

2. From outside the Keswick movement the same understanding of the origins of Keswick is standard. E. H. Johnson, *The Highest Life, A Story of Shortcomings and a Goal; Including a Friendly Analysis of the Keswick Movement* (New York: A. C. Armstrong, 1901) criticized Keswick at the

point of its perfectionist American roots. A similar critique was developed by J. B. Shearer, *Modern Mysticism; or, The Covenants of the Spirit, Their Scope and Limitation* (Richmond: Presbyterian Committee of Publications, 1905). Paul Fleisch traced the origins of the German *Gemeinschaftsbewegung* to the visits of R. P. Smith on the Continent. See Paul Fleisch, *Die moderne Gemeinschaftsbewegung in Deutschland* (Leipzig: H. G. Walmann, 1903, 2d ed. 1906); *Zur Gerschichte der Heiligungsbewegung*, Bnd. I: *Die Heiligungbewegung von Wesley bis Boardman* (Leipzig: H. G. Walman, 1910); *Die moderne Gemeineschaftsbewegung in Deutschland*, Bnd. I: *Die Geschichte der deutschen Gemeinschaftsbewegung bis zum Auftreten des Zungenredens (1875–1905)* (Leipzig: H. G. Walmann, 1912), reprinted in The Higher Christian Life Series, ed. D. W. Dayton (New York: Garland, 1985); "Der Heiligungslehre der Oxforderbewegung," *Neue kirchliche Zeitschrift* 35 (1924): 49–87; "Die Entstehung der deutschen Heiligungsbewegung vor 50 Jahren," *Neue kirchliche Zeitschrift* 38 (1927): 663–702. *Oxfordbewegung* (named after the Oxford Conference of 1875) came to denote a German theological *Tendenz* similar to that of Keswick. After the advent of Pentecostalism in Germany, Fleisch interpreted the new movement as a derivation of the *Oxfordbewegung* and American perfectionism, an analysis that has become standard in German scholarship as one sees in the recent volume by Dieter Lange, *Eine Bewegung bricht sich Bahn; Die deutschen Gemeinschaften im ausgehenden 19. und beginnenden 20. Jahrhundert und ihre Stellung zu Kirche, Theologie und Pfingstbewegung* (Giessen: Brunnen Verlag; Dillenburg: Gnadauer Verlag, 1979). B. B. Warfield, *Perfectionism* (New York: Oxford University Press, 1931), canonized Fleish's analysis for the Anglo-Saxon world in his monumental critique of perfectionism.

3. Proponents of the theory of the American roots include Steven Barabas, *So Great Salvation: The History and Message of the Keswick Convention* (London: Marshall, Morgan and Scott, 1952); David Bundy, *Keswick: A Bibliographic Introduction to the Higher Life Movements* (Occasional Bibliographic Papers of the B. L. Fisher Library, 1975); Melvin E. Dieter, *The Holiness Revival of the Nineteenth Century* (Studies in Evangelicalism 1; Meteuchen: Scarecrow Press, 1980); George M. Marsden, *Fundamentalism and American Culture; The Shaping of Twentieth-Century Evangelicalism: 1870–1925* (New York: Oxford University Press, 1980); Donald W. Dayton, *The Theological Roots of Pentecostalism* (Grand Rapids: Zondervan, 1987); David Bundy, "Keswick Higher Life Movement," *Dictionary of Pentecostal and Charismatic Movements*, ed. S. Burgess et al. (Grand Rapids: Zondervan, 1988), 518–19.

4. John Kent, *Holding the Fort: Studies in Victorian Revivalism* (London: Epworth Press, 1978), began to draw this interpetative consensus into question by exploring the social significance of Victorian revivalism. David Bebbington, *Evangelicalism in Modern Britain; A History from the 1730s to the 1980s* (London: Unwin Hyman, 1989), 151–80, traced various theological strands that influenced the development of Keswick. This essay was completed before Bebbington's book became available.

5. All details except as noted regarding William Pennefather and Mildmay come from Robert Braithwaite, *The Life and Letters of Rev. William Pennefather, B.A.* (New York: Robert Carter and Brothers, 1878). See also *A Retrospect of Mildmay Work during the Year 1887* (London: Mildmay, 1887).

6. Hy. Pickering, ed. *Chief Men among the Brethren*, 2d ed. (London: Pickering & Inglis, 1931), 12. This relationship is important for analyzing the flow of Darbyist ideology into the Evangelical wing of the Anglican Church.

7. Braithwaite, *Life and Letters*, 304–5 (emphasis in original).

8. Ibid., 305.

9. On the deaconess movement, and Pennefather's role in its English and American development, see Jane M. Bancroft, *Deaconesses in Europe and Their Lessons for America*, with an introduction by E. G. Andrews (New York: Hunt and Eaton; Cincinnati: Cranston and Stowe, 1889); Hariette J. Cooke, *Mildmay; or, The Story of the First Deaconess Institution*, 2d. ed. (London: Elliot Stock, 1893); Lucy Rider-Meyer, *Deaconesses, Biblical, Early Church, European, American, with The Story of the Chicago Training School for City, Home and Foreign Missions, and the Chicago Deaconess Home* (Chicago: Message Publishing Company, 1889) [note: Rider-Meyer was sent to England to examine Mildmay and other institutions by D. L. Moody in order to develop a model for the Chicago ministries]; C. Goldner, *History of the Deaconess Movement in the Christian Church* (Cincinnati: Jennings and Pye; New York: Eaton and Mains, 1903).

10. Braithwaite, *Life and Letters*, 253–56.

11. Cooke, *Mildmay*; Braithwaite, *Life and Letters*, 414: "He was surprised to find himself welcomed as 'a brother beloved' by foreign Christians, some of whom had been present at one or more of the various Conferences, while to others his name was familiar." On Fliedner, see, M. Gerhardt, *Theodor Fliedner, Ein Lebensbild* (Dusseldorf-Kaiserwerth: Diakonissenanstalt, 1933–37), and A. Sticker, *Theodor Fliedner der Diakonissenvater* (Kaiserwerth: Verlag der Diakonissenanstalt, 1950).

12. Bancroft, *Deaconesses in Europe*, 166–88; Rider-Meyer, *Deaconesses*, 41–44; Cooke, *Mildmay*, passim.

13. On the concept of lay ministry and the network that developed, see R. C. Morgan, *The Life of Richard Weaver, the Converted Collier* (London: Morgan and Scott, n.d.); Clyde Binfield, *George Williams and the Y.M.C.A.: A Study in Victorian Social Attitudes* (London: Heinemann, 1973); C. Binfield, *So Down to Prayers; Studies in English Nonconformity, 1780–1920* (London: J. M. Dent; Totowa, N.J.: Rowman and Littlefield, 1977); John Macpherson, *The Life and Labors of Duncan Matheson, the Scottish Evangelist* (New York: Robert Carter, 1876).

14. I have been unable to document the beginning of Pennefather's involvement in the Evangelical Alliance. See John W. Ewing, *Goodly Fellowship: A Centenary Tribute to the Life and Work of the World's Evangelical Alliance, 1846–1946* (London: Marshall, Morgan and Scott, 1946), 35, regarding

the 1896 Evangelical Alliance meeting at Mildmay. See also, Braithwaite, *Life and Letters*, passim.

15. George E. Morgan, *"A Veteran in Revival," R. C. Morgan: His Life and Times*, with an introduction by the Rt. Hon. Lord Kinnaird (London: Morgan and Scott, 1909), 46.

16. Morgan, *"Veteran in Revival,"* 47.

17. *Evangelical Alliance; Report of the Proceedings of the Conference held at the Freemasons's Hall, London, from August 19th to September 2nd Inclusive, 1846* (London: Partridge and Oakley, 1847); William Arthur, *Tongue of Fire* (London: Adam Hamilton, 1865). Arthur's volume was accepted as a classic statement of Wesleyan/Holiness ideology on both sides of the Atlantic. It became an important source for the early pentecostal movement in the United States, Britain, and on the Continent. Theodor Christlieb exemplifies the complex relationships between Mildmay and the Evangelical Alliance in Germany. See *Theodor Christlieb, D. D., of Bonn. Memoir by his widow and Sermons*, trans. T. L. Kingsbury and Samuel Garratt (London: Hodder and Stoughton, 1892), and Eugen Sachsse, "Christlieb, Theodor," *Realencyklopädie für protestantische Theologie und Kirche* 4, 1898, 1–4.

18. Ewing, *Goodly Fellowship*, 27–28.

19. *Evangelical Alliance Conference, 1873; History, Essays, Orations, and other Documents of the Sixth General Conference of the Evangelical Alliance held in New York, October 2–12, 1873*, ed. Philip Schaff and S. Prime (New York: Harper and Brothers, 1874).

20. *Evangelical Alliance Report . . . 1846*, 310–57, and passim. See also the letter sent to the conference by the Anti-Slavery Society of London, pages xxviii–xl.

21. "Oxford Conferences," *The Christian's Pathway to Power* 1:10 (2 Nov. 1874): 199–200.

22. *Adresses of Foreigne Visitors to the Brighton Convention* (n.p.: n.p., n.d.). This list, while helpful is far from complete.

23. Ami Bost, *Memoires pouvant servir à l'historie du réveil religeux des églises protestantes de la Suisse et de la France, et à l'intelligence des principales questions théologiques et ecclésiastiques du jour* (Paris: Librairie Protestante, 1854–55); Daniel Robert, *Les Églises Réformées en France (1800–1830)* (Paris: Presses Universitaires de France, 1961), 418–45; Hans Krabbendam, *Zielenverbrijzelaars en zondelozen; Nederlandse reacties op Moody, Sankey en Pearsall Smith*, Doctoraalscriptie, Leiden, 1988, 55; Marie Elizabeth Kluit, *Het protestantse Réveil in nederland en daarbuiten, 1815–1865* (Amsterdam: H. J. Paris, 1970), especially, pages 277–341, 348–50, 367–82; M. E. Kluit, *Nederlands Archief voor Kerkgeschiedenis* 45 (1963): 33–52; B. de Gaay Fortman, *Figuren uit het Réveil* (Kampen: J. H. Kok, 1980); Erich Beyreuther, *Die Erweckungsbewegung* (Die Kirche in ihrer Geschichte, ein Handbuch hrsg. K. D. Schmidt und E. Wolf, Bnd. 4, 1; Gottingen: Vandenhoeck & Ruprecht, 1963), R16–R22.

24. Krabbendam, *Zielenverbrijzelaars*, 55.

25. "Oxford Conferences," *Christian's Pathway to Power* 1:10 (2 Nov. 1874): 200; *Adresses of Foreigne Visitors to the Brighton Convention.*

26. Hannah Whitall Smith, *The Way to Be Holy* (London: Morgan and Chase, 1867), also published as, *God's Way to Holiness as Set Forth in the Scriptures* (Philadelphia: English Smith, 1868); Hannah Whitall Smith to Mary Whitall, 5 February 1868 alludes to the ongoing business relationship. A special thanks to Melvin E. Dieter, who provided the references to Richard Morgan and Mildmay in the correspondence of Hannah Whitall Smith. His edition of the correspondence will significantly impact the historiography of revivalism.

27. Hannah Whitall Smith to Frank Smith, 27 June 1869.

28. Ibid. Other letters fret over whether or not Richard Morgan will publish her material without alteration: see letters, Hannah Whitall Smith to Robert Pearsall Smith, 1 May 1873; 16 August 1873; 19 October 1873; 7 December 1873. She was angry when Morgan and Robert Pearsall Smith altered her work: Hannah Whitall Smith to Robert Pearsall Smith, 28 June 1873.

29. Thomas Hudson Bainbridge, *Reminiscences*, ed. Gerald France (London: C. H. Kelly, 1913), 55–56; *The King's Highway* 2: 10 (Oct. 1873): 346. See the obituary by John Westlake, "The Late Mr. Cuthbert Bainbridge," *King's Highway* 2:5 (May 1873): 176–78. See also, I. E. Page, *John Brash: Memorials and Correspondence* (London: C. H. Kelly, 1912).

30. Mary F. Boardman, *Life and Labours of the Rev. W. E. Boardman*, with a preface by the Rev. Mark Guy Pearse (New York: D. Appleton and Company, 1887), 134–36.

31. *Revival*, 11 (4 Nov. 1869): 1–2.

32. Boardman, *Life and Labours*, 136–41.

33. Ibid., 156–57.

34. *Signs of Our Times: A Serial of Prophetic Exposition, Jewish Intelligence and Revival News* (9 June 1875): 368.

35. Dwight L. Moody, *Life Words from Gospel Addresses* (London: J. Snow, 1875); D. L. Moody, *Power from On High; or, The Secret of Success in Christian Life and Christian Work* (London: Morgan and Scott, 1882). The American edition was *Secret Power; or, The Secret of Success in Christian Life and Christian Work* (Chicago: F. H. Revell, 1881).

36. Rufus W. Clark, *The Work of God in Great Britain: Under Messrs. Moody and Sankey, 1873–1875. With Biographical Sketches* (New York: Harper and Brothers, 1875); John Hall and George H. Stuart, *The American Evangelists, D. L. Moody and Ira D. Sankey, in Great Britain and Ireland* (New York: Dodd and Mead, 1875); E. J. Goodspeed, *A Full History of the Wonderful Career of Moody and Snakey, in Great Britain and America, Embracing, also, Mr. Moody's Sermons, as Preached in this Country and Abroad, Mr. Sankey's Songs, and Everything of Interest Connected with the Work* (New York: Henry S. Goodspeed, 1876); William R. Moody, *The Life of Dwight L. Moody* (New York: Fleming H. Revell, 1900).

37. James F. Findlay, *Dwight L. Moody; American Evangelist 1837-1899*, with a foreword by Martin E. Marty (Chicago: University of Chicago Press, 1869), 124-28. Morgan recalled meeting Moody for the first time, "One day in 1867, a plain, sturdy, stoutly-built young man came into our office on Ludgate Hill. He was about the Lord's business. He had heard of us through *The Revival*; and we were, so far as we remember, the first on whom he called in London" (Morgan, *"Veteran of Revival,"* 170-71). Emma Moody spoke of the relationship, Emma C. Moody to Anna Reese, 3 May 1867, Dwight L. Moody Papers, Yale Divinity School, Group 28, I, 8, 92: "Tomorrow we are going to Mr. Morgan's to stay over Sunday. I expect a pleasant time." The close involvement of Morgan in the Moody-Sankey campaign can be seen from the narrative of Morgan, *"Veteran of Revival,"* 169-88, as well as references in the unpublished *Journal of Mrs. Jane MacKinnon*, Dwight L. Moody papers, Yale Divinity School, Group 28, III, 14, 1, and was similarly recalled in G. Bennett to Will Moody, 12 March 1900, Dwight L. Moody Papers, Yale Divinity School, Group 28, I, 8, 95, who wrote of Morgan's responsibility for "communications." Douglas Russell to editor, *Life of Faith*, 28 December 1923, Dwight L. Moody papers, Yale Divinity School, Group 28, I, 8, 95, wrote of Moody working with Varley in Dublin. There are also references to H. Drummond and W. Haslam. The unpublished *Journal of Emma C. Moody, 1873-1875, Great Britain Campaign*, Dwight L. Moody Papers, Yale Divinity School, Group 28, III, 14, 2, provides only minimal relational details.

38. H. A. Ironside, *A Historical Sketch of the Brethren Movement* (Grand Rapids: Zondervan, 1942), 81-82. F. Roy Coad, *A History of the Brethren Movement. Its Origins, its Worldwide Development and its Significance for the Present Day* (London: Paternoster, 1968), 187-88, discusses the visit of Henry Moorhouse with Moody in Chicago.

39. Braithwaite, *Life and Letters*, 489.

40. *The Christian* 3 (11 Aug. 1872): 8-10.

41. Findlay, *Dwight L. Moody*, 149-50. Bainbridge was well aware of the American religious scene. See for example his reports of his travels, Cuthbert Bainbridge, "Over the Atlantic. Jottings of an American Tour," *King's Highway* 2:2 (Feb. 1873): 52-56. See also, Bainbridge, *Reminiscences*, passim.

42. Braithwaite, *Life and Letters*, 510-11. Aitken began his ministry as the curate of Pennefather at Midway; see Braithwaite, *Life and Letters*, 394-98. Aitken participated in the Oxford and Brighton Conferences: *Account of the Union Meeting for the Promotion of Scriptural Holiness held at Brighton, May 29th to June 7th, 1875* (Brighton: W. J. Smith; London: S. W. Partridge, 1875), 7. See also Aitken's discussion of Smith's "fall" in his letter to the editor, *Christian's Pathway to Power* 3:26 (1 Mar. 1876): 2.

43. Findlay, *Dwight L. Moody*, 150-91.

44. *Account of the Union Meeting . . . Brighton*, 47, 319.

45. Hannah Whitall Smith to Sarah Nicholson, 14 July 1873: "Mr. Smith continues to write most glowing accounts of his Christian work. In his last

letter he was in the midst of the Mildmay Conference; an annual meeting of all the principal Evangelical workers in Eng. Scot. & Ireland; and was holding crowded meetings of two, three, & four hours long, for the Higher Life, with clergymen etc. seeking to enter in!" On Smith's early weeks in England, see Alexander Smellie, *Evan Henry Hopkins, A Memoir*, with an introductory chapter by H. C. G. Moule (London: Marshall Brothers, 1920), 53–54; and, Boardman, *Life and Labours*, 156–60.

46. Hannah Whitall Smith to Mary Whitall, 8 February 1874.

47. Boardman, *Life and Labours*, 155–60. Fishbourne also served as a "referee" for Booths's mission in the late 1860s and early 1870s. Other Mildmay "referees," who can be identified as such, included Samuel Morley, J. H. Wilson, R. C. Morgan, and Samuel Chase. Catharine Booth also had discussions about women's ministry and personal holiness with R. C. Morgan. She convinced him of the validity of women's ministry and he frequently sponsored her and appeared on the platform with her. See F. de L. Booth-Tucker, *The Life of Catharine Booth, The Mother of the Salvation Army*, 3d ed. (New York, Chicago: Fleming H. Revell, 1892), 2:541–45, 620–21, and, Morgan, *"Veteran of Revival,"* 155–56, 294–302.

48. Hannah Whitall Smith to John and Mary Whitall, 1 July 1874.

49. Hannah Whitall Smith to Patricia Munsey, 24 June 1874. In a letter, Hannah Whitall Smith to Mary Whitall, 8 February 1874, Hannah indicates her mixed feelings about the Mildmay ministries and recounts a visit with Mrs. Pennefather: "Then the families are generally enormous, and there are four or five single ladies at home and it seems really necessary almost for two or three of them to go to a deaconess House. . . . I was thrown in with a good number of the Mildmay workers yesterday and I felt homesick all day afterwards. Perhaps it was a sense of my own shortcomings; I cannot tell, but I really was appalled. It may have been that to see women so cut off from home ties seemed unnatural to me. . . . I went to see Mrs. Pennefather yesterday at her request, but found her home sick in bed, so had to content myself with looking at and hearing about her 'work.' Now that her husband is dead, she had the great Conference Hall, an Orphanage, a Home for respectable Invalids, a Deaconess Home, a Probationer's Home, preparatory to the Deaconess Home, a Working Men's Hall, a Ragged School, a Boarding School, and all the poor of a large Parish under her sole care!! The money comes in by prayer, I believe."

50. "The Late Meetings 'For the Promotion of Spiritual Life,' at the Mildmay Conference Hall," *Christian's Pathway to Power* 1:2 (2 Mar. 1874): 38–39.

51. William Arthur, "The Beauty of Holiness," *Christian's Pathway to Power* 1:3 (1 Apr. 1874): 52–56.

52. "Evangelical Alliance Meeting, New York," *Christian's Pathway to Power* 1:4 (1 May 1874): 78–79.

53. Mrs. Pennefather, "The Secret of Loyal Service," *Christian's Pathway to Power* 1:7 (1 Aug. 1874): 126–28.

54. Hannah Whitall Smith to John and Mary Whitall, 1 July 1874; "The Mildmay Conference," *Christian's Pathway to Power* 1:2 (2 Mar. 1874): 140.

55. Edna V. Jackson, *Life that is Life Indeed* (London: James Nisbet, 1910). See also, Mrs. Edward Trotter, *Lord Radstock, An Interpretation and a record* (London: Hodder and Stoughton, n.d.), 30, and passim.

56. "A Week at Oxford, Aug. 31st to Sept. 7th, 1874," *Christian's Pathway to Power* 1:2 (2 Mar. 1874): 140; "The Oxford Meeting," *Christian's Pathway to Power* 1:8 (1 Sept. 1874): 158–59; R. P. Smith, "Union Meeting for the Promotion of Scriptural Holiness," *Christian's Pathway to Power* 1:8 (1 Sept. 1874): 160. A four-page brochure circulated by Robert Pearsall Smith, *Union Meeting, for the Promotion of Scriptural Holiness to be held at Oxford August 29th to September 7th, 1874* (London: Barratt and Sons, 1874), presented the reason for the meetings ("feeling of deep dissatisfaction with their present spiritual state"), suggested a "need for power," made comparisons with the "spiritual hunger" in America, and provided a list of persons cooperating with the meeting including Lord Farnham (Pennefather's brother), S. A. Blackwood, C. L. Braithwaite, W. H. Aitken, A. M. W. Christopher, W. Haslam, E. W. Moore, and H. Varley.

57. *Account of the Union Meeting . . . Oxford*, 326–36; Untitled report of the Oxford meeting, *Christian's Pathway to Power* 1:9 (1 Oct. 1874): 161–66.

58. *Account of the Union Meeting . . . Oxford*; See also Dieter, *Holiness Revival*, 166–69.

59. Notice of the "Conference for the Promotion of Scriptural Holiness" at Cheltenham was carried in *Christian's Pathway to Power* 2:12 (1 Jan. 1875): 12, and another at London, ibid. 2:13 (1 Feb. 1875): 24. These were but two of many.

60. "The Work of God on the Continent," *Christian's Pathway to Power* 1:10 (2 Nov. 1874): 189.

61. "France," *Christian's Pathway to Power*, 1:11 (1 Dec. 1874): 202; "The Work of God on the Continent: France," ibid. 2:14 (1 Mar. 1875): 57–58.

62. "The Work of God on the Continent: Germany," *Christian's Pathway to Power* 2:14 (1 Mar. 1875): 59–60.

63. "Letters from the Continent," *Christian's Pathway to Power* 2:14 (1 Mar. 1875): 80.

64. Ibid.

65. Untitled announcement, *Christian's Pathway to Power* 2:14 (1 Mar. 1875): 60. For contemporary analyses of R. P. Smith in Germany, see, Johannes Jungst, *Amerikanischer Methodismus in Deutschland und Robert Pearsall Smith. Skizze aus der neuesten Kirchengeschichte*, mit einem Vorwort von W. Kraft (Gotha: Friedrich Andreas Perthes, 1875) and, Fr. Reiss and Joh. Hesse, *Die Oxforder Bewegung und ihre Bedeutung fur unsere Zeit. Referat, im Auszug vorgetragen auf einer Conferenz in Stuttgart den 25. August 1875* (Basel: Bahnmaier's Verlag, 1875).

66. "Work on the Continent," *Christian's Pathway to Power* 2:16 (1 May 1875): 95.

67. Untitled article, *Christian's Pathway to Power* 2:17 (1 June 1875): 101–2.

68. "Convention at Brighton, May 29th-June 7th, 1875," *Christian's Pathway to Power* 2:16 (1 May 1875): 100; "Convention at Brighton for the Promotion of Scriptural Holiness, May 29th to June 7," *Christian* no. 274 (Thurs., 29 Apr., 1875): 11. See also F. E. Longley, *An Account of the Ten Days Convention for the Promotion of Scriptural Holiness Held at Brighton, 29 May to 7 June 1875* (London: Depot for the English and American Literature of the Higher Christian Life, 1875).

69. *Adresses of Foreigne Visitors to the Brighton Convention.*

70. *Account of the Union Meeting . . . Brighton;* Dieter, *The Holiness Revival,* 174–79. A severe critique was leveled by J. C. Ryle, *A Letter on Mr. Pearsall Smith's Brighton Convention by the Rev. John C. Ryle, dated 25 May 1875* (Stradbroke: J. C. Ryle, 1875). Exemplary of sympathetic reports on the Continent is E. Gebhardt, "Die allg. Konferenz zur Beforderung schriftgemasser Heiligung zu Brighton, England," *Wachterstimmen* (July 1875): 108–10.

71. Hannah Whitall Smith, *The Christian's Secret of a Happy Life* (New York: Revell, 1875), was published in serialized form in the *Christian's Pathway to Power.*

In a letter, Hannah Whitall Smith to Robert Pearsall Smith, 5 October 1873, Hannah comments, "As to Morgan, it is just what I would have expected from him, and I really do not see why thee need to care so much. He always was shaky, and poor fellow, it is too much to ask of him, without a satisfactory experience of it, to advocate an unpopular truth." Richard Morgan stood firmly against perfectionism after 1875. See the narrative of Booth-Tucker, *The Life of Catharine Booth,* 541–45, and the essays previously published in *The Revival* and *The Christian,* collected as Richard C. Morgan, *The Outpoured Spirit and Pentecost* (London: Morgan and Scott, 1907).

72. "The Devotional Meetings for the Promotion of Spiritual Life," *Christian's Pathway to Power* 3:28 (1 May 1876): 99–100; "The Devotional Meetings for the Promotion of Spiritual Life," ibid. 4:40 (1 May 1877): 100.

73. *Memoir of T. D. Harford-Battersby,* 141–44. See also 90, 122–24.

74. Braithwaite, *Life and Letters,* 431.

75. *Memoir of T. D. Harford-Battersby,* 149.

76. Ibid., 153–60.

77. J. D. [*sic*] Harford-Battersby , "Keswick Union Meetings for the Promotion of Practical Holiness," *Christian's Pathway to Power* 2:19 (2 Aug. 1875): 160.

78. Figgis is an interesting case study of the intersecting set of the Evangelical Alliance and Mildmay. See Westbury-Jones, *"Figgis of Brighton",* 111–18, 163, 196–202, for descriptions of his participation in both groups.

79. *The Mildmay Conference, 1892. Report of the Addresses, corrected by the Speakers* (London: John F. Shaw, n.d.) includes addresses by E. A. Stuart, Andrew Murray, G. H. C. MacGregor, Evan Hopkins, H. W. Webb-Peploe, inter alia; *The Mildmay Conference 1900. Subject: Praise. Report of the Addresses, corrected by the Speakers* (London: John F. Shaw, n.d.)

contains addresses by Hubert Brooke, H. W. Webb-Peploe, W. H. Griffith Thomas, Evan Hopkins, C. G. Moore, James Sibree, and Mrs. Howard Taylor, inter alia.

80. W. Y. Fullerton, F. B. Meyer, A Biography (London: Marshall, Morgan and Scott, n.d.); F. B. Meyer, Reveries and Realities: or, Life and Work in London (London: Marshall, Morgan and Scott, n.d.); F. B. Meyer, The Bells of Is; or, Voices of Human Need and Sorrow (London: Marshall, Morgan and Scott, n.d.). The relative significance of the Mildmay and Keswick events can be seen by the press coverage: "The Keswick Convention," Christian no. 602 (11 Aug. 1881): 8–9; "The Mildmay Conference, June 22nd, 23rd, and 24th 1881," ibid. no. 596 (30 June 1881): 13–30, ibid. no. 597 (7 July 1881): 10–21, ibid. no. 598 (14 July 1881): 8–10.

81. Fleisch, Die moderne Gemeinschaftsbewegung in Deutschland, 3d. ed., 1912; Lange, Eine Bewegung, 17–53.

82. Dieter, Holiness Revival, 172–74.

83. Theodor Jellinghaus, Das völlige, gegenwärtige Heil durch Christum. Bnd. I: Rechtfertigung allein durch Christum; Bnd. II: Heiligung allein durch Christum (Berlin: J. D. Prochnow, 1880).

84. P. Jellinghaus, Zum 25 jährigen Bestehen der Bibelschule 1885–1910 (n.p.: n.p., 1910).

85. Robert Turnball, Le Réveil et les Églises réformées, une confrontation dans les années trente (Master's thesis, New York University, 1980); Robert Mandrow, Historie des protestants de France (Toulouse: n.p., n.d.); Samuel Mours, Un siècle d'évangelisation en France, 1815–1914 (Collection "Essais sur l'histoire du protestantisme français": 2; Flavion: Éditions de la librairie des éclaireurs unionistes, 1963); Samuel Mours and Daniel Robert, Le Protestantisme en France du XVIIIeme siècle a nos jours (1685–1970) (Paris: Librairie Protestante, 1972), 249–75.

86. David Bundy, "Pentecostalism in Belgium," Pneuma 8 (1986): 41–56; and, D. Bundy, "The Making of a Pentecostal Theologian: The Writings of Louis Dallière, 1922–1932," EPTA Bulletin 7 (1988): 40–68, argue that the origins of Pentecostalism in France and Belgium cannot be understood apart from the Anglo-Saxon "higher-life" tradition and its interaction with the Réveil tradition.

87. Wilfrid Monod, "La nuée de témoins" (Paris: Fischbacher, 1929).

88. Martinus Cohen Stuart, Evangelische Alliantie; Verslag van de vijfde algemene vergadering, gehouden te Amsterdam, 18–27 augustus 1867 (Rotterdam: n.p., 1867)

89. Krabbendam, Zeilenverbrijzelaars, 64–65. On the context of the perception and reception of R. P. Smith in the Netherlands, see Kluit, Het Protestantse Réveil in Nederland.

90. Krabbendam, Zeilenverbrijzelaars, 68.

91. Frans Lion Cachet, Tien dagen te Brighton; Brieven aan een vriend (Utrecht: van Peursen, 1875).

92. Adresses of Foreigne Visitors to the Brighton Convention, 12–13; Krabbendam, Zeilenverbrijzelaars, 70.

93. Edited by A. H. L. de Bel, twelve fascicles appeared between November 1875 and January 1877; see, Krabbendam, *Zeilenverbrijzelaars*, 83–84.

94. Krabbendam, *Zeilenverbrijzelaars*, 86–109.

95. There were protests against this trend, resulting, for example, in the Southport Convention. See, *To the Uttermost; Commemorating the Diamond Jubilee of the Southport Methodist Holiness Convention, 1885–1945*, ed. J. Baines Atkinson (London: Epworth Press, 1945).

96. Findlay, *Dwight L. Moody*, 190–93; Dieter, *Holiness Revival*, 185–86.

97. Findlay, *Dwight L. Moody*, 342–43.

98. Emma Dryer, "Reminiscences of the Founding of Moody Bible Institute," (unpublished ms., 1916) cited in Findlay, *Dwight L. Moody*, 343; Fullerton, *F. B. Meyer*, 41.

99. Fullerton, *F. B. Meyer*, 40 (emphasis in original). Two letters from Meyer to Moody's secretary and son-in-law, A. P. Fitt, dated 2 May 1899 and 1 February 1907, are preserved in the Dwight L. Moody Papers, Yale Divinity School, Group 28, I, 2, 50.

100. Fullerton, *F. B. Meyer*, 29–45; Ernest R. Sandeen, *The Roots of Fundamentalism; British and American Millenarianism, 1800–1930* (Chicago: University of Chicago Press, 1970), 176–80; Meyer, *Reveries and Realities*, 16–25.

101. See, for example, *Northfield Echoes* 4 (1897), passim.

102. Sandeen, *Roots of Fundamentalism*, 176–87.

103. J. B. Culpepper, "The Keswick Movement," *Pentecostal Herald* 11:3 (Wed., 23 Jan. 1899): 6. A similar analysis had been proffered by Daniel Steele, "The Keswick Doctrine," *Illustrated Christian World* no. 99 (Mar. 1897): 5, at the same time that Asbury Lowrey, "Full Salvation Not Full," *Illustrated Christian World* no. 99 (Mar. 1897): 5, was arguing against articles in *The Christian* criticizing the concept of sinless perfection.

104. W. B. Godbey, *Keswickism* (Louisville: Pentecostal Publishing House, n.d. [1909]).

105. A. M. Hills, *Scriptural Teaching and Keswick Teaching Compared* (Manchester: Star Hall, n.d. [1912]).

106. Bundy, *Keswick*, 44–47.

107. Sandeen, *Roots of Fundamentalism*, 180. A thorough study of the life and influence of Charles G. Trumball and the *Sunday School Times* is an important desideratum for American religious studies.

108. Warfield, *Perfectionism*, 561–611; *Victory in Christ; A Report of Princeton Conference, 1916* (Philadelphia: Board of Managers of the Princeton Conference, 1916); *The Victorious Life; Messages from the Summer Conferences at Whittier, California, June; Princeton, New Jersey, July; Cedar Lake, Indiana, August; including also some messages from the 1917 Conference at Princeton and other material* (Philadelphia: Board of Managers of the Victorious Life Conference, 1918).

109. Marsden, *Fundamentalism*, 141–95.

# 8

# Restoration as Revival: Early American Pentecostalism

———— ✦ ————

EDITH L. BLUMHOFER

ON 18 APRIL 1906, a severe earthquake rocked San Francisco. Material aid poured in from around the world. Meanwhile, a small congregation gathered in a nondescript frame building known as the Apostolic Faith Mission in Los Angeles pondered the meaning of the quake and the devastation that followed. They readily concluded that the San Francisco earthquake was God's judgment on sinful humankind, the first of a series of natural disasters that would usher in the endtimes.[1] Los Angeles, they prophesied, would be shaken next. But first, there would be a revival that would offer all in the city an opportunity for salvation. The end was near, they warned; they knew, because the revival "was now in progress" and they were one of its manifestations.[2]

Participants in the newly formed and racially mixed congregation that met daily at the Apostolic Faith Mission identified with the fledgling pentecostal movement that was slowly disentangling itself from the various turn-of-the-century popular evangelical subcultures that had shaped much of its spirituality and practice. Pentecostalism emerged as a discrete movement over a long period. It is convenient and appropriate to note 1 January 1901 as a significant date in the process. On that New Year's day, which also marked the dawning of a new century, during a religious service at an independent Bible school in Topeka, Kansas, one Agnes Ozman requested prayer for the baptism with the Holy Spirit. In response to prayer and the laying on of hands, she spoke in tongues. From that date, the school's leader, itinerant evangelist Charles Fox Parham, taught publicly what he had probably concluded earlier: tongues speech would always evidence an experience of baptism with the Holy Spirit.

The subject of baptism with the Holy Spirit had fascinated Amer-

ican and European evangelicals for at least several decades.[3] Many
believed that Spirit baptism should be a crisis experience and a normal
part of the Christian life. Some regarded it as a work of grace,
stressing its cleansing, purifying aspects; others commended it as an
enduement with power essential for effective evangelizing and a victorious Christian life. Some posited various signs, but none before
Parham unequivocally advocated a uniform initial evidence. That
insistence became the core around which American pentecostalism
emerged.

But this premise was not the essence of early pentecostalism.
Parham rallied his followers to an all-encompassing sense of identity
and purpose. Before reaching his conclusions about Spirit baptism,
Parham had called his work in Topeka (which from 1898 included a
mission, a healing faith home, and a publication) "The Apostolic
Faith." During the 1890s, he had become intrigued with restorationist
notions, convinced that he lived in the last days and that God was
about to restore New Testament faith and practice in a brief, intense
revival before the end of the world. With the restoration of tongues
speech in January 1901, he considered that all the components of the
New Testament church were evident in his ministry. He set out to
announce the Apostolic Faith as a restoration with eschatological
meaning: it was the "latter rain," the revival that would immediately
precede Christ's return.

From the beginning, then, pentecostals had a different sense of
revival than had most other Protestants. They did not pray for revival
with the same intentions as their contemporaries: rather, they *were*
revival. Their movement's existence marked God's sovereign restoration, and they were a "sign people," evidence that God's Spirit was
being poured out copiously to prepare the world for judgment. They
prayed for more intense, sustained, and extensive "showers," but they
believed that the revival for which they and others had long yearned
had come with the birth of their movement. They announced revival
and saw themselves as both its evidence and its agents.

This confidence nurtured audacity: pentecostals dared to believe
that they had become the focal point of God's contemporary work
in the world. "The Lord," one noted, "had found the little company
at last, outside as always, through whom he could have right of
way."[4] Their lack of social status and religious influence reinforced
their convictions: they insisted that God always worked "without the
camp"—outside institutions, especially religious ones. "Los Angeles
seems to be the place, and this the time, in the mind of God, for
the restoration of the church to her former place, favor and power,"

participant Frank Bartleman reflected. "The fullness of time seems to have come for the church's complete restoration."[5]

American pentecostalism focused briefly on Azusa Street, but it spread rapidly to other centers of influence where men and women shared a distrust of denominations and the yearning for restoration. People from abroad visited the Azusa Street Mission and carried its message around the world. The revival that pentecostals heralded featured similar assumptions and behavior wherever it emerged. Some of these were rooted in an identity that has long been abandoned by most American pentecostals, but they once shaped the movement's essence.

## Features of Pentecostalism as Revival

Their conviction that they were agents of restoration of the apostolic faith molded early pentecostal expectations about revival. As restorationists, pentecostals believed that the best had already been realized: perfection meant a return to the norms of an earlier era, and pentecostals proudly described their movement as the return of "old-time religion." It represented "Bible salvation," a restatement of the "full gospel" unparalleled since the early church. D. W. Kerr, a pentecostal pastor in Cleveland, Ohio, called it "the climax in the process of . . . recovery of truth since John Wickliffe gave us the Bible."[6]

As champions of "the restoration of the faith once delivered unto the saints," pentecostals hoped to transcend the church's history and traditions and "leap the intervening years crying 'Back to Pentecost.'"[7] The New Testament, then, illumined by the Holy Spirit in immediate revelation (described by one as "God shedding new light on the old Word") guided their expectations about the features of revival. These, they admitted, were broader than those of other Christians: "As a result of our contending for this same faith once delivered to the saints, we are beginning to be enlarged in expectation, we are now expecting . . . signs to follow the ministry of the saints, and even to learn that the dead are being raised."[8]

A strong call to unity through experience echoed from their pulpits and publications. Envisioning a return to early Christian norms, they asked members of "denominational churches" pointedly, "Why not just be Christians?" Impatient with tradition and creeds, they often found submission to church authority intolerable and insisted that God had long since abandoned organized religion. They summoned true believers to "come out" from human denominations and to identify with the restoration of the true faith. The "come outist" urge thrived in a movement that marshalled people whose restorationist inclinations had often already prompted their separation from denominations.[9] The *Apostolic Faith* editorialized: "We . . . are seeking to displace dead forms and creeds and wild fanaticisms with living, practical Christianity."[10] Pentecostals, then, intended to reconstitute believers everywhere along "Bible lines."

Pentecostalism as revival emphasized much traditional popular evangelical teaching but exhibited little interest in formal doctrine or theology. The movement's message was intended to be experienced rather than systematized. Many of its early adherents had been influenced by the Wesleyan tradition's affirmations of "felt" religion.[11] As components of the restored "full" gospel, pentecostals identified confession, repentance, and restitution; salvation by faith in Christ; sanctification; the baptism with the Holy Spirit evidenced by tongues; divine healing; the life of faith; and the imminent return of Christ.[12] But this typical listing of teachings was by no means complete. Reports, testimonies, and exhortations indicate that they fully expected miracles to authenticate their witness. Healings, provisions, raising the dead, "words of wisdom and knowledge" revealing "the secrets of the heart," tongues speech in human languages reportedly understood by foreigners, insights into the future—these and other unconventional "signs" regularly attested the restoration of the faith. And overarching all of them was the conviction that the end was here.

Biblical rhetoric typically replaced concrete doctrine when pentecostals described their beliefs. In October 1911, for example, the *Whole Truth*, published by the Church of God in Christ, summarized that group's creed: "Our rule or discipline is the Bible; our ordinances are those taught us in the Bible. As Jesus said, man shall not live by bread alone, but by every word that proceedeth out of the mouth of God. Matt. 4:4."[13] The movement, one of its earliest adherents averred, stood for "the restoration of Apostolic faith, power and practice, Christian unity, the evangelization of the whole world preparatory to the Lord's return, and for all of the unfolding will and word of God."[14] Since it possessed the "full message" and the "real Endowment of the Holy Ghost," its success was assured.

Their celebration of the Holy Spirit's power and presence within and among them helped transform the way pentecostals perceived reality. Accustomed to thinking of themselves as indwelt by Christ, they yielded to impressions and subjective "leadings" as well as to prophetic utterances and expressions of "gifts" of wisdom and knowledge. Life "in the Spirit" offered new insights, reordered priorities, and absorbed one's energies. And it was emphatically unpredictable: "[The Holy Spirit] does not always want you to be doing the same thing," one enthusiastic adherent admonished. "He does not want things to run in a groove; He wants liberty to have a diversity of operations in the Spirit."[15] When pentecostals gathered, it was often uncertain who would preach; singing, too, was expected to be "led by the Spirit," often without the use of hymnals.[16] Sometimes the faithful alleged that the Spirit directly and perceptibly controlled the smallest details of their lives: "A sister who was baptized, when she came to change her clothing, attempted to put on her jewelry again, but the Spirit would not let her, so she left it off. So the Spirit has been working in harmony with the Word, teaching His people how to dress according to the Bible."[17] Some claimed divine directions to abstain from coffee, tea, and pork products. "God's chosen ones," Abbie C. Morrow wrote, "are coming to be altogether satisfied with God's 'good' natural gifts, Jas. 1:17. These are fruits, grains, vegetables and nuts."[18] Prophecies and messages decrying "church amusements" and "worldly" behavior were commonly accepted as the Spirit's message to the restored church. Carnality—or neglect of the Holy Spirit—posed the community's most ominous threat.

A focus on "liberty" or "freedom in the Holy Ghost" accounted in part for early pentecostal aversions toward organization and their insistence on the authority of the Holy Spirit in both individuals and corporate gatherings. They chided the majority of American Christians who in countless ways opted for "anti-Christ" rather than the Holy Spirit. "Look at [anti-Christ] in the Wesleyan Methodist Church," one wrote in 1906, "taking work out of the hands of the Holy Ghost by voting for preachers, thus giving the devil a chance to vote out a Holy Ghost preacher."[19] The movement as a whole acknowledged no human leader: "There is no man at the head of this movement. God Himself is speaking in the earth."[20]

The movement kept adherents in a state of heightened anticipation, for it offered spiritual renewal that never ended. Spirit baptism, they were told, inaugurated them into a life of growing awareness of God's presence and purpose. As they often sang, there was "always more to follow."[21] The conviction that they had been granted special insight into God's plan for the present and future energized people with little vested interest in this world's affairs. As they welcomed and worked toward what they perceived as a divine restoration, they encouraged one another: "This work is of God," they often reminded one another, "and cannot be stopped. While our enemies scold, we pray and the Lord works, and the fire burns."[22]

The certainty among pentecostals that their movement represented history's final renewal was nurtured by religious events abroad.[23] Especially in 1904 and 1905, a revival in South Wales captured the attention of much of the evangelical world. Accounts of tumultuous religious gatherings heartened Americans to anticipate similar stirrings in their ranks. Books like S. B. Shaw's *Great Revival in Wales* circulated eyewitness accounts, newspaper reports, and evaluations by such noted evangelicals as G. Campbell Morgan and F. B. Meyer.

By all accounts, the Welsh revival defied description. It ignored the methods usually associated with revival. Spontaneity and seeming disorder replaced promotion, scheduling, regular preaching, financial planning, and systematic evangelistic outreach. In several important ways, the revival modeled what American pentecostal restorationists believed the endtimes revival (or "showers of latter rain") would be like.

First, accounts emphasized the presence and power of the Holy Spirit and illustrated "obedience to the Holy Spirit" in unconventional behavior. Second, participants described events in Wales as an endtimes Pentecost (or "the first showers of the latter rain").[24] They regarded the movement as the prelude to the final worldwide awakening they believed was indicated in the Bible. Third, revival accounts popularized terminology pentecostals later found meaningful, and they gave those terms specific experiential connotations just as the pentecostal movement gained wider attention in the United States.

As in American pentecostal missions, during the Welsh revival, no one knew for certain who—if anyone—would preach. The revival "anticipated the preacher," the (London) *Times* reported. "The people met and poured out their souls in prayer and praise for hours before the preacher came, if he came at all."[25] The services were generally in Welsh. They frequently began with prayer, Bible reading, and hymn singing, and sometimes they proceeded to a sermon. At any time, however, the congregation would "burst forth—apparently without lead or concert, but all and at once"—into singing.[26] Worshipers fell to their knees in prayer or stood to confess sin or offer praise. Congregations engaged in corporate audible prayer or sang repeated choruses of worship. When the excitement was "at its highest," a *Times* reporter noted, "the outbursts were not successive, but literally simultaneous."[27] Hours passed—sometimes eight or nine hours—before services disbanded.

A phenomenon that received considerable press was the alleged use of classical Welsh by "ordinary farm servants, common plough boys and practically unlettered youths," which the faithful maintained was prompted by the Holy Spirit.[28] J. Morris Jones, Professor of Welsh at the University College of North Wales, was quoted as admitting that these individuals attained "diction . . . more chaste and beautiful than anything I can hope to attain to."[29] The *Times* cited as an example a young girl who spontaneously prayed aloud before some 2,000 people. In the course of her prayer she recited scripture and old Welsh hymns as well as her own thoughts "in the purest idiomatic classical Welsh" that "would have done credit to the most scholarly theologian of the Welsh pulpit."[30]

The *Times* noted as well immediate social effects of revival, applauding reduction in alcoholism and a substantial increase in contributions to support libraries and recreation halls as alternatives to saloons. A decline in numbers of arrests brought approval from magistrates. Efforts to conserve such gains generated numerous social programs. Many stories of repentance followed by restitution circulated. For a time, at least, the revival contributed to increased sobriety, industry, repaid debts, and mended relationships.[31] The prominent British journalist W. T. Stead sensed hopefulness: "On all sides there was the solemn gladness of men and women upon whose eyes has dawned the splendour of a new day."[32]

A long list of notable evangelical preachers visited Wales; most left without participating. R. A. Torrey, G. Campbell Morgan, Salvation Army founder William Booth, and F. B. Meyer cited unwillingness to intrude upon a divine visitation. "It is Pentecost continued, without a single moment's doubt," Morgan reported. "The meetings are absolutely without order characterized from the first to the last by the orderliness of the Spirit of God."[33]

Some who were involved in the Azusa Street Mission in 1906 had corresponded with participants in the Welsh revival and had been encouraged to expect revival in Los Angeles.[34] In other centers that would soon identify with the emerging pentecostal movement, the Welsh revival occasioned renewed fervor in prayer for worldwide revival. Its eschatological emphasis helped make evangelicals with endtimes restorationist yearnings receptive to pentecostal terminology and enthusiasm. Before news of the Welsh revival reached American evangelicals, a few thousand Americans at best identified with Charles Parham and the endtimes restoration he called "The Apostolic Faith." But the Welsh revival strengthened his appeal by popularizing terminology about the "latter rain" and apparently validating his view that an intense endtimes worldwide revival was underway.[35] The Welsh revival influenced and coincided with another revival duly reported in the United States and associated with the work of a highly visible Indian woman, Pandita Ramabai, who enjoyed immense popularity among American Protestants.[36] Reports from India, like those from Wales, filled evangelical papers and confirmed to pentecostals that the revival was worldwide in its extent.

In the United States, the view of history and anticipation of the future inherent in the endtimes expectations amplified by the Welsh revival and Pandita Ramabai's experiences characterized early pentecostals and set them apart from most other evangelicals. For the growing ranks of the faithful, events at Azusa Street and in other early pentecostal centers simply verified these revivals' message: the "latter rain" had begun to fall.

## Pentecostalism as Sign

Pentecostals were not the first American evangelicals to use biblical imagery about rain to express their yearnings or identify their place in history. The words "latter rain" had been bandied about with growing frequency in the decades prior to the emergence of pentecostalism. Advocates of Wesleyan views on holiness and participants in the quest for a "higher" Christian life sometimes expressed their convictions about coming revival in terms of the "latter rain." A. B. Simpson, founder of the Christian and Missionary Alliance, for example, anticipated a day when "the deserts of the earth would be watered by showers of abundant latter rain." That rain, he insisted, alone would facilitate the worldwide evangelistic outreach to which he dedicated his life. Evangelicals who pursued the experience of baptism with the Holy Spirit were familiar as well with the biblical passages that described the last days as a time of revival as well as judgment.

If the terminology of the latter rain was familiar, the pentecostal application of the concept was not. Pentecostals were well aware of their innovations. One A. J. Rawson, describing his services at a mission in Lynn, Massachusetts, wrote: "We are fully committed to this Pentecostal revival, or 'Latter rain' work, and that makes our work on peculiar lines."[37] Intrinsic to pentecostal self-understanding was a carefully articulated view of the contemporary significance of Old Testament prophecies of the "latter rain."[38]

The "days of heaven on earth" foretold in Deuteronomy 11 were being fulfilled in their movement, they asserted. Passages like Joel 2 and Zechariah 10:1 helped define their worldview. The most detailed identification of the pentecostal movement as "latter rain" came from the pen of David Wesley Myland, a former Christian and Missionary Alliance official who embraced pentecostalism in 1906.

In May 1909, Myland was the featured speaker at a pentecostal convention in the large and (among pentecostals) influential Stone Church in Chicago. His addresses, duly recorded in the church's publication, the *Latter Rain Evangel*, consisted of lengthy expositions of Old and New Testament passages that, he maintained, validated the contemporary "outpouring" as the prophesied "latter rain." Myland drew parallels between the natural course of events in Palestine and the spiritual momentum of pentecostalism, citing rainfall charts that indicated increasing rainfall in Palestine, especially between 1890 and 1900, and noting as well the significance of growing contemporary pressure for a Jewish homeland. Such events represented *literal* fulfillments of prophecies, just as pentecostalism represented their *spiritual* fulfillment: "If it is remembered that the climate of Palestine consisted of two seasons, the wet and the dry, and that the wet season was made up of the early and latter rain, it will help you to understand this Latter Rain Covenant and the present workings of God's Spirit. For just as literal early and latter rain was poured out upon Palestine, so upon the church of the first century was poured out the spiritual early rain, and upon us today is being poured out the spiritual latter rain."[39]

The convergence of pentecostal teaching and Zionist activities, as well as the coinciding of literal and spiritual fulfillments, Myland assured pentecostals, "betokened in a remarkable way that the closing days of the Dispensation are upon us."[40]

During the first decade of the century, similar views appeared in other publications, especially those sponsored by the *Christian and Missionary Alliance*. In 1907, Alliance founder A. B. Simpson had encouraged the notion that the latter rain was "due": "We may ... conclude that we are to expect a great outpouring of the Holy Spirit in connection with the second coming of Christ and one as much greater than the Pentecostal effusion of the Spirit as the rains of autumn were greater than the showers of spring. . . . We are in the time ... when we may expect this latter rain."[41]

The persuasion that "literal Israel" and "spiritual Israel" were simultaneously each "coming into its own possessions" generated awe and excitement.[42] The message was often presented as an empowering of the socially and economically marginalized. Myland assured them: "God sent this latter rain to gather up all the poor and outcast, and make us love everybody. . . . He poured it out upon the little sons and daughters, and servants and handmaidens. . . . God is taking the despised things and base things, and being glorified in them, and the meetinghouse—the river of God—is full of water."[43]

Myland was aware of the extensive yearning for revival among turn-of-the-century evangelicals and explained widespread criticism of pentecostalism as rooted in a misunderstanding about revival "rains." The church had prayed for "ordinary rain" but had been overwhelmed by the "latter rain"; and because the revival had not met expectations, it had become a source of controversy rather than unity. While most Americans ignored or rejected the "latter rain," those who had received it had been initiated into an unprecedented life of heaven on earth—"heavenly tongues, heavenly songs, heavenly choirs, heavenly interpretation, heavenly inspiration, heavenly fellowship." They participated in the realization of God's plan for the ages, the return of "perfection and perpetuity to this fallen world." The latter rain was intended "to get the last crop or fruit" ready for harvest. It unfolded God's plan—salvation history—and would soon usher in "the eternal kingdom of our Lord Jesus Christ."[44]

Participants did not need a full grasp of Myland's rationale to share his enthusiasm. One T. McLain in Cleveland, Tennessee, expressed a typical view: it was simply "the rain of the Holy Ghost," and it had made a difference in his life. "When I was in a justified state," he mused (referring to his Christian life before Spirit baptism), "I thought I would like to have lived in the age of the Apostles; but I have come to the conclusion I'd rather live in the time of the latter rain."[45] Life at the edge of time appealed to many: "Beloved, we are on the verge of a climax," wrote one excited convert in Crewsville, Florida.[46]

As indicators of the progress of God's endtimes calendar, pentecostals were not expected to attempt to influence their culture. They were citizens of another kingdom, "pilgrims and strangers" on earth; Myland called them God's "little messengers" distributing invitations to the Marriage Supper of the Lamb. Reveling in "days of heaven on earth," they assigned far more significance to prophecy as history of the future than to the molding influences of history and culture. Their identity, they assumed, was rooted in the future rather than in the past. All else paled before the certainty that Christ would burst through the clouds at any moment.

Pentecostals frequently appropriated other biblical metaphors to underscore their identity as a sign of the endtimes: especially popular were "evening light" and "midnight cry." Each had been used in popular evangelicalism prior to the emergence of pentecostalism, but pentecostals assigned them new significance.

"But it shall come to pass that at evening time it shall be light."
These words from Zechariah 14:7 shaped a view of history that
pentecostals shared with participants in segments of the holiness
movement. Holiness and pentecostal expounders of this text disagreed
on when the true "light" had come, but they concurred that in their
day it was shining.

"The dark and cloudy day has passed. We are now in the evening
of this wonderful gospel age. . . . The full blaze of light beamed forth
from the Pentecostal chamber . . . in the early morning of the gospel
day. . . . We can expect nothing less in glory and power in the evening
light than broke out over the eastern hills in the early morning of
the gospel age."[47] With this explanation, A. J. Tomlinson, general
overseer of the Church of God, Cleveland, Tennessee, introduced his
newly titled publication, the *Evening Light* in 1910. Like other pentecostals, Tomlinson believed that the purity and power of the early
church (which had lasted some 270 years) had given way to a "long
dreary Papal night." The Reformation had ushered in "a cloudy day."
Pentecostals believed that with their movement's restoration of the
apostolic faith, "the mists [had been] cleared away" and "the sun
would go down no more." Once again, the "light" of the gospel shined
brightly. Pentecostal songwriter R. E. Winsett put it as follows:
"Christians awake! See the light has come, / Shining in evening as
clear as morn; / Christians awake! Now awake and behold evening
light."[48]

"Truth crushed on earth shall rise again," Tomlinson exulted. "His
church shall shine out with the brilliancy of her infancy. . . . Behold
her as she is finally pure and spotless, and presented to Himself a
glorious church, not having spot, or wrinkle, or any such thing."[49]

Another typical descriptor for pentecostalism was the term "midnight cry." This alluded to a New Testament parable of ten virgins
awaiting the arrival of a bridegroom who appeared at midnight,
heralded by the call: "The bridegroom cometh; go out to meet him."
From this perspective, pentecostalism was "the Bridegroom's messenger," announcing Christ's return to a mixed group of slumbering
and wakeful Christians worldwide. It called the church to anticipate
the immediate return of the heavenly bridegroom with lamps
"trimmed and burning."[50] Countless messages in tongues were interpreted to indicate the imminence of Christ's return.[51]

"What do such congregations as this mean here and there over
the world?" the leadership at the Azusa Street mission asked late in
1906. "Jesus is coming back to take His bride. How long is it going
to take? The way this wonderful power is spreading over the world

today, not very long."[52] Some ventured to set dates: in Lynn, Massachusetts, a congregation, heeding several prophecies, anticipated the end in 1908.[53] Most preferred simply to focus their hopes on an event they described in simple, everyday language—"going home." Their uncertainty about their worldly tomorrows was in sharp contrast to their confidence about their heavenly future.

Early pentecostals proclaimed an alternative version of the emerging popular dispensationalism that taught the "secret rapture" of the church before the onset of seven years of judgment called "the tribulation." They typically insisted that the baptism with the Holy Spirit was necessary for a place in the "bride of Christ." Charles Parham, the movement's earliest leader, taught that Spirit baptism represented a "sealing" that offered the only escape from the "plagues and wraths" of the last days that "unsealed" Christians would experience together with unbelievers.[54]

"He that hath wrought us for the selfsame thing is God," quoted D. W. Kerr. "This selfsame thing is the climax, the last crisis, that is, the translation." The rapture was "the thing to which God had called" pentecostals.[55] The latter rain, another ardent pentecostal evangelist in Boston concurred, had been sent "to ripen up a people ready for translation."[56] Those who had not received the baptism with the Holy Spirit evidenced by tongues speech would not "go up" in the rapture but would endure the horrors of the tribulation. "Jesus could not translate a people from a lower plane than Pentecost," one teacher insisted.[57] Kerr outlined the early pentecostal insistence on the relationship between Spirit baptism and the rapture: "The beginning is the speaking in tongues, and then come the other blessed and wonderful experiences which are all symptoms of the rapture, and then the Lord Himself shall descend from heaven with a shout . . . then we which are alive . . . shall be caught up . . . in the clouds to meet the Lord in the air."[58] Pentecostal experience, then, offered the only escape from impending disaster. Through pentecostalism, God was "thundering forth His last appeal."[59]

As both revival and sign, pentecostalism represented a solemn challenge to participants and an ominous warning to humankind. For pentecostals, it meant that responsibility for the progress of God's purpose on earth rested with them: "Oh, Pentecostal Saints, upon you devolves the whole of present realization for God. He must, He does depend on you for all. To work out His purpose in the earth at this time, He must depend on you."[60] Those evangelicals who resisted the "latter rain," pentecostals believed, would suffer "a terrible spiritual desolation and uselessness."[61] And to the impenitent, they offered only the certainty of "the flaming judgment seat."[62]

In pursuing an understanding of the times in which they lived, early pentecostals opted for an identity that focused outside of time, dealing in eternal verities and divine schemes. When Christ's coming failed to materialize, everyday affairs intruded, and the pentecostal ethos gradually changed.[63] But the conviction that their experience made them pilgrims and strangers on earth, energized in time by eternal powers that transcended time, once made them insist that pentecostal experience transformed this life into a foretaste of heaven: "I have found a heaven below, / Living in the glory of the Lord!"[64]

Pentecostals' early confidence that they were shaping history's climax fueled a profound burst of evangelistic activity that established pentecostalism as an enduring presence on the American religious scene.

## NOTES

1. See, for example, "Testimony and Prophecy," *The Apostolic Faith,* October 1906, 2; Bennet F. Lawrence, *The Apostolic Faith Restored* (St. Louis: The Gospel Publishing House, 1916), 74.

2. *Apostolic Faith,* September 1906, 1.

3. Many prominent evangelicals published books on the subject. See, for example, R. A. Torrey, *The Baptism with the Holy Spirit* (New York: Fleming H. Revell, 1895); A. J. Gordon, *The Ministry of the Spirit* (New York: Fleming H. Revell, 1894); C. I. Scofield, *Plain Papers Concerning the Work of the Holy Spirit* (New York: Fleming H. Revell, 1899); Andrew Murray, *The Full Blessing of Pentecost* (New York: Fleming H. Revell, 1908); A. B. Simpson, *The Holy Spirit, or Power from on High* (New York: Christian Alliance Publishers, 1895); Asa Mahan, *The Baptism of the Holy Ghost* (New York: W. C. Palmer, Jr., 1870).

4. Frank Bartleman, *How Pentecost Came to Los Angeles* (Los Angeles: n.p., 1925), 44.

5. Ibid., 89. Already during the Azusa Street Mission's first year, however, observers noted the divisiveness that seemed inherent in the mission's message. Late in 1906, Joseph Smale, a Los Angeles minister well known to the pentecostals, noted: "In the city there are already four hostile camps of those who unduly magnify the tongues, which prove that the tongues have not brought Pentecost to Los Angeles. When Pentecost comes, we shall see the union of the Lord's people." Joseph Smale, "The Gift of Tongues," *Living Truth,* January 1907, 40. Early opponents of pentecostalism frequently cited its failure to promote unity.

6. D. W. Kerr, "The Selfsame Thing," *Trust* 13 (Aug. 1914): 3–4.

7. Lawrence, *Apostolic Faith Restored*, 12.

8. Mrs. E. A. Sexton, "The Faith Once Delivered to the Saints," *The Bridegroom's Messenger* 3 (1 Aug. 1910): 1.

9. Many concurred with the sentiments of John P. Brooks, whose book, *The Divine Church* (El Dorado Springs, Mo.: Witt Printing Co., 1960), was first published in 1891. It became a handbook for turn-of-the-century separationists, insisting on the basic incompatibility of religious organizations and spiritual movements.

10. *Apostolic Faith*, September 1906, 2.

11. The testimony of one C. W. Bass in Goldsboro, North Carolina, is typical: "Well praise God for old-time heart-felt salvation." *Apostolic Evangel*, 15 May 1918, 2. Pentecostals sang holiness songs that emphasized experiential faith. With Mrs. C. H. Morris, for example, they "[knew] God's promise [was] true" primarily because they had "trusted and tested and tried it" rather than because an immutable God had uttered it. Mrs. C. H. Morris, "I Know God's Promise Is True," *The Best of All* (n.p., n.d.), no. 40.

12. *Apostolic Faith*, November 1906, 2.

13. *The Whole Truth* 4 (Oct. 1911): 2.

14. W. F. Carothers, "The Apostolic Faith Movement," *Word and Work* 29 (Apr. 1907): 117.

15. Elizabeth Baker, *Chronicles of a Faith Life* (Rochester, N.Y.: The DuBois Press, n.d.), 65; see also A. W. Orwig, "Program vs. the Holy Ghost and Vice Versa," *Bridegroom's Messenger* 7 (June 1914): 4.

16. F. A. Atwater, "Visions and Messages Given Gertrude Smith," *Word and Work* 29 (Sept. 1907): 236. See also Glen A. Cook, "Purge Out the Leaven," *The Good Report* 1 (1 Nov. 1913): 4.

17. *Word and Work* 30 (Jan. 1908): 5.

18. Abbie C. Morrow, "Health and Hygiene," *Word and Work* 29 (Aug. 1907): 217.

19. W. C. Montague, "Anti-Christ: Where Is He Found?" *The Household of God* 2 (Sept. 1906): 1.

20. "A Crisis at Hand," *Household of God* 5 (May 1909): 5.

21. P. P. Bliss, "More to Follow," *Gospel Hymns 1–6* (Chicago: Biglow and Main, n.d.), no. 22.

22. *Household of God* 3 (Nov. 1907): 10. Sometimes such "scolding" meant physical harassment. For example, see "A Dastardly Deed," *Free Methodist* 40 (2 July 1907): 27.

23. For an example of the connection pentecostals saw between the Welsh revival and their movement, see Julia Morton Plummer, "The Bridegroom Cometh," *Word and Work* 30 (Mar. 1908): 76.

24. See especially Jessie Penn-Lewis, *The Awakening in Wales* (New York: Fleming H. Revell, 1905).

25. *Times* (London), 13 February 1905, 9d.

26. *Times* (London), 3 January 1905, 12b.

27. Ibid.

28. *Times* (London), 31 January 1905, 7c.

29. Ibid. Criticism of the view that such speech was supernaturally enabled appeared in *The Times*, 4 February 1905, 8c.

30. *Times* (London), 31 January 1905, 7c.

31. *Times* (London), 3 January 1905, 12b; 31 January 1905, 7c; 6 February 1905, 8d; W. T. Stead, "The Story of the Awakening," *The Story of the Welsh Revival* (New York: Fleming H. Revell, 1905), 62.

32. Stead, "Awakening," 61.

33. G. Campbell Morgan, "The Lesson of the Revival," *Welsh Revival*, 37.

34. Bartleman, *Pentecost*, 35–38.

35. See especially Penn-Lewis, *Awakening in Wales*, and Evan Roberts, "A Message to the World," *Welsh Revival*, 5.

36. See Pandita Ramabai, *The Baptism of the Holy Ghost and Fire* (Kedgaon: Mukti Mission Press, 1906): "There are many indications that the time of the outpouring of the Holy Spirit is fully come" (4); "Those who know the Lord most intimately are constantly being reminded by the Holy Spirit that His coming draweth nigh" (71).

37. A. J. Rawson, "Apostolic Faith Mission," *Word and Work* 30 (Jan. 1908): 17.

38. A succinct summary of pentecostal latter rain views is "Latter Rain," *Word and Work* 30 (Jan. 1908): 11. The insistence that pentecostalism was "latter rain" was confirmed for the faithful by tongues and interpretation. For example, see "What Meaneth This Speaking in Tongues?" *The Latter Rain Evangel* 1 (Oct. 1908): 15.

39. D. W. Myland, *The Latter Rain Pentecost* (Chicago: Evangel Publishing House, 1910), 1.

40. Ibid., 106.

41. A. B. Simpson, "What is Meant by the Latter Rain?" *The Christian and Missionary Alliance*, 19 October 1907, 38. See also W. C. Stevens, "The Latter Rain," *Word and Work* (July 1908): 17; May Mabette Anderson, "The Latter Rain and Its Counterfeit," *Living Truth*, June, July, August 1907.

42. Myland, *Latter Rain*, 30.

43. Ibid., 53, 49, 45.

44. Ibid., 20, 29, 6.

45. T. L. McLain, "The Latter Rain," *The Evening Light and Church of God Evangel* 1 (1 Mar. 1910): 5.

46. Marion T. Whidden, "Latter Rain Revival," *Evening Light and Church of God Evangel* 1 (1 Mar. 1910): 3.

47. "Apology for Above Title," *Evening Light and Church of God Evangel* 1 (March 1910): 1.

48. R. E. Winsett, "Evening Light," *Songs of the Coming King*, ed. R. E. Winsett (Ft. Smith, Ark.: privately published, 1922): no. 124. Winsett appended the following words: "We are truly living in the evening light of time . . . and the church is returning to apostolic faith and doctrine." William G. Schell, "Biblical Trace of the Church," and Daniel Warner, "The Evening

Light," *Songs of the Evening Light*, ed. Barney E. Warren and Andrew L. Byers (Moundsville, W.Va.: 1897), nos. 20, 1.

49. "Apology," 2.

50. See "The Midnight Cry," and "Behold the Bridegroom Cometh", *Bridegroom's Messenger* 13 (Apr. and May 1920): 1.

51. See, for example, "Work in Corinna, ME," *Word and Work* 30 (Jan. 1908): 19; "The Second Chapter of Acts," *Apostolic Faith*, October 1906, 2; "Jesus Is Coming," *Apostolic Faith*, September 1906, 4; "The Last Call is upon Us," *Bridegroom's Messenger* 12 (Sept. 1919): 4.

52. "Hallelujah for the Prospect," *Apostolic Faith*, October 1906, 4.

53. Mrs. A. F. Rawson, "Apostolic Faith Mission," *Word and Work* 30 (Feb. 1908): 49.

54. Charles Parham, *A Voice Crying in the Wilderness* (n.p., 1910), 86.

55. Kerr, "Selfsame Thing," 4.

56. S. G. Otis, "Work in Boston and Vicinity," *Word and Work* 29 (June 1907): 177.

57. Baker, *Chronicles of a Faith Life*, 130.

58. Kerr, "Selfsame Thing," 8.

59. M. R. Tatman, "God's Saturday Night," *The Midnight Cry* 12 (Oct. 1925): 3. See also "Organization," *The Gospel Witness* 1 (1915): 14. The experience of Spirit baptism as "sealing" for the rapture presupposed that baptism had been preceded by an experience of "crucifixion of self." This death to self, in theory at least, was usually evidenced by tongues speech, since Spirit baptism was assumed to indicate "the full reign of Christ within the soul." See Edith Blumhofer, *Pentecost in My Soul* (Springfield, Mo.: Gospel Publishing House, 1989), 18.

60. Frank Bartleman, *Word and Work* 30 (Jan. 1908): 20.

61. W. C. Stevens, "The Latter Rain," *Word and Work* 30 (July 1908):1.

62. "The Future," *Word and Work* 30 (Mar. 1908): 1.

63. There was some dissatisfaction with "latter rain" typology fairly early. See, for example, "False Report," *Midnight Cry* 6 (Mar. 1919): 4.

64. These lines from a song by A. B. Simpson, a wistful pursuer of pentecostal experience, who was mentor to an impressive number of early pentecostals, were sung by pentecostals with deep conviction. "Living in the Glory," *Hymns of the Christian Life* (Harrisburg, Pa.: Christian Publications, 1962), no. 268. Similar language can be found in many songs early pentecostals sang. See, for example, Mrs. C. H. Morris, "I Know God's Promise is True," *The Best of All* (n.p., n.d.), no. 40: "Eternal life begun below / Now fills my heart and soul."

# 9

# Christian Revival in China, 1900–1937

✦

## DANIEL H. BAYS

Revivalism . . . is a distinctly American phenomenon, dating from the mid-eighteenth century and relating to one or a series of services, often highly emotional, designed to stimulate renewed interest in religion.
—Stuart C. Henry[1]

As I ENDEAVORED to put what I know of twentieth-century Chinese Protestant "revivalism" into a wider international context, I was struck by the above claim of Professor Stuart C. Henry. Until about 1900 there certainly was no visible Chinese analogue to the revival movements led by Edwards, Whitefield, Finney, Moody, and others that had punctuated the American scene for over 150 years. The Chinese Protestant church, on the contrary, was still so small and scattered that as late as the 1890s one might wonder if there was sufficient momentum to survive, let alone to revive; there were about 37,000 Protestants in 1889.[2] These Christians were the product of arduous foreign missionary efforts over the previous sixty to seventy years, and were spread about the country in slowly growing small congregations jointly served by the missionaries and native Christian workers. The sparseness of the Protestant community, plus the lack of a rapid nationwide communication and transportation system until nearly 1900, makes it unsurprising that "revivals" in the church of China were small in scale and localized, without national publicity or impact.

Within a few years after 1900, however, revivals reminiscent in tone and size of those of Finney and Moody were occurring in China. A major reason for this was the dramatically altered climate of receptivity to Christianity in China. Few nations have as dramatic an event to mark the passage from one century to the next as China had in the Boxer uprising (or Boxer Rebellion) of 1900, which had as one of its goals the extirpation of Christianity and Christians from China. Much changed soon after the Boxer affair played itself out in tragic obscurantist violence, and the nation was subjected to a humiliating foreign occupation and heavy reparations in 1900–1901. There ensued a substantial opening to the West, with new Chinese government educational and economic initiatives and significant political reform.[3] And, for the first time, there was a quantum jump in interest in Protestant Christianity. Christian mission schools grew rapidly, as did the church; from still far fewer than 100,000 baptized Christians in the late 1890s, the church reached 178,000 members in 1906.[4] Many Chinese Christians saw Christianity as the answer to China's national dilemma of weakness and underdevelopment; it offered as well a personal religious identity. A much larger Christian community after 1900, therefore, was one of the conditions that made revivalism possible.

Another factor in the emergence of Chinese revivalism was what one might call the "internationalization of revivalist expectations"—in particular, the worldwide publicity given to the Welsh revival from 1904. Just as Christians hoping for mass revitalization in the United States looked to Wales, so too did many in China. In 1906, reporting on events in his district, Dr. A. D. Peill, a north China missionary, wrote: "At last it has come, the 'Revival' we have sought. . . . We cast longing eyes on Wales no more."[5]

It is inherently a bit unfair, and inevitably somewhat inaccurate, to point to a single event or person as the embodiment of a major trend at a time when, in the context of new post–1900 Christian growth and high expectations, many missionary and Chinese Christian leaders alike reported signs of spiritual quickening.[6] Nevertheless it seems clear that the first revival to gain nationwide publicity in China and international repute outside China was the Manchurian revival of 1908. Its central figure was Jonathan Goforth, an unprepossessing Canadian who in 1888 had been the first Canadian Presbyterian sent to China.[7]

The Canadians carved out a small mission field in the northern part of Henan province, just above the Yellow River in the heart of the north China plain. For over a decade, Goforth and his colleagues worked to build a modest network of churches in this area. Then, in 1900, they found themselves in the middle of the Boxer turmoil and were fortunate to escape with their lives; Goforth himself was badly beaten en route to safety. After returning to China in late 1901,

Goforth was restless and dissatisfied with both his own spiritual state and the progress of his work; the churches he tended seemed dead. He, like others, avidly read reports of the Welsh revival, and in 1905 he began to study the works of Charles Finney, resolving to try to implement Finney's principles.[8] Other missionaries and Chinese church workers as well were starting to experience and write about spiritual renewals in their churches, schools, and hospitals.[9] The combination of more dynamic church growth and the "expectation," perhaps, had its effect. Another factor may have been the apparently increasing practice (it had been done before 1900, but not extensively) of inviting missionaries or Chinese evangelists from other parts of China to visit a local area for a few days of consecutive meetings. These visits would be preceded by a period of concentrated prayer by the hosts in order to prepare for anticipated spiritual renewal among local Christians. The hope and expectations may often have fathered the experience.

Reports from Korea also energized expectations. As Goforth related it: "the religious world was electrified by the marvelous story of the Korean Revival."[10] When reports reached China, the Canadian Presbyterian foreign mission secretary was in China, and he invited Goforth to accompany him to Korea to investigate. The two of them made a short visit, were profoundly impressed, and then returned to China by the northern route through Manchuria.[11] There they stopped briefly to report on their Korean experiences in the Scottish/Irish Presbyterian missions in Manchuria. So eagerly was the news received that Goforth was invited back, and he returned to Manchuria early in 1908 for an extended tour of speaking engagements. It was the dramatic response to this speaking tour that constituted the "Manchurian Revival," establishing Goforth's reputation as a revivalist and drawing nationwide Protestant attention.

To summarize a complex phenomenon, the general pattern in Manchuria was that Goforth would speak, then there would be a mass expression of contrition for sins and confession, all in an emotionally charged atmosphere. Goforth was by all accounts not a stemwinder of an orator; he would speak plainly of sin, the need for repentance and confession, and the power of the Holy Spirit. His audiences were largely Christian. Then he would conclude by inviting prayer. Within the context of congregational prayer, first a few, then many, confessed their sins and long-harbored resentments, begged forgiveness, and broke down emotionally. Frequently elders of the church, or even pastors, participated in this confession, thus legitimizing it for all.[12]

As this happened, another phenomenon emerged, one new to most witnesses, of united mass prayer, the voices rising and falling and blending, although each one's words differed. Clearly, emotional release was a major part of this experience. A sympathetic account, calling this "the greatest spiritual movement in the history of missions in China," described how people would confess "with sobs, shrieks, and groans," falling on their faces, until "their separate cries were merged and lost in the swelling tide of general weeping."[13] The same account noted that "strange thrills coursed up and down one's body," and that everywhere could be heard "the agony of the penitent, his groans and cries and voice shaken with sobs." Those who confessed "seemed to find peace, and their faces shone." Some "were exalted to ecstasies, or . . . saw visions." All this was strong stuff for staid Scotch-Irish Presbyterian missionaries to countenance. No wonder that Christians all over China were struck by such accounts.

It is easier to report this phenomenon than to analyze it. Salient features included a high state of expectation, with Wales and then nearby Korea as examples; weeks or months of purposeful prayer for revival; and the combination of individual and mass repentance and individual and group prayer, all in a context of stress on the power of the Holy Spirit to cleanse and renew the converted and to save any unbelievers. In many ways, this resembled American holiness camp meetings, or even the early Pentecostal revivals. The long-term results were not particularly spectacular, however; though there was some evidence of gain in zeal and commitment in the churches, Manchuria did not dominate Chinese Christianity because of its 1908 revival.[14]

These events of the years just before 1910, in Manchuria and in other places on a lesser scale, inaugurated an era in which the full-time revivalist or evangelist became fairly commonplace in China. The Chinese church had grown and matured sufficiently to continue to support such revival activities; many within the churches wanted to promote regular revival, and after 1910 several individuals, some Chinese as well as foreigners, became more or less full time revivalists/evangelists.

Jonathan Goforth was himself one of these. After the Manchurian revival, he worked nearly full time at meetings all across China until his furlough in 1909–10, during which time he achieved further notoriety, some of it skeptical of his "emotional" methods, in Canada and in England. Back in Henan between 1910 and 1917, he worked part-time as a traveling revivalist, and partly in his old local field, where he was increasingly frustrated by the growth of "modernist" ideas among his colleagues. After 1917 his home board authorized him to move at will around China. In the late 1920s, he opted to reestablish his work in the Presbyterian missions in Manchuria, where he finished his China career in 1935.[15] Interestingly, Goforth at the end of his career remained committed to the same revival methods he had "discovered" soon after 1900. In 1929, Goforth helped arrange a few weeks' revival meetings featuring Wang Zai (Leland Wang), a well-known Chinese evangelist, and Paul Rader, a U.S. revivalist from the Chicago area. According to Goforth, Rader preached intensely on "sin, only sin" as the obstacle to a full Christian life, and often "the whole audience would be in tears." This resulted in "touching confessions and . . . a wave of spontaneous prayer which seemed to pass over the entire audience." It all reminded him of Manchuria in 1908.[16]

It is important to return to the period around 1910, for about then a major new component of revivalism in modern China appeared—native Chinese evangelists and revivalists. In the years before 1910 it was not unknown for capable Chinese pastors or church workers to lead meetings of spiritual renewal, or successful local evangelistic meetings.[17] However, there were as yet no nationally or even regionally known Chinese revivalists. The first to gain national stature was Ding Limei.[18]

Ding, born in 1871, was a second generation Christian and an outstanding 1892 graduate of Calvin Mateer's Christian academy in Shandong province.[19] He worked as a teacher, then as a pastor in his native province for many years; like Goforth, he had a narrow escape from the Boxers in 1900. As a pastor in the years after 1900, he urged young men in Christian middle schools and colleges to choose Christian work as a career, and to make a spiritual recommitment to underpin that vocational choice. A turning point in his career came in 1909–10. Still a pastor, Ding visited his alma mater, now called Shandong Union College, in the spring of 1909. In a series of meetings, there occurred such a revival of Christian dedication in the student body that over 100 students committed themselves to enter the ministry.[20] Over the coming months Ding had a comparable impact on other Christian schools in north China. Then in 1910, at the annual meeting of the North China Young Men's Christian Association, there was organized a "Chinese Student Volunteer Movement for the Ministry," with Ding as its full-time traveling secretary. This was clearly modeled on the Student Volunteer Movement for Foreign Missions, originating in the 1880s in the United States and likewise affiliated with the YMCA.

For the next several years Ding traveled all over China, holding evangelistic-revival meetings, especially in Christian mission schools. He had considerable impact on many students between approximately 1910 and 1918.[21] Although referred to by some as "the Moody of China" (when not called "the Apostle of Shantung"), it seems that Ding as a revivalist was far different in style from Moody or Goforth. His target was usually students, and I have seen no references to his using emotionalism as a device; indeed one author claims he eschewed it.[22] This was undoubtedly an appropriate posture to use with young intellectuals. The enthusiastic response he received from students, and the success he had in helping some of them to choose the significant career choice of the ministry as opposed to secular employment, is evidence of the relative openness to Christianity on the part of many young Chinese intellectuals at this time. These years could later be seen as a halcyon period, between the eras of anti-Christian prejudices of the late imperial period (especially pre–1900) and the anti-imperialist emotions of the 1920s. The student responsiveness, and thus Ding's revivalistic success, probably related in part to Ding's direct contention that a dedicated life of Christian service would improve China's sorry national state.[23]

The years 1911 to 1919, bracketed by the political watersheds of the Republican Revolution and the May Fourth Movement respectively, were probably the high point of joint Sino-foreign mass evangelism and revivalism in modern China.[24] The unequivocal freedom of religious belief contained in the new Republican constitution promulgated after the overthrow of the Manchu dynasty, and the optimism that republican political forms modeled on those of the West might help solve China's problems, contributed to continued receptivity to Christianity and the growth of the Christian movement. During these years China attracted a number of international evangelists and revivalists. United States YMCA Student Volunteer Movement speakers John Mott and Sherwood Eddy made several trips to China, speaking to large crowds of a thousand and more in major cities, and directing their appeal to the students in Chinese government schools and the Chinese urban middle class. Mott, who made repeated trips to China beginning in 1897, first enjoyed a mass response in 1907, then again in 1913. Eddy's first foray was in 1911, and he returned frequently until the 1930s, with Mott in 1913 and then alone in 1914, 1918, and thereafter.

The work of Mott, Eddy, F. N. D. Buchman, and other visitors during these years, though it had mass appeal, was more "evangelistic" than "revivalistic" in nature, being directed mainly toward non-

Christians. It was solidly part of the Sino-foreign "mainstream" of missionary-run institutions—the old established missions, the China Continuation Committee (deriving from the Edinburgh Missionary Conference of 1910), and the YMCA. During these years revivalism in China seems in retrospect to have been a seamless fabric. Men such as Ding, Goforth, and the visiting luminaries Mott and Eddy certainly did not see themselves working at cross-purposes.

A closer look, however, reveals developing tensions. One was theological/experiential. On one hand was the "Christianity as personal salvation and service to nation and mankind" strand of Mott, Eddy, and Ding Limei, which as the years passed put increasing stress on service and decreasing stress on an intense personal experience of faith and renewal. Another strand put the emphasis quite the other way around, elevating above all else the need for not only personal faith and a personal experience of repentance and redemption, but also (more implicitly) a need for lifelong occasional renewal and rededication—that is, "revival." This tension arose in Goforth's career and resulted in his leaving his mission after 1917 to be a full-time evangelist/revivalist. The tension is also apparent in comparative accounts of the harrowing experiences of those undergoing the half-day meetings of the Manchurian revival of 1908 and the descriptions of how in Ding Limei's revival meetings soon thereafter (although the observer reported "a great outpouring of the Holy Spirit") Ding used "blackboard and neatly prepared charts" and carefully kept track of the time, so that the meeting would not run too long.[25] Soon the tension would erupt internationally, appropriately beginning in China and quickly manifesting itself in the United States and England as the "fundamentalist-modernist controversy."[26] By the 1920s, for the most part in China, as elsewhere, it was "fundamentalists" who insisted on the need for "revivalism," and "modernists" who could do without it, at least in traditional form.

Another growing tension between 1911 and 1919 was between native Chinese Christian leaders and foreign missionaries, reflecting the rising force of Chinese nationalism. In addition to Ding Limei, several capable Chinese pastors, YMCA secretaries, Christian educators, and church administrators rose to respected positions in the Sino-foreign Protestant establishment.[27] Yet that establishment itself, having grown large and ponderous over the decades, did not accommodate rapidly or recognize commensurately these leaders: it remained dominated by the foreign mission groups, most of them American. In turn, the foreign mission structures, automatically dragging with them their Chinese participants, remained part and parcel of the "unequal treaty system" under which, for example, every foreign missionary in China came under the treaty provisions of extraterritoriality.

These two tensions—that of religious experience and national identity—both erupted dramatically in the 1920s. The latter was the first to do so, beginning in the student-led May Fourth Movement of 1919 as the first stage of a wider mass nationalism that in short order made all the prominent symbols of foreign presence and exploitation in China into targets for vituperative denunciation.[28] The Christian church, including its foreign leaders, its schools and hospitals, its Chinese pastors and parishioners, all became targets.[29] Almost overnight, it seemed to many Christians in China, many Chinese, especially the student class, turned from honest curiosity about Christianity to emotional and irrational hostility. The mass audiences once attracted by Mott, Eddy, and Ding Limei disappeared. More students chose to excoriate Christianity than to investigate it. Ding's career entered a period of relative obscurity in the 1920s. All this did not happen overnight, but it did occur over just a few years, from about 1919 to 1927. By 1927 new, strongly anti-imperialist forces (the Chinese Communist and Guomindang parties) were changing the political landscape of China. Foreigners, including missionaries, were alarmed and most fled for their lives in the spring of 1927, temporarily abandoning their stations; Chinese Christian leaders were bewildered, isolated and resentful at their own inevitable association with foreign "imperialism" in the eyes of radical students and political activists; common Chinese Christians were demoralized, many becoming less visible or altogether inactive.

Yet during these years of apparent disaster for the Christian movement in China, revivalism continued, and even gained momentum, growing to impressive proportions in the late 1920s and 1930s, after the political scene had stabilized again. How did this occur? Several shifts in the components of revivalism made it possible. One shift was away from the emphasis put on the student class by Ding, Mott, and Eddy, and back to the church-based community of those already converted and whomever else of any social class that could be drawn to a meeting, sometimes by dramatic public relations techniques (for example, gongs, banners, and street parades inviting onlookers). Common folk in both urban and rural areas—whoever would come—became the targets of evangelistic and revival endeavors as students and intellectuals became, for a time, preoccupied with the religion of radical nationalism.

A second shift in surviving revivalism occured because, in the midst of the developing fundamentalist-modernist split, fundamentalists and their allies proved stronger than was anticipated. Their ranks were substantially reinforced during the period 1900–1920. The mainstream ("liberal" or "modernist") denominational mission establishment remained firmly in control of the great majority of important institutions of the Sino-foreign Protestant community in China: the large urban church edifices; the schools and hospitals; the administrative positions interfacing with Chinese government and foreign consular authorities; and the influential monthly magazine, the *Chinese Recorder.*[30] Yet their days were numbered. The fastest-growing mission groups in the first two decades of the century included the Southern Baptists, various evangelical Scandinavian groups, and especially the China Inland Mission, holiness and "higher life" groups such as the Christian and Missionary Alliance, Seventh-day Adventists, and a whole host (hundreds by the late 1910s) of independent missionaries, almost all of whom were fundamentalists (in the 1920s sense) and many of whom were Pentecostals.

The proliferation of new missions, most of them small and sectarian, meant an infusion of eager (though often ill-prepared and naive) missionaries unencumbered by institutional preoccupations and intensely concentrated upon spiritual regeneration for themselves and for Chinese Christian converts, all in a context of strong premillennialist expectations. This meant, among other things, much less structure, somewhat more fire, brimstone, and Second Coming; and a fair dose of adventuresome creativity on the China mission scene by the 1920s, along with a high dropout rate among the enthusiastic newcomers. There was also a distinct new ingredient of Holiness/Pentecostal stress on the Holy Spirit and the gifts of the Spirit in some quarters, and a generally high stress on the importance of revivalism across the board in the fundamentalist/evangelical sector. In short, by the 1920s, the menu for a potential Chinese Christian seems to have become far more varied, and perhaps more interesting, than it had been only a few years before.

In this sector of revivalistic Christianity, the force of nationalism was making telling marks by the 1920s, creating a new generation of independent Chinese Christian leaders and organizations. Actually, this process of establishing independence had been underway for some time. Independent Chinese Christian leaders (that is, those who consciously broke away from or distanced themselves from the foreign missionary structures) had been active since the early 1900s. Early in the twentieth century the Shanghai Presbyterian pastor Yu Guozhen and several colleagues formed an all-Chinese organization called "The Chinese Christian Union" (Jidutuhui). In about 1906 they

formed an independent, all-Chinese congregation, and in the following years other churches in the region followed suit in order to become
independent of missions. By 1910 they had a newspaper, *Zhongguo
Jidutu bao* ("The Chinese Christian"), which later became *Sheng bao*
("The Sacred News"). Out of this group a federation of churches
emerged by the 1920s called the China Jesus Independence Church
(Zhongguo Yesujiao zilihui); in 1920, this federation had over 100
member churches, an annual national meeting, and full bylaws, in
addition to its own newspaper.[31] It continued to grow in the 1920s.
Many of its member churches were formerly Presbyterian or Con-
gregationalist; they were largely urban middle-class Chinese. Beginning in 1912, a comparable movement in north China produced a
smaller but similar federation of independent churches centered in
Shandong province but also well represented in the cities of Beijing
and Tianjin.[32]

These independent churches were on the whole evangelical but
not necessarily ardently fundamentalist in nature; many of them
participated in the revival campaigns of the late 1920s and 1930s,
but their theology did not impel them to be leaders in revivalism.
They evidence the beginnings of independence movements in the
larger Protestant community.

Another, radically sectarian, independent Chinese church was
taking shape by the late 1910s. It was Pentecostal in belief and practice, and militantly antiforeign in stance; its relations with foreign
missions were laden with friction (as opposed to the relations with
missions of the two federations mentioned above, which were fairly
amicable if not close). This was the True Jesus Church (Zhen Yesu
jiaohui), formed in north China in 1917–19. In the 1920s it grew most
rapidly in central interior provinces like Henan and Hunan. It was
exclusivist and "revivalist" in nature—revivalist both in terms of
spiritual renewal and in its insistence that Chinese Christians renounce
their old churches and acknowledge the sole legitimacy of the True
Jesus Church and its unique dogma. This dogma represented a mix
of "unitarian" (that is, "Jesus only") Pentecostalism and Seventh-day
worship. Its exclusivism did not permit its revivalism ever to have a
wide or ecumenical impact, though its proselytizing effects were
widely felt, and thoroughly resented, by mission churches.[33]

In the 1920s, as revivalism continued to be important only in
certain sectors of the Protestant community in China, there were a
few foreign revivalists who continued to come to China and find a
responsive audience. These included holiness revivalists such as Seth
Cook Rees, who came to China in 1922 and 1926, and Paget Wilkes

of the Japan Evangelistic Band, men with a very different appeal from that of Mott and Eddy in the 1910s.

Meanwhile, amid the general hostility to imperialism and Christianity, a new generation of Chinese Christian leaders were coming of age. Many of them were born in the years just before or after 1900 and were more willing to strike out on their own and form independent Christian ministries than their elders like Ding Limei had been. It was these men, and a few women as well, who would dominate revival activities in China in the 1930s, rendering obsolete the role of foreign revivalists among Chinese Christians. Several of these individuals warrant individual biographies, and a few have been studied; here I can do no more than describe briefly the careers of some of them.[34]

Wang Mingdao (1900–1991) is perhaps the best known in the West because of his public resistance to the authorities in the 1950s and subsequent long imprisonment before his release in 1979. Wang had a salvation experience and soon thereafter a Pentecostal experience around 1920, although later he backed away from full Pentecostalism. A stern and rather dogmatic man, often critical of missionaries and vociferously opposed to "liberal" theology, Wang was a powerful, effective speaker and teacher. From the late 1920s he spent about half of every year on the road conducting revivals and evangelistic meetings in evangelical and fundamentalist churches, even after building his own church in Beijing. Wang did not create new churches nationwide but worked closely with others. He also edited and published a popular quarterly Christian magazine for over two decades.[35]

Ni Duosheng ("Watchman Nee," 1903–72) is another name familiar to many Christians around the world, because many of his works have been translated and published abroad since the 1930s. From the mid-1920s onward, Ni, strongly influenced by Brethren ideas (especially premillennialism) but also by a holiness stress on the Holy Spirit, was an effective teacher. His revival or evangelistic meetings were not large-scale ones: they were often held in homes, but his emphasis on the spirituality of the deeper Christian life drew many followers. Antagonism toward missions and foreign Christians often characterized his ministry. Seldom invited by or working within established congregations, his followers usually formed new groups, in effect forming a new nationwide denomination with headquarters in Shanghai called the "Assembly Hall" (Juhuichu) or "Little Flock" (Xiaoqun).[36]

Wang Zai ("Leland Wang," 1898–1975) was an older colleague of

Ni Duosheng in Fuzhou in the early 1920s, who became a traveling revival speaker with a popular music ministry. He made international contacts early in his career, and by the 1930s had formed an evangelistic association that took him frequently to Hong Kong, Southeast Asia, and North America.[37]

Some of the most dramatic and flamboyant revivalists of the decade before 1937 were associated at one time or another with the "Bethel Bands" of the Bethel Mission in Shanghai. The Bethel Mission was an independent and self-sustaining holiness enterprise (hospital, church, Bible training school) founded by Phoebe and Mary Stone, two Chinese sisters who were medical doctors, and by Jennie Hughes, an American. All three had been in the Methodist mission, but had left the mission in the early 1920s because of its "modernism."[38]

Through holiness networks, Bethel developed a linkage with Asbury College in Kentucky, and sometimes hosted traveling international holiness evangelists like Seth Cook Rees. But Bethel made its mark by sending out ardent Chinese young men and women from its training institute to conduct revival meetings at whatever churches would welcome them. Several of the young people who emerged from these "bands" proved gifted with eloquence and music. Five young men, including two who would later become stirring revival speakers in their own right, Song Shangjie ("John Sung") and Ji Zhiwen ("Andrew Gih"), set off in early 1931 as the unknown but ambitiously named "Bethel Worldwide Evangelistic Band." By 1935, when the band dissolved, they had traveled over 50,000 miles, visited 133 cities, and held almost 3,400 revival meetings at churches of all denominations.[39]

Andrew Gih went on to become a well-known revivalist in Hong Kong and overseas Chinese communities until his death in the 1980s. John Sung, immediately after leaving the Bethel Band at the end of 1934, became the most controversial of Chinese revivalists during the next two years, until the invasion by Japan. Sung (1901–44), the son of a Fujian pastor, studied in the United States from 1919 to 1927, receiving a Ph.D. in Chemistry at Ohio State University in 1926. He then went to Union Theological Seminary in New York, where he had a religious and psychological crisis due to the clash between his traditional Christian beliefs and the higher Biblical criticism and liberal theology that surrounded him at Union. He ended up in a sanatorium for several months in 1927, after denouncing his teachers and local pastors, then returned to China freshly reconverted to the tenets of his childhood—a fundamentalist, in the new terminology of the period.[40]

Sung developed a unique, abrasive style of forceful or "rude" revivalism. He was a creative Bible expositor and good song leader, but he was also ruthlessly direct and acerbic in his denunciations of those with whom he disagreed, especially "liberal" theologians and pastors. In calling Christians to be truly born again, and to confess old sins, make restitution and be cleansed, he was not unusual; and thousands responded to his call for revival. Sung also developed a stress on healing in his revivals. His meetings were often quite emotional, even spectacularly so. But he also did not hesitate to denounce the pastors and leaders of denominational churches even as they sat before him in his meetings in their churches. In one place in 1935 he urged local Christians to boycott the upcoming meetings of the old evangelist Sherwood Eddy on one of Eddy's last trips to China. This behavior, both as a member of the Bethel Band from 1931 through 1934 and then as a lone revivalist until 1937, not surprisingly alienated many Christians, foreign and Chinese alike.[41] Yet Sung must be reckoned probably the single most powerful figure in Chinese revivalism in the mid–1930s. Although eventually barred by some churches, he was highly esteemed by many others.

An especially noteworthy instance of revival in China before the Sino-Japanese War of 1937 was the "Shantung Revival" of the early 1930s. Shandong (Shantung) province, in the heart of north China, had long been a major mission field of the U.S. Presbyterians and Southern Baptists, as well as of the English Baptists. It had also produced many native sectarian religious movements over the centuries, as well as the "Boxers" in 1899–1900, and some early leaders of the sectarian Christian True Jesus Church in 1919. At least two factors combined to create the revival of the 1930s.

One stemmed from the work of a freelance Norwegian missionary, Marie Monsen, a Pentecostal or near-Pentecostal, who had had a major impact upon Shandong Southern Baptists beginning in the late 1920s. From 1930 to 1932, many Southern Baptist and other missionaries and Chinese Christians in parts of Shandong were not only "born again" for the first time, but large numbers of them had a "definite experience of the baptism of the Holy Spirit," in the words of Mary Crawford, one participant.[42] It seems clear that the revival meetings brought Pentecostal experiences to many: Crawford's account describes people being hurled to the ground unable to rise, "holy laughter and praise," all-night meetings, "the Holy Spirit moving as an audible wind," involuntary sounds in prayer, and so forth, as well as many miraculous healings.[43]

Another factor on the Shandong scene in the early 1930s was an avowedly Pentecostal movement that, unlike Monsen's efforts, was largely under the direction of Chinese leaders. This movement began in 1930, with a traveling Chinese revivalist from the south, and soon resulted in several Chinese pastors (most of them from the U.S. Presbyterian Shandong mission) embracing the experience and forming a loosely structured new group, the "Spiritual Gifts Society" (Lingen hui). This in effect constituted a new church for those who eventually left their former churches due to hostility toward their newfound Pentecostalism.

On the whole, the Presbyterian missionaries among whose flocks this revival occurred suspected or opposed it and their reports fed two long articles, featured in the missionary press in Shanghai, on the Lingen hui and the alleged chaos it created.[44] In these articles, "excesses" of superstition and irrationality were recounted; "vagaries of the leaders" and "primitive psychology" or "dangerous phases" were noted, as well as "misuse of the Bible"; talk of "manna" appearing, or claims of "communication with the dead" are attributed to its enthusiasts; reports of the meetings described them as a "liturgy of disorder" and "pandemonium."[45] We have no accounts to balance this from the Chinese who were in favor of it; the movement was largely rural, and the people involved left no known written records of it. It apparently waned after the mid-1930s.

A watershed for Chinese history, and Chinese Christianity as well, followed the revivalist "high tide" of the 1930s, with its varied components like the Bethel Band and John Sung stirring older urban churches, while Shandong missionaries and rural Christians were experiencing their respective versions of revival. Full-scale war with Japan beginning in 1937 meant a new set of conditions for missions and the Chinese church. Thus 1937 is an appropriate stopping point for a historical survey that includes both mission and native revivalism.

The devastation of the wartime years, 1937–45, was followed by the chaos of the civil war, 1946–49, and then by the radically restricted conditions for Christianity imposed by the new Communist government after 1949, including a period from about 1965 to 1980 when all religious activities were forbidden. Indeed, severe situational or governmental limitation on the sort of activities associated with revivalism was the rule rather than the exception for nearly half a century, from 1937 until the early 1980s.

Yet the public reemergence of Christianity in China after 1980 revealed some striking continuities with the earlier period of revivalism described in this essay. Older Christians renewed themselves and proudly reestablished their public identity as believers; new, younger converts produced dynamic traveling evangelists and revival leaders who nurtured growing churches, especially in the rural areas; and a strong stress on the Holy Spirit in much of the revivalism of the 1980s called to mind the prominent Pentecostal strand in revivalism after 1920.[46] China has a dynamic Protestant Christian community today, larger by several times than the one that existed in 1949, although the foreign missionary presence in China was totally eliminated by the new Communist state in the early 1950s. One of the interesting features of this community is its resumption of revivalism. The seeds for this continuity were sown in the first third of the twentieth century.

Two general observations emerging from this survey deserve to be highlighted. First, Chinese revivals were extensive between 1900–1937, and on the surface they seem similar in many ways to the American and British revivalist tradition as it evolved in North Atlantic Protestantism from the late nineteenth into the early twentieth century. This included variously Moody-style, holiness, and Pentecostal revivals. Why was this so? Was the North Atlantic model a valid, universal one? Were missionary expectations of the format and content of revivals sufficient to determine the forms and themes that revivalism took in China? Or are Christian revivals part of a broader, transcultural human religious phenomenon, which expressed itself naturally in China?

Second, revivalism in China, while originating in the Sino-foreign sector run by the missionaries, eventually came to be dominated by Chinese leaders, many of them independent from and even antagonistic toward the foreign mission establishment. Many theologically conservative or fundamentalist mission groups retained a stress on revivalism through the 1930s, but they increasingly invited Chinese leaders to conduct their revival meetings. The obvious question that should be posed, one which might also apply to other non-Western cultures, is whether revivalism is a handy and effective means for indigenous Christian leaders to break free of domination by missions. The tentative answer in the Chinese case is that, in the first part of the twentieth century, it was. This may also indicate the long-term historical significance of the phenomenon of revivalism in a global Christian context.

## NOTES

1. Stuart C. Henry, "Revivalism," in *Encyclopedia of the American Religious Experience,* ed. Charles H. Lippy and Peter W. Williams (New York:

Scribner's, 1988), 2:799. The author thanks the Henry Luce Foundation and the University of Kansas General Research Fund for supporting this research.

2. Kenneth S. Latourette, *A History of Christian Missions in China* (London: Society for the Propagation of Christian Knowledge, 1929), 479.

3. See Daniel H. Bays, *China Enters the Twentieth Century* (Ann Arbor: University of Michigan Press, 1978).

4. D. MacGillivray, ed., *A Century of Protestant Missions in China, 1807-1907* (Shanghai: Presbyterian Press, 1907), 669.

5. *Chinese Recorder*, June 1906, 344.

6. However, in my opinion, J. Edwin Orr's *Evangelical Awakenings in Eastern Asia* (Minneapolis: Bethany Fellowship, 1975), 34ff., overdramatizes and overcategorizes what were essentially local events.

7. For a basic biography and general features of the Manchurian revival, see Rosalind Goforth, *Goforth of China* (Minneapolis: Bethany Fellowship; originally published 1937), and Alvyn J. Austin, *Saving China: Canadian Missionaries in the Middle Kingdom, 1888-1959* (Toronto: University of Toronto Press, 1986), chapters 2, 6.

8. Jonathan Goforth, *By My Spirit* (London: Marshall, Morgan and Scott, n.d.), 23-25.

9. *Chinese Recorder*, June 1906, 344-50; *Chinese Recorder*, July 1906, 410-14. Several other instances of spiritual renewals in 1906 are noted in Orr, *Evangelical Awakenings*, 34-36.

10. Goforth, *By My Spirit*, 28.

11. Jonathan Goforth, *When the Spirit's Fire Swept Korea* (Grand Rapids: Zondervan, 1943).

12. This description is culled from J. Goforth, *By My Spirit*, chapter 3; *Chinese Recorder*, June 1908, 330-35, 339-42; *Chinese Recorder*, September 1908, 523-26; Austin Fulton, *Through Earthquake, Wind and Fire: Church and Mission in Manchuria, 1867-1950* (Edinburgh: Saint Andrews Press, 1967), 48-51.

13. Noted by Dr. W. Phillips in *Chinese Recorder*, September 1908, 524.

14. Fulton, *Through Earthquake*, 51.

15. Career summary from R. Goforth, and from the finding aids to Collection 188, Goforth Collection, Billy Graham Center (hereafter BGC) Archives, Wheaton College, Wheaton, Illinois.

16. J. Goforth and James McCammon, "A Foretaste of Revival Blessing in China," *The Life of Faith*, 25 December 1929, 1611-12, in Goforth Collection, BGC Archives.

17. Various sources, especially the *Chinese Recorder*, have scattered references to local Chinese speakers having some impact from the late 1890s on.

18. The best biography of Ding is in Zha Shijie, *Zhongguo Jidujiao renwu xiaozhuan* (Concise biographies of Chinese Christians) (Taipei: China Evangelical Seminary Press, 1983), 107-12. Also, C. E. Scott, "Ding, the Apostle of Shantung," *Missionary Review of the World* 34:2 (1911): 125-27; Wei Waiyang, "Ding Limei Lijie xiongdi hezhuan" (A combined biography of

Ding Limei and Ding Lijie), *Xiaoyuan* 22:2 (Feb. 1980): 62–65; an autobiographical article by Ding is in *Chuandao jingyan tan* (Preaching experiences) 1 (1925): 25–29.

19. For Mateer and his school, see Irwin T. Hyatt, Jr., *Our Ordered Lives Confess: Three Nineteenth-Century American Missionaries in East Shantung* (Cambridge: Harvard University Press, 1976), chapters 7–9.

20. See sources in note 18; also "A Revival in the Shantung College," *Missionary Review of the World* 33:4 (Apr. 1910): 244–45.

21. The writings of later, important Chinese Christian leaders provide testimony to this impact. See, for example, Xie Fuya, *Xie Fuya wannian wenlu* (The later writings of Xie Fuya) (Taipei: Chuanji wenxue, 1977), 286.

22. This is Ma Kezheng and Xin Yifu, "Qingmo de budao gongzuo yu fuxing yundong (1900–1911)" (Evangelism and revivalism in the late Qing period, 1900–1911), *Zhongguo yu jiaohui* 33 (1984): 14. For a report by a missionary who accompanied Ding on one tour, see O. Braskamp, "The Evangelist Ding Li Mei: The Moody of China," *Chinese Recorder*, July 1916, 497–500.

23. See Ding's openly patriotic appeal as reported by Braskamp, "Evangelist Ding Li Mei," 498.

24. For an overview of these years, see Ma Kezheng and Xin Yifu, "Minchu banian zhi budao shigong yu fuxing yundong (1911–1919)" (Evangelism and revival in the first eight years of the Republic, 1911–1919), *Zhongguo yu jiaohui* 35 (1984): 15–20. Much useful information is also in Zha Shijie, "Minguo Jidujiaohui shi (1), 1911–1917" (History of Christianity in the Republican period, part 1: 1911–1917), *Guoli Taiwan daxue lishi xuexi xuebao* 8 (1981): 109–45.

25. Braskamp, "Evangelist Ding Li Mei," 497–98.

26. For basic documentation on the China mission field's role in the early controversy, see Joel A. Carpenter, ed., *Modernism and Foreign Missions: Two Fundamentalist Protests* (New York: Garland, 1988). The first of these documents is a famous 1921 *Princeton Theological Review* article by W. H. G. Thomas.

27. Zha Shijie, *Concise biographies*, has profiles of several of these people.

28. This phenomenon is one of the commonly stressed themes in the scholarly literature on twentieth-century Chinese history, from textbooks to monographs.

29. The anti-Christian movement of the 1920s, while always mentioned, is seldom studied in detail. A recent monograph by Jessie G. Lutz, *Chinese Politics and Christian Missions: The Anti-Christian Movements of 1920–1928* (Notre Dame: Cross Cultural Publications, 1988), does an excellent job on this theme.

30. For an important, recent, and massive biography of the editor of the *Chinese Recorder* from 1912 to 1937, Frank Rawlinson, by his son, see John L. Rawlinson, *Rawlinson, the Recorder and China's Revolution*, 2 vols. (Notre Dame: Cross Cultural Publications, 1989).

31. The story of this church and its leaders is a fascinating one, although I cannot pursue it here. Important sources are: Zhao Tianen, "Zili, ziyang yu jiaohui zengzhang" (Independence, self-support, and church growth), in Chinese Coordinating Committee of World Evangelism, ed., *Shijie huaren jiaohui zengzhang yantaohui huibao* (Proceedings of the conference on world Chinese church growth) (Hong Kong, 1981), 231–36; also Chabei Shanghai church, ed., *Zhonghua Jidujiaohui Chabeitang liushi zhounian xintang luocheng jinian tekan* (Sixtieth anniversary volume of the new church building of the Chabei Christian church) (Shanghai, 1948).

32. Zha Shijie, "History of Christianity in the Republican period," 135, and Qu Zhengmin, "Meiguo zhanglaohui he Shandong zilihui shilue" (The American Presbyterian mission and the Shandong independent church), *Shandong wenxian* 11:1 (1985): 19–37. One of the Tianjin leaders of this federation was Zhang Boling, founder of the prestigious Nankai University.

33. See Daniel Bays, "Indigenous Protestant Churches in China, 1900–1937: A Case Study from the Pentecostal Sector" (unpublished article, 1988). The True Jesus Church, which I interpret partly in terms of the heritage of Chinese sectarian folk religion, was almost certainly the largest of the independent Chinese Protestant churches from the 1920s to the early 1950s, when it was demolished and its leaders jailed. It is still very active in Taiwan and among Chinese communities around the world.

34. Brief biographies of twelve Chinese revivalists and evangelists are included in Gustav Carlberg, *China in Revival* (Rock Island, Ill.: Augustana, 1936). Six are highlighted, and many more are mentioned, in Z. K. Zia, "Chinese Evangelists in Modern China," *Chinese Recorder*, January 1935, 46–48.

35. Wang's autobiography, first published in 1950, is *Wushinian lai* (These fifty years) (Hong Kong: Bellman, 1982). It is partially translated by Arthur Reynolds in *A Stone Made Smooth* (Sholing, England: Mayflower, 1981). A short biography appears in Leslie Lyall, *Three of China's Mighty Men* (London: Hodder and Stoughton: Overseas Missionary Fellowship, 1973).

36. Angus Kinnear, *Against the Tide* (Wheaton: Tyndale, 1978) contains a serviceable biography of Nee; see also Lyall, *Three of China's Mighty Men*. There are a host of Chinese-language publications from Hong Kong and Taiwan, with a solid overall biography in Zha Shijie, *Concise biographies*, 305–40.

37. Zha Shijie, *Concise biographies*, 267–78.

38. Little has been written in any language on Bethel. The organization still exists in Hong Kong.

39. Ji Zhiwen later wrote several books. See Andrew Gih, *Launch Out into the Deep* (London: Marshall, Morgan and Scott, 1938); *Twice Born—and Then?* (London: Marshall, Morgan, and Scott, Ltd., 1954); *Into God's Family*, rev. ed. (London: Marshall, Morgan, and Scott, Ltd., 1955); also Ji Zhiwen, *Fuxing de huoyan* (Fire of revival) (Hong Kong, 1957).

40. See Sung's own story in Song Shangjie, *Wode jianzheng* (My testi-

mony) (Hong Kong: Bellman, 1962; originally published 1936). Also, Li Yiling, *Song Shangjie zhuan* (The life of John Sung) (Hong Kong: Christian Communications Ltd., 1962); and Leslie Lyall, *Flame for God: John Sung and Revival in the Far East* (London: OMF, 1954).

41. In addition to the sources in note 40, see Z. S. Zia, "Indigenous Evangelism and Christian Unity," *Chinese Recorder,* July 1936, 408–12. Sung is clearly the target here.

42. Mary Crawford, *The Shantung Revival* (Shanghai: China Baptist Publication Society, 1933), 40. See also C. L. Culpepper, *The Shantung Revival* (Dallas: Baptist General Convention of Texas, 1968), and Marie Monsen, *The Awakening: Revival in China, a Work of the Holy Spirit,* trans. Joy Guiness (London: China Inland Mission, 1961).

43. Although a Baptist herself, Crawford's account does not use the term "tongues," or even "Pentecostals," but everything else is there. She concludes (104) with the plea, "O friends, let us turn back to Pentecost." When he published his memoir in 1968, C. L. Culpepper, who participated as a young missionary, deleted many of Crawford's explicit and harrowing descriptions.

44. See "Indigenous Revival in Shantung," *Chinese Recorder,* December 1931, 767–72; and Paul R. Abbott, "Revival Movements," in *China Christian Year Book, 1932–33* (Shanghai, 1934), 175–92, much of which deals with the Shantung events. But see one favorable short editorial report in *Missionary Review of the World,* February 1933, 67, quoting from a letter by a young American missionary on the scene. *Missionary Review of the World* was published in the United States.

45. "Indigenous Revival in Shantung," 769–70, 772; Abbott, "Revival Movements," 182, 186–87.

46. For some interpretive thoughts on the Chinese Christian scene today, with a bibliographical survey, see my article, "Chinese Popular Religion and Christianity before and after the 1949 Revolution: A Retrospective View," *Fides et Historia* 23.1 (1991), 69–77. For a solid history of Chinese Christianity, with considerable detail on the last forty years, see Bob Whyte, *Unfinished Encounter: China and Christianity* (London: Collins, 1988).

# 10

## Revival and Revolution in Latin America

———————◆———————

EVERETT A. WILSON

LATIN AMERICA's rapidly growing evangelical movements have given rise to contradictory explanations of their origins, effects, and significance. While a wide range of religious and secular publications have dealt with these revival movements, most treatments have been preoccupied with policy rather than analysis. Moreover, writers are likely to adopt at least an implicit position about the legitimacy of North American overseas missions and their role in either supporting or resisting social revolution. Critics have represented theologically conservative missions as defenders of United States hegemony in the region and guarantors of the status quo, while evangelicals intensify their efforts, convinced of theological mandates.[1] Assessments that make either of these two positions mutually exclusive may tend to the polemical, self-serving, and ethnocentric, prescribing remedies for Latin Americans without consulting them.

Any North American evaluation of Latin American Protestantism must appreciate both the vast differences that history has produced in the religious perspectives of the two cultures and the difficulty of reconciling North American political interests with Latin American spiritual needs. The sardonic lament often heard in Latin America says, "Poor Mexico, so far from God and so close to the United States." There can be no mistaking the Latin Americans' quest for control over their own destinies, as suggested by geographer Preston James's anecdote of the two engineers who were inspecting a recently completed hydroelectric project in a South American country. One, a North American, waves his hand in a wide gesture over the imposing dam and asks his Latin counterpart, "Well, what do you think of it?" The Latin American replies pensively, *"Es bueno, pero no es nuestro"* [It may be good, but it isn't really ours]. For several millions of Latin American evangelicals, many of whom have claim to little else, their faith, at least, is genuinely theirs.

There can be little reason to doubt that there is some correlation between the Latin American turbulence of recent decades and evangelical growth. Much evangelical increase appears to have been preceded by natural disasters, civil violence, and deteriorating economic conditions. Growth has also been notable among alienated, marginal groups excluded from the benefits of national life. However pleased North American conservatives may be with the reported evangelical strength in these republics, they must not fail to recognize that revival has occurred within the context of the masses' profound struggle to find a secure and rewarding life. It is not excessive to portray these movements as a response to social pathology, a protest against a traditional system that deserves to be denounced as unequal, unjust, and unresponsive. If Latin American evangelicals are typically cautious and pragmatic in their political involvements, it may be because they consciously reject the avowed premises and methods of the revolutionary left and are reluctant to compromise their institutional independence. Their aloofness should not be interpreted necessarily as support for either U.S. foreign policy or the status quo.

Evangelicals perceive themselves as initiators in the spiritual reconstruction of their own nations, and rely little on foreign help. Brazilian missionaries, for example, have long been at work in Uruguay, Paraguay, and Bolivia in substantial numbers, and Puerto Rican evangelists are found virtually everywhere in Latin America.

Self-conscious of their successes—sometimes having read church growth literature—numbers of Latin American evangelicals have suggested with no small delight that perhaps they should help their North American counterparts evangelize the United States. According to a story that circulated in Central America several years ago, a country pastor who had come to the capital city to attend a Jimmy Swaggart stadium crusade was asked what he thought of the effort. Dazzled by the bright lights, the excitement of the crowds, and the upbeat music, the pastor conceded that the event was marvelous. Truly *hermano* Swaggart was an outstanding man of God. The pastor was deeply disturbed, however, by the rudeness of the brown-haired Yankee who, from the beginning of the evangelist's sermon, followed him all over the stage, duplicating every step and gesture. No sooner would the evangelist get out a sentence or two in Spanish, complained the pastor, than that *gringo* would interrupt him to say something unintelligible in English!

The growth of Latin American evangelical groups must be seen from the perspective of the tens of thousands of pastors and lay leaders who have found in the movement opportunity to express their own frustrations, aspirations, and initiatives and, in the process, have made the evangelical movement more than an episode of spiritual renewal. Acting in a vacuum of leadership, evangelicals have produced the largest popularly initiated effort at social organization in the region, in the aggregate with more than 100,000 congregations, and with bureaucratic organization, personnel and material resources, and mechanisms for meeting the individual and collective needs of their adherents. It may be that except for national governments and the Roman Catholic church, no institution has the resources of the combined evangelical churches, and no other voluntary associations constitute such an extensive network of popular communication and influence.[2]

## Revival

By any standard of assessment, the evangelical revival in Latin America is impressive. Most recent compilations identify 36,000,000 evangelicals, double the number twenty years ago and growing at rates that appear in keeping with projections of as many as 60,000,000 evangelicals by the year 2000.[3] There is also ample evidence that these groups are spiritually alert, theologically sound, and morally vigorous.[4] If, as their critics claim, they are legalistic, inbred and suspicious of change, and made up largely of representatives of the poorest and most alienated sectors, they have often paid a high personal price for their faith and are enthusiastic and committed.

These groups tend to be self-renewing because of the form of their organization. Members are required to participate actively in a variety of demanding responsibilities. Their conduct is subject to scrutiny both by church members and the non-evangelical community. Lapses in conduct are often disciplined, especially in small congregations where personal integrity and dedication count far more than a member's social standing. Attrition rates are high in congregations where peer pressure is strong, but where merely getting to a meeting place may require considerable effort and sacrifice, the surviving members are likely to be stalwart. If the poor and disadvantaged make up the largest part of the congregations, business and professional people among their ranks pay an even higher price for their convictions in the form of voluntary exclusion from social circles that would afford them advantages. In addition, the market approach to membership recruitment assures energetic, imaginative efforts to extend the evangelical movement. Lay leaders are often encouraged to establish their own congregations, and the availability of competing denominations requires pastors to vindicate their leadership recurrently. The resulting fragmentation of evangelicals into cells keeps churches small but structurally strong. Churches are often networks of extended families and work associates. The aggregate growth of these groups into an impressive grass-roots movement demonstrates the suitability of their beliefs for contemporary Latin Americans, people with few options who are suffering the effects of social disintegration.

For the evangelical groups to thrive as they have, there must be more to their motivation and appeal than simply emotional gratification. Evangelical churches appeal to their adherents' vital interests and exact from them a serious commitment. The growth of the evangelical movement in Colombia during the era referred to as *la violencia* (from 1948 into the 1960s, when as many as 300,000 persons were murdered by opposing political factions) demonstrated the believers' tenacity and the relevance of their faith for crisis.[5] While the Colombian example is extreme, most evangelicals must overcome some disabilities for their faith. Persistent growth, however, assures constituent renewal and reinforcement of the groups' values and convictions. Meanwhile, evangelical communities increasingly enjoy recognition and growing resources. In nine of the nineteen Latin American republics and in Puerto Rico the proportion of evangelicals in the national populations is reported in double digits. In Guatemala, evangelicals make up as many as 25 percent of the population.[6] Yet, the difference in the size of evangelical communities in these countries suggests that dissimilar social conditions and cultural climates are responsible for varying rates of evangelical growth. Brazil and Chile account for more than two-thirds of the total evangelicals in Latin America while, on the other hand, the proportion of population claimed by evangelicals in seven republics is less than 3.5 percent. Mexico and Cuba, perhaps best thought of as special cases, have identified, respectively, 3.1 and 2.5 percent of the national population as evangelical. If political repression explains the difficulty faced by Cuban evangelical churches, what explanation can be given for Mexico, where Protestantism has been active since the 1840s and where 15 percent of all North American evangelical missionaries in Latin America are deployed?[7] It would seem that evangelical growth has much to do with the perceptions of adherents who find satisfaction and security in these often spontaneous movements.

The emergence of other popular religious movements also suggests that evangelical growth in the hemisphere owes much to the social and cultural climate of contemporary Latin America. If conservative Christian groups are flourishing in Brazil, for example, spiritists by some estimates are growing even faster.[8] These syncretistic movements may be considered by many North Americans to be superstitious and pragmatic devices for coping with an uncertain existence, but cults of the saints and *curanderismo* are part of reality in the insecure world of most Latin Americans.

It must be concluded that Latin American revivals derive in large measure from the anxieties and aspirations of emergent peoples. There is little indication that growth has regularly followed notable evangelists or particular denominations. Although a disproportionate number are in the pentecostal tradition (perhaps three of every four), the groups represent a wide range of theological and denominational positions. All evangelical groups seem to be effective to the extent that they communicate the gospel in the idiom of the people. Evangelical churches are a means of stabilizing existence for large numbers of Latin Americans who are caught in various stages of transition from a traditional to a modern world. To the extent that evangelical believers have become convinced of a new view of reality, one that in fact is not remote from the medieval Catholic view of the prevailing folk culture, they have facilitated their entry into the modern world and have asserted their claim to a share in the benefits of contemporary life.[9]

## Revolution

The context of evangelical growth in Latin America may not be assumed to be a stable social order. No sector of Latin American society is exempt from tension, threats, and eroding power. Unpredictable markets, an inadequate infrastructure, declining values of export goods, and a series of related problems keep economic development tenuous. Moreover, even considerable real progress is undermined by net population growth rates as high as 3 percent per year, wiping out many temporary gains. Internal migration in virtually every republic continues to crowd cities with unskilled workers and their families. The republics' health, educational, and housing needs far exceed their ability to satisfy them, making enterprising individual initiative and forms of self-help such as those provided by evangelical churches necessary for survival.

If social revolution, exacerbated by the East-West struggle, has been the focus of controversy in the hemisphere since World War II, scholars have shown remarkable consensus in identifying deteriorating social conditions as the prime issue in the region. Development programs like the Alliance for Progress moved to avert impending social upheaval in a kind of hemispheric Marshall Plan in the 1960s. The nature of the problem, Brazilianist Charles Wagley pointed out in the case of that country, was that Brazil had "entered on a transformation which began during the early years of the century, has been felt with increasing intensity since 1930, and has not yet run its course." This vast change, which he called "the Brazilian revolution," was at once an economic, a political, and a social process. "It has not taken the form of armed rebellion or civil war, nor is it expressed in a set of consciously planned policies and ideals such as those that developed out of the Mexican Revolution of 1910," he wrote. "Rather, it has happened, and is still happening largely without plan or ideology, except as each political administration attempts to solve the more urgent problems which arise out of this process of change. From an essentially agrarian, rural, semi-feudal, and patriarchal society, Brazil is now in the process of becoming a modern, industrial, urban-centered capitalistic society. Brazil is midway in a process of changing from its 'traditional' structure of the nineteenth century to a 'new' Brazilian society of the future. The process is painful and often costly."[10]

In 1965 the churchmen François Houtart and Emile Pin noted similarly that "a significant development in present-day Latin America is the entry of the masses into the deep and moving stream of social change. Until recent years, only a relatively small part of the population was involved; the social transformations were operating almost exclusively within the upper echelons. Today the whole society is in movement. The changes in society formerly had little effect on the basic social structures of most of the Latin American countries, for it was being absorbed by the elites. Now it is passing to the masses."[11] The typical Latin American congregation, struggling as it is for stability in an insecure and hostile world, has little notion of theories of social change. Nor do the congregants care much about the interests of other social sectors. They do know, however, their own immediate interests and respond to what appear to be effective means of survival, including participation in vigorous, demanding evangelical movements.

## Revival *or* Revolution

Overseas missionary interests seem all too willing to accept credit for evangelical growth in Latin America. At work in most of the republics since the turn of the century, North American Protestants have contributed substantially to these churches. There can be little doubt also that the recent investment has been massive, in the tens of millions of dollars in personnel, programs, equipment, and funds.[12] Interestingly, the evangelicals' claim to notable success in Latin America has largely stood unchallenged by the same unsympathetic groups that view them as the cause for much popular resistance to revolution. In arguing that American dollars are responsible for the rise of evangelical groups, and that American religious missions are tools of North American foreign policy, the political left has concurred in attributing effectiveness to the missions agencies. These claims may need to be substantiated by the kinds of questions that emerge in church growth theory. For example, do available reports confirm the correlation between investment and growth? Do the statistics themselves, largely arrived at by formulas rather than by enumeration of memberships, find confirmation in field studies? Given the differences in rates of growth between countries and their various geographical, cultural, social class, and ethnic subdivisions, what correlation exists between these differences and rates of growth? By and large, however, the answers to these and similar questions are readily available.

Existing data indicate quite clearly that the groups that have experienced the largest, most impressive growth are those that have received the least assistance from the North American sending agencies. While it may be true that strategic, necessary functions have been served by foreign groups, their expenditures may not be justified purely on numerical grounds. On the other hand, there is clear evidence that most of the evangelical work in Latin America depends little on the sending agencies and foreign budgets, no matter how strategic they may seem. As early as 1969 the *Latin American Church Growth* study attributed two-thirds of the total communicant evangelical membership in the region to indigenous groups with about 10 percent of the foreign personnel.[13] The organizations that accounted for more than three-quarters of the missionaries, the mainline denominations and faith missions, had constituents that totaled fewer than a quarter of the membership. The 1982 *World Christian Encyclopedia* revealed that the indigenous groups continue to grow at rapid rates.[14]

These tendencies are further reflected in the numbers of personnel associated with specific missions. The group in Brazil that claims the largest evangelical constituency, 11,000,000 members, reports only eleven missionary couples, most of whom are engaged in education and publications.[15] The same source indicates that in Guatemala, where evangelicals report the highest per capita rate of evangelicals

in Latin America, the largest single denomination reports five missionary couples, two of whom are in their first term and the remaining
at or beyond retirement age. In another example, the Chilean evangelicals, who have been nationally directed from the beginning of the
century, remain an effective and representative movement despite considerable criticism from both progressive and conservative extremes.

If interpretation of the Latin American evangelical revival hinges
on the issue of the movement's role in advancing or resisting change,
the considerable publicity given General José Efaín Ríos Montt, Guatemala's "born-again" president (1982–83), provides an appropriate
case study. Conservatives rushed to the defense of Ríos Montt against
the criticisms of the left, contending that the general represented a
bulwark against Communism and a model of evangelical influence
in Latin America.[16] The ideological left, in the meantime, largely
accepted this ascription of evangelical leadership to the general and
blamed him for the policies that, they alleged, may have been responsible for greater violence and dislocation in the Guatemalan countryside than had occurred under his predecessors.[17] Accordingly,
evangelicals have been berated for policies deemed brutal by observers
and irritating to Guatemalans who resented the influence of Ríos
Montt's intimate spiritual advisers in the Verbo Church, a North
American missionary agency that had influenced his conversion five
years previously. Ríos Montt's policy of "guns and beans," alleged
by some analysts to be inspired by U.S. policy in Viet Nam, and
his disregard of courtesies that would normally have been paid to
the visiting Pope John Paul II, further drew the lines of debate.

Upon closer examination, however, it appears that neither side
was justified in its judgments of Ríos Montt and North American
religious influence in Latin America. The Church of the World, a
relatively recent group to join the already large number of evangelical
organizations in Guatemala, was hardly representative. It remains a
fairly small group of professional and business people whose life-
style and perspectives are unlike the proletarian, peasant, and Indian
populations among whom the evangelical churches have flourished.
Guatemalan evangelicals, flattered by the attention they received,
nevertheless faced the awkwardness of being identified as pawns of
a foreign religious organization. The leader of the Evangelical Alliance
confided to a visiting North American that the evangelical cause in
the country would have been better served had Ríos Montt not
become a symbol of evangelicalism.[18] In the meantime, Ríos Montt's
biography indicates that he is hardly representative of Guatemalan
evangelicals. A career soldier raised as a Roman Catholic, and whose

brother was a Catholic bishop of Guatemala, Ríos Montt's career after his conversion was politically little different from what it had been before.[19] In their enthusiasm for finding, respectively, a champion and a scape goat, neither side assessing Ríos Montt's role duly reflected on his uniqueness or on the origins of his policies. The vitality of the Guatemalan evangelical groups both before and after his administration suggests that little was gained or lost by the general's brief tenure of office. The evangelical movement had already been a presence in Guatemala for a century and owed little to his contribution. Similarly, the relatively small impact of sensational moral failures recently revealed about North American evangelists suggests that evangelical roots lie deep in the subsoil of Latin American society, no matter how much the growth seems to respond to North American nurturing. There is little reason to assume that evangelical growth represents a polarized case of "revival or revolution" in Latin America. While the revival is genuine and owes much to catalytic North American influence, it has from the beginning been essentially an expression of national religious insurgence. Having begun as a radical rejection of the status quo, Latin American evangelicalism responds to social impulses that are deeper and more comprehensive than those generally attributed to the movement by either its critics or its supporters.

## Revival *and* Revolution

What then is the role of evangelical groups in Latin America's process of change? Is it possible that these groups, consisting of persons who have defied the existing system, are either tools of foreign imperialism or, on the other hand, sectors committed to the status quo? Organizationally effective and largely made up of the poor and disadvantaged, are they unable to represent their own interests or would they be reluctant to do so? Are they oblivious to demands for social justice or to the indictments of the oligarchy and repressive military governments? Are they insensitive to the future of their families and their communities?

In answer to these questions it must be recognized that the evangelicals represent a mosaic of diverse and tentative groups. As people in transition they are to a considerable extent without power, outsiders unaccustomed to making demands. But case studies indicate that they nevertheless are part of the emerging national system. There is no reason to believe that they will fail to respond to the mainstream of their national popular political currents or hold policy opinions that are unique to evangelicals. Certainly, there is reason to believe that as a group they do not always concur with their North American counterparts. Nor does their evangelical faith exempt them from the concerns of economic deterioration and exploitation. They face the same options and circumstances that face other people of their social standing. As marginal elements, they have seldom been asked their opinions. They resort to available sources of self-help assistance and, like their peers, often view the establishment with distrust.

Several propositions help to clarify the posture of Latin American evangelicals. First, they make an overt statement of their rejection of the establishment when they adopt their new faith. In most cases this is an avowal of responsibility for their own well-being and a denial of dependence on the established church, including the moral authority of the traditional religion and the dominant social classes. For many, the independence and initiative of the act of identifying with evangelicals is mirrored in the rigorous and preemptive influence of the religious movement on their personal and family lives. Such people are hardly passive or reactionary. Intrinsically they aspire to a new order that better provides for their needs. Economic opportunities, social acceptance, and education are major concerns they share with their non-evangelical counterparts.

Second, the years during the rapid evangelical growth have been characterized by the rise and waning of populist politics in Latin America.[20] Various leaders who have emerged since World War II, notably Juan Perón in Argentina and Gestulio Vargas in Brazil, have promised a "new deal" for the common man, generally based on the redirection of national resources to promote education, medical services, public housing, minimum wages, and a variety of projects identified with the masses. Lázaro Cárdenas in Mexico in the 1930s, Jacobo Arbenz in Guatemala in the 1950s, Acción Democrática in Peru in the 1960s, and other leaders and movements have demonstrated the readiness of the masses to support programs that promise a better future. Although Fidel Castro polarized Latin American political ideology in the 1960s, corruption, incompetence, opportunism, and disillusionment have taken an even greater toll than radicalism on mass national movements. Populism is not likely to vanish soon from the region's politics, but the people generally are too skeptical to place confidence in political messiahs. The oligarchy, often absent and recalcitrant, and the United States, sometimes intrusive in economic and military policies, become targets of revolutionary resentment. But in the light of extensive disillusionment with recent political experiments, and without viable programs of structural change, the call for revolution, especially for the marginal populations, has more the ring of romantic adventurism than of promise.

Third, it appears that the Latin American political left offers little for the millions who have been attracted to evangelicalism. For these believers, the use of violence is not acceptable, more for practical than for moral reasons. There could be little identification of most rural, peasant peoples with the urban leaders of revolution. Apart from the often not-so-latent antipathies of the common people toward urban professionals, identification with insurgence simply exposes a highly vulnerable population to reprisals from one or the other fighting factions. For the urban poor, as well, radical leadership is not likely to engender confidence by simply proclaiming a new era, calling for sweeping changes, and rationalizing production. The intrusion of government into the affairs of most Latin Americans is likely to be met with stubborn resistance, whether the government is run by the military or by Marxists. Moreover, whatever other options are available to Latin Americans, those offered by Cuba are untenable, given the need to sell out to foreign control. "Had there not been a Cuba," it was said in the 1970s after the failure of policies that left Cuba dependent on the Soviet Union, "the United States should have created one." Government generally in these cultures does not merely represent abstract bureaucracies, but persons whose goodness, badness, favor, and disfavor take concrete form. Commitment to an abstract notion of revolution carried out by leaders whom these groups are not likely to trust appears to be an unlikely option.

Fourth, nationalism remains the most viable and appealing ideology for most Latin Americans. Despite the vast inequalities found in every Latin American republic, commonalities prevail, making the forging of a national system the first concern of most people. National—not ideological—salvation is the hope of the vast majority of Latin Americans. Witness the lack of peasant enthusiasm for Che Guevara's liberation of Bolivia in 1967, when little support was given by the local peoples—or even by the Bolivian Communist Party, with whom Che had little communication. Animosities between neighboring Nicaragua and Costa Rica, for example, owe at least as much to traditional aversions based on history and race as to political ideologies. Mexicans and Guatemalans are not less skeptical of each other, divided as they are by history and culture. Ecuador and Peru have fought destructive wars over disputed common boundaries, as have El Salvador and Honduras, Chile and Peru, Bolivia and Paraguay, Argentina and Chile.

If bitter territorial disputes and even genocide have been the negative aspects of nationalism, visions of a national system that would more efficiently and effectively exploit natural resources and funnel revenues into the construction of a modern system of production and distribution lie at the base of most expectations for the future. Possessive, pragmatic, and individualistic, the emergent groups are suspicious of comprehensive ideologies and blueprints for the future that leave control to other sectors. Beyond satisfaction of their immediate material needs and increased representation, policies that bring control close to home and reliable government are the hope of the masses. If evangelicals have political goals, they lie within these nationalistic aspirations.

Given this perspective on national development, evangelicals may be expected to act pragmatically. As the revivals progress, internal tensions between the movement's spiritual and social objectives may become increasingly apparent. Meanwhile, evangelicals are emerging as a recognizable force. A recent profile of Latin American evangelicals written by Paul Pretiz for the Latin America Mission portrays these believers well. Pretiz points out that the image of evangelicals has changed since the early twentieth century when Protestants appeared to be ideologically progressive, supportive of education, efficiency, integrity, and enlightenment. By the 1950s evangelicals seemed to be undermining traditional authority and were believed to be revolutionary. Now, however, as evangelicals are criticized for placing personal salvation before social revolution, they appear politically to support the status quo. Protestant sects are even alleged to receive U.S. government sponsorship and CIA funding. As Pretiz writes, "Studies and general observation indicate that evangelicals are usually perceived as honest and sober. They are seen as people who put in a good day's work and who try to help a neighbor. For these reasons employers may even prefer an evangelical. People may often admire evangelicals whose lives really are changed. There is recognition, sometimes grudgingly given, that evangelicals are good people." He concludes, "Perhaps evangelical Christians are politically naive and out of step with the local culture. Perhaps they are often poorly educated and from a despised social level. But with all of their alleged failings, evangelicals often provide the salt in Latin American society, and it is beginning to take effect."[21] Whatever the rhetoric of revolution, the facts make a strong case that Latin American evangelicals are committed to taking control of their own destinies and are themselves effective agents of social change.

## NOTES

1. Notable examples of polarized interpretations of Latin American evangelicalism may be found in publications supportive of either revolutionary movements or conservative North American overseas missions. Representative of the former include Deborah Huntington, "The Prophet Motive," *North American Congress on Latin America Report on the Americas* 18 (Jan.-Feb. 1984): 4–11. The entire issue, entitled "The Salvation Brokers: Conservative Evangelicals in Central America," is of interest, as is Sara Diamond, "Holy Warriors," *NACLA* 22 (Sept.-Oct. 1988): 28–37. A corresponding article favorable to North American missions in Central America is Dan Wooding, "Experiment in Righteousness," *Christian Life* 44 (June 1983): 2–22. Specialized journals like *Global Church Growth* and *The International Bulletin of Missionary Research*, as well as many denominational and missions publications, are written with similar assumptions.

2. See Everett A. Wilson, "The Central American Evangelicals: From Protest to Pragmatism," *International Review of Mission* 77 (Jan. 1988): 94–106.

3. Recent comprehensive statistics on Latin American evangelicals have been compiled by William Taylor, executive secretary of the Missions Commission of the World Evangelical Fellowship, and published in the *Atlas of Comibam* (1987).

4. This is the premise of C. Peter Wagner, *Look Out! The Pentecostals are Coming* (Carol Stream, Ill.: Creation House, 1969). A less sanguine view is presented in Samuel Escobar, "What's Happening to the Fastest Growing Church in the World?" *His* 34 (Oct. 1973): 8–11.

5. Cornelia Butler Flora, *Pentecostalism in Colombia, Baptism by Fire and Spirit* (Cranbury, N.J.: Associated University Presses, 1976) and Donald C. Palmer, *Explosion of People Evangelism* (Chicago: Moody Press, 1974) analyze evangelical growth during *la violencia*.

6. This statistic, often found in print, appears to be based on the reported combined adult memberships multiplied by a factor of four to account for children and nonmember adults in the evangelical community.

7. Taylor, *Atlas of Comibam.*

8. Park Renshaw, "A New Religion for Brazilians," *Practical Anthropology* (July-Aug. 1966): 126–32.

9. Sheldon Annis, *God and Production in a Guatemalan Town* (Austin: University of Texas Press, 1987) and Bryan S. Roberts, "Protestant Groups and Coping with Urban Life in Guatemala City," *American Journal of Sociology* 73 (May 1968): 713–67.

10. Charles S. Wagley, "The Brazilian Revolution," in *Social Change in Latin America Today,* ed. Richard Adams et al. (New York: Vintage Books, 1960), 178.

11. François Houtart and Emile Pin, *The Church and the Latin American Revolution* (New York: Sheed and Ward, 1965), 58.

12. For a discussion of missionary finances, see *Mission Handbook: North*

*American Protestant Ministry Overseas* 12th ed. (Monrovia, Calif.: Missions Advanced Research and Communications Center, 1979), 59–63.

13. William R. Read, Victor M. Monterroso, and Harmon A. Johnson, *Latin American Church Growth* (Grand Rapids: William B. Eerdmans Publishing Company, 1969).

14. David B. Barrett, *World Christian Encyclopedia* (New York: Oxford University Press, 1982).

15. Data supplied by the Foreign Missions Department of the Assemblies of God, Springfield, Missouri.

16. Tom Minnery, "Why We Can't Trust the News Media," *Christianity Today* 28 (13 Jan. 1984): 14–21.

17. Huntington, "Prophet Motive."

18. Guillermo Galindo Ordoñez, Guatemala City, 4 June 1987.

19. Joseph Anfuso and David Sczepanski, *Efraín Ríos Montt: Siervo o Dictador* (Guatemala City: Gospel Outreach, 1983).

20. Michael L. Conniff, ed., *Latin American Populism in Comparative Perspective* (Albuquerque: University of New Mexico Press, 1982).

21. Paul Pretiz, "The Gospel People," *Latin America Evangelist* 66 (Oct.-Dec. 1988): 18–19.

# 11

## American Revivalism from Graham to Robertson

### DAVID EDWIN HARRELL, JR.

As IN OTHER AREAS of athletic accomplishment, the roster of the all-time, all-American revivalist Hall of Fame begins with New Englanders and ends with southerners. The stars of the eighteenth century were Englishman George Whitefield and New Englander Jonathan Edwards; the leaders of the nineteenth century were Charles G. Finney, born in Connecticut and reared in New York, and Dwight L. Moody whose home was Chicago. The acknowledged captain of God's team in the early twentieth century was an Iowa farm boy and Chicago White Stocking outfielder, Billy Sunday.

The present generation of superstars are southerners. The South was not completely unfazed by the spasms of religious fervor that brought earlier preachers to the attention of God and their fellow Americans. But through much of its history, the South had its own encounter with God. By the twentieth century the region had become the Bible Belt, a section seemingly immune to the ravages of modern thought and deviant religious expression, one of the most thoroughly churched societies in American history. "Everywhere in the South," wrote the sardonic H. L. Mencken, "except in a few walled towns . . . the evangelical sects plunge into an abyss of malignant imbecility." Mencken labeled the South "The Sahara of the Bozart" and surmised that "there are single acres in Europe that house more first-rate men than all the states south of the Potomac; there are probably single square miles in America."[1] Southern preachers were as aware of their cultural dissonance as was Mencken. In 1939 a southern pentecostal editor noted that "the average bootlegger in the 'Bible Belt' has as great a respect for God Almighty and real religion as many of the high salaried divines who decorate New York's modernistic pulpits."[2] American revivalists were welcome in the pre–World War II South;

they were honored there; they could refresh their spirits and refill their quivers there; but the battle was elsewhere. The South did not need revival—the South was the national campground.

Southern-born revivalists have rewritten the record books in the years since World War II. With due respect to the heroes of history, who can deny that the new generation of revivalists are bigger, stronger, and more skilled than the champions of the past? Billy Graham has been nearly everywhere and has been personally beheld by more people than any human who ever lived. Oral Roberts has placed his pulsating right hand on the heads of over one million persons—not to speak of those who have touched their television sets or some other point of contact. Jerry Falwell revitalized American fundamentalists; Jimmy Swaggart, even in his hour of considerable distress, sang, preached, and wept on television sets from Baton Rouge to Beijing; and Pat Robertson almost made Christians out of the Republican party's leaders after the Iowa primary in 1988.

Graham's roots are in the sturdy farming stock of North Carolina, Robertson and Falwell were reared in the Virginia Piedmont; Roberts and Swaggart are products of the pentecostal subculture in Oklahoma and Louisiana. Behind these headline names are scores of other former and current southern big league prospects—Kenneth Copeland and James Robison of Ft. Worth, Charles Stanley of Atlanta, and Rex Humbard of Akron, Ohio, who entered the Lord's work as a member of the singing Humbard family in Little Rock. Perhaps it would be tasteless for me to point out that Jim Bakker was nearly the only Yankee in the big religion business in the 1980s.

To be sure, a few nonsouthern preachers have reached the level of national visibility in recent years—most notably Robert Schuler in southern California. And southern revivalists have reaped unprecedented harvests of souls and gold outside the South. Viewed individually, Graham, Roberts, Falwell, Swaggart, and Robertson each represents the exportation of a particular religious message. Their individual stories highlight the uniqueness of each independent ministry and tell something about the constituencies that made their successes possible. Taken together, these evangelists are symbols of a general troubling of the soul of the South.

Billy Graham was reared in the staunchly Calvinistic Reformed Presbyterian church, but his mother was mightily impressed by the preaching of Methodist revivalist Bob Jones, Sr., and when Graham came of age she packed him off to the Jones compound in Cleveland, Tennessee.[3] Jones's austere Bible school was too much for Graham's ebullient personality, and he soon headed north to Wheaton College where folks were a little more good natured about their love of Jesus. He graduated there in 1943. Graham's journey away from the South foreshadowed his later career. He returned to the South to accept ordination in the Southern Baptist church, and he has retained vestiges of his southern upbringing. Tall, handsome, and gracious, Graham remains the height of southern charm; Calvinistic assumptions mingle incongruously with his sunny disposition. He has retained a genuine respect for virile southern fundamentalism, though he has little stomach for it.

But Graham's career has never been particularly connected with the region of his birth. As he rose to the forefront of American evangelists in the 1950s and 1960s, he appeared less and less a southerner. By the end of the 1950s he was under attack from Bob Jones, John R. Rice, and other separatist fundamentalists and had become the spokesman for a more irenic and cerebral evangelical orthodoxy. His institutional connections became uniformly Midwestern; millions of letters addressed simply to Billy Graham, Minneapolis, Minnesota, found him annually. With Graham's support, Wheaton College became the evangelical Harvard; the Chicago suburb that surrounds the school is now the home of *Christianity Today*; the college houses a lavish research library known as the Billy Graham Center; and there are a host of other evangelical institutions associated with Wheaton.

In the 1980s, Billy Graham stood squarely in the center of American evangelicalism. An amorphous empire that geographically spreads rather evenly across the nation, evangelicalism has become the mainstream of American religion. Sitting atop this Evangelical Empire sits a former North Carolina farm boy. His evangelical kingdom has become increasingly complicated and unruly; Graham himself is frequently criticized and denounced by evangelicals on his left and his right, but few individuals in modern history have so consistently held the esteem of so many of their fellow Americans.

Billy Graham's break with separatist fundamentalism in the late 1950s opened the way for the emergence of another world-class fundamentalist evangelist. Jerry Falwell is nearly twenty years younger than Graham, and whether his lifetime batting average will approach Billy's remains to be seen.[4] He is, however, the most visible symbol of another groundswell in modern southern religion. Falwell grew up in Lynchburg in the foothills of the Appalachians. Valedictorian of his high school class, he completed two years of an engineering curriculum before renouncing worldly ambition and heading for Baptist Bible College in Springfield, Missouri. After graduating in 1956, he returned to Lynchburg, rented the abandoned Donald Duck Bottling building on Thomas Road and started a congregation with thirty-five members. In the first year his congregation grew to 864 members. By the end of the 1980s, like all of the major television ministries, his was operating on a nine-figure budget. His list of friends and enemies expanded once again with the founding of the Moral Majority in 1979.

Falwell is the brightest star of post–World War II separatist fundamentalism, a virile genre of religion that has boomed in the twentieth-century South. Deeply stung by Graham's defection to neo-evangelism in the 1950s, fundamentalists withdrew, as they had in the 1920s, to build churches that resembled fortified enclaves. Many liberals assumed at the end of the 1950s that the declining influence of such prominent conservatives as Carl McIntire and Billy James Hargis signaled the end of fundamentalism.

In the late 1950s the actual doctrinal differences between evangelicals and separatist fundamentalists were slight; in recent years both movements have become genuinely diverse. The three chief marks of the fundamentalist were an emphasis on separation from liberalism (a stance that called for constant guerilla warfare against mainstream churches), a condemnation of "worldliness," and an objection to a growing evangelical interest in social justice.[5] The heart of separatist fundamentalism was militancy, spiritual toughness. It was a masculine, macho movement that railed against softhearted, effeminate Christianity. The problem with Graham and the evangelicals was that they were "unable to stand the sight of blood and the sound of abuse."[6] Fundamentalists loved Billy Sunday; they often quoted the old ballplayer's favorite litany: "I'm against sin. I'll kick it as long as I've got a foot, and I'll fight it as long as I've got a fist. I'll butt it as long as I've got a head. I'll bite it as long as I've got a tooth, and when I'm old and fistless and footless and toothless, I'll gum it till I go home to Glory and it goes home to perdition."[7] Falwell told a 1979 audience: "One thing fundamentalists do better than anything else is fight. It's all we know how to do, and if there isn't an issue, we'll start one."[8] Fundamentalist rhetoric bristled with military terminology (attacking, battling, troops, Christian soldiers, and boot camps) as well as athletic allusions.

The fundamentalist army of the 1970s was trained in the ubiquitous Bible colleges that came to cover the land after World War II. Moody established his prototype Bible institute in 1886, and by 1940 over 160 had been founded throughout the nation. The most important of these early schools in the South were Bob Jones's college, a seminary established by J. Frank Norris in Ft. Worth, and John Brown University. When Mencken came south in the 1920s he was amazed by the omnipresence of Bible schools: "You will find one in every mountain valley of the land, with its single building in its bare pasture lot, and its faculty of half-idiot pedagogues and broken-down preachers. . . . The aspirant came from the barnyard, and goes back in a year or two to the village. His body of knowledge is that of a bus driver or a vaudeville actor."[9] Mencken's yokels knew exactly what they were doing; they were training for the war to come. The fundamentalist Noel Smith wrote to Norris in 1947: "Once this generation of seriousminded young men get it into their heads that Fundamentalism means to go to Ft. Worth [to Norris's seminary] and learn how to study the Bible, to win souls, to organize them into a church, and build the largest Sunday School and church in their communities, and that the logical alternatives to Fundamentalism are doubt, uncertainty, defeat and Communism—once that idea sinks clearly into their heads, we are really going to see something."[10]

These young Christian soldiers built huge Bible-believing churches in the 1950s and 1960s, most of them Independent Baptist, a disproportionate share of them in the South. Their churches were fortified enclaves; the young warriors became warlord pastors. Jack Hyles's Independent Baptist Church in Hammond, Indiana, claimed the largest membership in the country—once setting a record for Sunday school attendance with 100,000 present and on another occasion baptizing 960 new converts in a single service. Lee Robertson's Highland Baptist Church in Chattanooga left the Southern Baptist Convention in 1956 and, by the end of the 1970s, claimed over 50,000 members in seventy branches. The church operated Tennessee Temple University and supported 496 missionaries. Virtually every southern city and town, including Lynchburg, Virginia, came to have such a church.

The model preacher for the rejuvenated southern fundamentalism was J. Frank Norris, the "Texas Tornado," whose bulldog temperament and two-fisted preaching inspired a generation; he was, in Falwell's words, "the epitome of an independent, fundamentalist Baptist."[11] Norris pastored First Baptist Church in Ft. Worth from 1909 until his death in 1952 and for fifteen years was also pastor of a huge congregation in Detroit. Norris's career was marred by acrimonious personal disputes with his friends and a trail of violence that began in 1912 when his church was burned. Norris was indicted, tried, and acquitted on charges of perjury and arson. His church burned again during the Depression, and in 1926 he was indicted and tried for first-degree murder after shooting D. E. Chipps four times during an altercation in the pastor's study. He was acquitted under the Texas statutes of self-defense. All this dampened Norris's reputation with sissies and Episcopalians, but the self-conscious fundamentalist community of the 1950s honored him for his fearless denunciations of sin. His confrontation with the enraged Chipps, after all, had taken place just after Norris had preached a sermon to a packed house entitled, "The Ten Biggest Devils in Ft. Worth, Names Given."[12]

It was in this embattled Christian environment that Jerry Falwell grew to be the brightest and the best. His mentor at Baptist Bible College in Springfield was G. Beauchamp Vick, long Norris's assistant in Detroit until the stormy Texan turned on him. Falwell has the look of a cherub, but deep inside him is the hard flint rock of ages.

It is still too early to judge the lasting impact of the southern-led fundamentalist revival. Arch-fundamentalists of the Bob Jones variety have returned to isolation, convinced that they have "lost the battle" but "kept the faith." They condemn Falwell as a traitor and apostate. Falwell, on the other hand, has glimpsed a broader world. A man of keen intellect and unquestioned courage, he has heard the sound of voices saying he may be the next Billy Graham. But his adventuresome spirit has demanded that he repeatedly build new constituencies.

Oral Roberts is more controversial, more complicated, and more southern.[13] Born just a few months before Billy Graham in 1918, he has carried through life the brand of the "holy roller," with all that such scars do to one's psyche. Roberts's grandfather parceled out small farms to each of his seven sons, but after a few years of scratching a feeble subsistence from the red sandy hills of Pontotoc County, Ellis Roberts and his wife, Claudius, received a call from above. In an old-time shouting, brush arbor meeting they were baptized in the Holy Ghost. Ellis sold his farm (missing the subsequent oil boom), bought a portable organ, and preached pentecost all over southeastern Oklahoma. A gentle man, he walked to his meetings, trusting the Lord for his support. Claudius and the children worked in the neighbors' fields and came to know hunger—depression Okies.

Oral's two older brothers rebelled against their pentecostal upbringing—disgusted by the grinding poverty imposed on the family by their equally deprived supporters and cut by the snickers of city sophisticates in Ada. Oral tried to escape; at fifteen he ran away to Atoka to finish high school, study law, become governor, and play basketball for the Atoka High Wampus Cats. He collapsed during a game, was taken home and diagnosed as tubercular. The rest of the story is hagiography—told by Oral thousands of times and published millions—the despondent youth was bedridden for 163 days thinking that he would die; he first underwent a conversion experience in which his father was transformed into the image of Jesus, and then a miraculous healing under a tent in Ada.

On the evening of his healing, while Oral was riding to the tent, God spoke audibly to him, as he was to do rather regularly in the years ahead, and told him that he would bring healing to his generation. Unlikely as the message seemed to the frail youth in 1935, subsequent events have shown that God knew what he was talking about. After about a year of recuperation (Oral's healing was instant but his recovery was gradual), he spent twelve years preaching in the small Pentecostal Holiness Church in the South. Then, in 1947, in a step that required audacity and faith, he resigned his pastorate and launched an independent revivalistic career. During the next twenty years he preached healing and deliverance from Miami to Tacoma, from San Diego to Bangor, on Indian reservations, in Israel, and in over fifty other nations. His big tents (seating 3,000 in 1948 and 18,000 in 1968) crisscrossed the nation like Barnum and Bailey. Night after night Oral called sinners to repentance with astonishing results; at his peak, over one million souls sought the Lord under Oral's tent each year. At about 10:30 each evening, in the incandescent canvas haze, Oral began to lay his throbbing right hand on the sick, sometimes gently, but more often violently, vice-like, commanding the foul demon of fear and disease to come out. Stretching far into the morning hours, broken by periods when Oral retired backstage to wait on the Lord and have a chocolate milk, not a soul leaving the enchanted premises—sometimes 50, sometimes 300, sometimes 5,000 sought wholeness through his healing touch.

While Billy Graham climbed steadily in the esteem of his fellow Americans, Oral constantly battled the image of the sleazy con-man. He was labeled a fraud, a charlatan, and a "fake-healer"; his tent was set afire in Australia and he fled the country; even his fellow southerners considered him "faintly berserk" and the whole pentecostal subculture "overheated cults." In the mid–1950s, in a much more ominous development, the National Council of Churches, with the support of the *New York Times*, and much of the national press, tried to ban him from television.

Roberts's reputation began to improve in the early 1960s. While he was having dinner in a restaurant with Pat Robertson, God told him to build a university. There was the usual impolite guffawing about a college-drop-out-faith-healer becoming a college president, but in the long run, it appeared once again that Oral had heard correctly. The buildings were impressive, if somewhat bizarre, the kids were clean-cut, and the ORU basketball team made it to Madison Square Garden. Oral's prayers for the sick were increasingly confined to his partner's meetings on campus; he even seemed to apply a friendlier touch to these neatly dressed donors. He joined the Methodist church in 1968 and soon returned to television in prime-time in the company of Jerry Lewis, Jim Durante, and a host of other trusted Americans.

Then, in 1975, Roberts's reputation once again began to turn sour. When he announced plans to add graduate schools in business, dentistry, theology, law, and medicine to his university, he infuriated some of the strongest professional cliques in the nation. Furthermore, his financial needs became so acute that he resorted to the most high-pressure fund raising techniques of his career. In the 1980s, God's messages to Oral increased in frequency, urgency, and grandeur as the revivalist neared the end of his career.

The Oral Roberts story is a classic tale of the exportation of southern culture. For the first fifteen years of his public ministry, Roberts was a part of an ecumenical pentecostal revival that had its strongest base of support in the South and that drew its talent almost entirely from the sons of southern share-croppers and marginal farmers. Each night the tents filled with gaunt, tanned, hard-handed men and fat, dour, unpainted women come in search of a miracle. The grayer heads were the pioneers of the pentecost; they brought with them sons and daughters with pockets full of dollars earned in the shipyard and wartime factories. They dreamed of exporting worldwide miracle revival, and Oral became the foremost salesperson of their faith.

The pentecostal revival burst out of the South with a vitality that took it across the nation and around the world. The charismatic movement that followed the revival came to be much larger than Roberts, marked by the outbreak of tongues-speaking in the Episcopal Church in 1960 (thereafter more politely referred to as glossolalia or the prayer language) and in the Catholic church in 1966. Oral tried to position Oral Roberts University in the center of the dynamic movement, though that became increasingly difficult to do. Nonetheless, from Manila, to Singapore, to Nairobi, to Santiago and Helsinki, the world of the 1970s and 1980s was saturated with the message that "something good is going to happen to you."

The gospel that found such worldwide favor was a hopeful, Christian affirmation that one is never too low to look up.[14] God is a good God, even though all of life may seem to deny it; one should expect a miracle, particularly if more conventional means have proven ineffective. The proof of the message lay in one's direct encounter with the supernatural through the baptism of the Holy Spirit, a "filling" that allows one to communicate immediately, directly, and frequently with God, bypassing intervening specialists and elites, including physicians. It was a message that had sustained the battered, defeated, poor whites (and blacks) of the South. It had offered them peace, healing, and the hope of prosperity—it offered wholeness.

As the pentecostal message exploded out of the South in the 1950s and 1960s it found a ready audience among the poor around the world. And, increasingly, there were listeners among the frustrated middle class, particularly those alienated by the aloofness and fallibility of modern medicine, who had lost confidence in the mediating elites who controlled their lives. The search for intuitive truth in the charismatic movement was not unlike the subjective cravings of the counterculture. And in much of the Third World, charismatic revivalism meshed with local supernaturalism to revolutionize the religious geography of Asia, Africa, and South America. A timid, stuttering, tubercular little boy from Pontotoc County, still a bit of a joke in genteel Christian circles, had been elevated to sainthood by millions of the world's poor.

Like Billy Graham, Oral Roberts grew through the years. He consciously changed more than most preachers, and so did his pentecostal contemporaries. The kernels of their message remained unchanged—the emphasis on the Holy Spirit, the value of speaking in tongues, and God's miracle power—but even these were redefined and clarified. And the cultural changes that accompanied the spread of the Holy Spirit into the traditional churches were immense. Modern charismatics are joyfully upwardly mobile; they are a runaway spiritual Amway movement, a Dale Carnegie course with a language requirement. In the years since World War II, the South has taken the Holy Ghost to the world, and the apostles who took it brought the world back to the South.

The worldwide pentecostal and charismatic revival that Oral Roberts rode to fame and fortune had become so diverse by the 1970s that those who spoke in tongues often did not speak to one another. The road ahead was clearly forked. Down one fork proceeded the old-time pentecostals, bursting the seams of megachurches but laden with the theological baggage of three generations of unsophisticated biblical exegesis. Another byway was clogged with an array of charismatic Christians who shared little with one another save the miraculous warmth of the Holy Spirit. Those paths continued to diverge for two decades.

In the 1970s and 1980s, Jimmy Swaggart became the foremost international salesperson of traditional pentecostalism.[15] His most loyal support came from the swelling ranks of the Assemblies of God. Like all pentecostal preachers of his generation, Swaggart believed that being "spirit-filled" was only one part of the full gospel message. He bristled at the suggestion that Roman Catholics were led by the Holy Spirit. Preaching old-fashioned morality, fervent premillennialism, and unabashed anti-Catholicism, Swaggart became the most widely known Protestant preacher of the twentieth century. He introduced three-fourths of the world to southern gospel music, the best camp meeting preaching since Bill Sunday, and orthodox pentecostal theology—all packaged in the best technology of the 1980s.

Swaggart was an archetypal product of the pentecostal culture he came to represent and promote. Born in Ferriday, Louisiana, in 1935, his family was among the pioneers of pentecost in the midst of the southern depression. Swaggart and his cousins, Jerry Lee Lewis and Mickey Gilley, grew up in a cultural hothouse that spawned country and rock music as well as spirit-filled religion, where honky-tonks and whorehouses competed with cinder block churches and brush arbor revivals. Few southerners made clear-cut choices between these options.

Jimmy Swaggart became the priest of his clan. He used his considerable musical and preaching talents to bring himself to the attention of his fellow pentecostals, who, like him, now dressed in $500 suits to sing the old hymns of longing for escape from the hardships of life. For a decade and a half, Swaggart became an informal voice of the Assemblies of God, negotiating a truce with that church's hierarchy that could not have been made in the 1960s. It was an uneasy alliance; the pentecostal denominations had always been threatened by the huge independent ministry that fleeced their flocks but granted to church leaders no theological or ecclesiastical control. But the rewards of the Swaggart-Assemblies of God alliance were so lucrative for both sides that the decision to discipline Swaggart after the Debra Murphy revelation was painfully difficult.

In the long run, Swaggart's fall was the most disruptive of the religious scandals of the 1980s. It permanently shattered the relationship between the premier pentecostal revivalist and the clientele that had supported his ministry. The scandal forced Swaggart to become an anti-ecclesiastical outsider and to build a new base of support. On the other hand, since the Swaggart debacle, the traditional pentecostal message has had no national television presence, nor are the pentecostal denominations again likely to sanction the rise of such powerful independent ministries from inside the churches.

Pat Robertson's southern credentials are impeccable.[16] The son of a Virginia senator, a graduate of Washington and Lee, reared in a village made famous by the ghosts of Robert E. Lee and Stonewall Jackson, in 1985 Robertson was selected by the readers of *Charisma* magazine as the leading charismatic in the world. It was an odd choice by some measures, placing Robertson ahead of such world-class evangelists as Oral Roberts, Jimmy Swaggart, and Kenneth Hagin. Here was a religious movement led by an individual who in some ways did not think of himself as an evangelist and was certainly not a conventional revivalist.

Robertson was, in fact, as different from the stereotype revivalist as his charismatic constituency was from the fundamentalist and pentecostal subcultures. A Southern Baptist by birth and by ordination, Robertson was well-bred, well-educated, and a fairly careful student of historic evangelical theology. Like millions of other Protestants and Roman Catholics who experienced the moving of the spirit after 1960, Robertson brought to his charismatic experience a respect for historical theology and a cultural sophistication that separated him from the likes of Roberts and Swaggart. If Robertson learned how to speak to pentecostals, he always imagined that he was a part of the broader evangelical community. And if Robertson was infatuated by the miraculous moving of the spirit, he mixed that enthusiasm with a search for theological order and an interest in the social and political meanings of Christianity. Robertson's clientele included both pentecostals searching for a more traditional and responsible understanding of their faith and the millions in the nation, who, like him, added the baptism of the Holy Spirit to an older conservative religious base.

The southernness of Robertson, like that of Graham, appears largely in his origins. He received his legal training at Yale and his theological education and his Holy Spirit baptism in New York. In the Republican primaries in 1988, Robertson's charismatic sympathizers were as likely to be found in Iowa as in Alabama. Still, it seemed fitting that the first twentieth-century, white American to combine leadership roles in religion and politics should be a son of Dixie.

The vision of a united, triumphant revivalism that was promoted by religious television in the 1970s and momentarily materialized in the political campaign of 1980 was a distortion of reality. That unnatural apparition vaporized in the wake of the PTL scandal. For the most part, modern American revivalists did not know one another and did not like one another. Militant fundamentalists viewed Graham as an apocalyptic monster, and they regarded Oral Roberts as a genuine lunatic. Many evangelicals were chagrined to be linked with such political conservatives as the Moral Majority. Pentecostals were as concerned as ever about the loose majority and theological error of traditional Protestants and Catholics; charismatics were embarrassed by the anti-Catholic tirades of Jimmy Swaggart and the fact that God seemed so personally and vocally concerned about Oral Roberts's welfare. The superstars of modern revivalism always have had distinct fan clubs. Jessica Hahn simply reminded them that they had always had good reasons for not liking one another.

Each of these men is the fruit of a religious message ripe for the marketplace. Graham is the product of the Baptist-Methodist-Presbyterian hegemony that for a hundred years reigned as the folk church of the South. Falwell became the leader of rejuvenated southern fundamentalism, the best of the Bible school preacher boys. Roberts led post–World War II pentecostals out of the rural backwater on to an international stage. Jimmy Swaggart became the spokesperson for orthodoxy in the booming pentecostal movement of the 1970s, and Pat Robertson was the acknowledged leader of that collage of charismatic Christians who embraced the Holy Spirit in the ballrooms of Hilton Hotels. In short, each of the revivalists launched his career from a solid home base. In each case the religious community that supported him had lost some of its sectarian disdain for the world, had a membership with the money and the expertise necessary to support mass evangelism, and remained deeply committed to old religious truths.

These leaders of modern revivalism were all products of an upwardly mobile South; sociological theories on status anxiety explain much about their views and their successes. Since 1945 the South has lived with delicious religious tensions. The rapid social and economic change within the region, accompanied by the breakdown of old cultural patterns, has created strains similar to those noted by anthropologists in primal cultures, where they are generally accompanied by religious revivals and revitalization movements. A generation of religiously schizoid southerners has tried to pull together an agrarian, religious world view and a college education. They have been torn between their love for their simple God-fearing parents and the dazzling world that beckoned them. The repercussions of their own religious struggles have reverberated throughout the world and returned to

them again. These have been years of creative genius in the South—
as collapsing New England birthed Edwards and Hawthorne; as an
introspective Midwest gave us Moody and Twain; the South in transition produced not only Graham, Falwell, Roberts, Swaggart, and
Robertson, but Faulkner, Warren, and Wolfe. If it is not the power
of God that is afoot, it is no less than messages from deep in the
bellies of introspective and troubled people. Like decaying Israel
under Ahab, like profligate New England when Winthrop's grandsons
came of age, the recent South has been the land of the prophets.

To a remarkable extent, the television religion of the 1980s was
southern fundamentalist and pentecostal—no ritual or holy water,
no liturgy or Latin, just fundamentalist preaching and promoting and
pentecostal picking and praying. It was camp meeting time. The
faces, the accents, the sermons were all familiar. But they were not
altogether familiar. The most talented of the prophets made their way
to the court. Their aspirations became grander, their manners slicker,
their messages a bit less ferocious. From Billy Graham to Pat Robertson we have witnessed the southernization of American revivalism
and the Americanization of southern religion.

## NOTES

1. H. L. Mencken, *A Mencken Chrestomathy* (New York: Alfred A. Knopf,
1974), 184.

2. "Here and There," *Pentecostal Holiness Advocate* 23 (7 Dec. 1939): 2.

3. Three useful studies on Billy Graham are William G. McLoughlin,
*Billy Graham: Revivalist in a Secular Age* (New York: Ronald Press, 1960);
Marshall Frady, *Billy Graham: A Parable of American Righteousness* (Bos-
ton: Little, Brown, 1979); and William Martin, "Billy Graham" in *Varieties
of Southern Evangelicalism,* ed. David Edwin Harrell, Jr. (Macon, Ga.:
Mercer University Press, 1981), 71–88.

4. A thoughtful treatment of Jerry Falwell is Francis FitzGerald's article,
"A Disciplined, Charging Army," *New Yorker,* 18 May 1981, 53ff.

5. George Marsden has done much to clarify the history of American
fundamentalism in two books: *Fundamentalism and American Culture: The
Shaping of Twentieth Century Evangelicalism, 1870–1925* (New York: Oxford
University Press, 1980), and *Reforming Fundamentalism* (Grand Rapids:
William B. Eerdmans Publishing Company, 1987). For insights into fundamentalists' own understanding of the distinctions that separated them from
other evangelicals, see Jerry Falwell, ed., with Ed Dobson and Ed Hindson,
*The Fundamentalist Phenomenon* (Garden City, N.Y.: Doubleday and Company, Inc., 1981), 173–75; and George W. Dollar, *A History of Fundamentalism in America* (Greenville, S.C.: Bob Jones University Press, 1973), 192.

6. Dollar, *History of Fundamentalism,* 85.

7. Quoted in Falwell, *Fundamentalist Phenomenon*, 108.

8. Sermon, Birmingham, Alabama, Civic Center, 30 July 1979.

9. Mencken, *Chrestomathy*, 79.

10. Letter dated 1947, J. Frank Norris Papers, Southern Baptist Archives, Nashville, Tennessee.

11. Falwell, *Fundamentalist Phenomenon*, 92–95.

12. For an assessment of Norris's standing among fundamentalists, see Dollar, *History of Fundamentalism*, 123–35. A good dissertation on Norris is Clove G. Morris, "He Changed Things: The Life and Thought of J. Frank Norris" (Ph.D. diss., Texas Tech University, 1973).

13. For an extensive treatment of Roberts, see David Edwin Harrell, Jr., *Oral Roberts: An American Life* (Bloomington: Indiana University Press, 1985).

14. An article examining the basic content of pentecostal and charismatic preaching is David Edwin Harrell, Jr., "Divine Healing in Modern American Protestantism," in *Other Healers*, ed. Norman Gevitz (Baltimore: Johns Hopkins University Press, 1988), 215–27.

15. The best source of information on Swaggart's life is Jimmy Swaggart with Robert Paul Lamb, *To Cross a River*, 3d ed. (Baton Rouge: Jimmy Swaggart Ministries, 1984).

16. For an examination of Robertson's life, see David Edwin Harrell, Jr., *Pat Robertson: A Personal, Religious and Political Portrait* (San Francisco: Harper and Row, 1987).

# 12

# Writing about Canadian Religious Revivals

✦

GEORGE A. RAWLYK

RELIGIOUS CONVERSIONS have actually occurred; peoples' lives have apparently been profoundly and permanently changed—sometimes gradually and sometimes suddenly and traumatically. Conversions still take place and so do religious revivals—spiritual awakenings often involving large numbers of men, women, and children. In fact, since the 1730s, millions of North Americans have been deeply affected by the religious revivals that have frequently, like epidemics, swept through entire communities and sometimes entire regions and even entire countries.

For the past quarter century I have been particularly interested in Canadian revivals and revivalists—especially in the eighteenth and nineteenth centuries and especially in the Atlantic region of Canada. I have learned, often painfully, that despite the frequency and intensity of many of these revivals over a 200-year period, and despite the remarkable number of Canadians touched directly or indirectly by them, there is a large Canadian academic price to pay for writing with sympathy and empathy about the revivals and revivalists. For example, in a critical review of one of my books on Canadian revivals, a former graduate student and coauthor argued that my work, in fact, significantly strengthened the cause of right-wing North American fundamentalism and, moreover, was a betrayal of my commitment to Democratic Socialism.[1] Where he saw these major themes in *Ravished by the Spirit*, I really do not know, but he obviously saw what he wanted to see. Another leading Canadian historian wondered why I was wasting my time writing about religious revivals. Did I not realize how irrelevant the evangelical tradition actually was within the context of Canadian history? As he looked at the Canadian past through a lens carefully ground by both suspicion and opposition to things religious, he could only see in history what seemed practically relevant and important to him today.[2] And according to his secular Whig bias, which is now, without question, the Canadian authorized version of the past, evangelical religion in its various manifestations must be ruthlessly and unceremoniously relegated to some dark and distant corner of historical oblivion.

Even a superficial reading of my most recent works—*Ravished by the Spirit* (1984) and *Wrapped up in God* (1988–89)—will discern the influence of Anthony Wallace, Victor Turner, and George Marsden. Sometimes Wallace's influence seems primary; at other times Turner's seems primary. And then there is Marsden, almost everywhere, but nowhere explicitly recognized. Yet despite what to some might be my growing dependence on Wallace, Turner, and Marsden, I hope that I have not been shackled or intellectually stultified by their work. I have attempted to use their insights with care for descriptive rather than analytical purposes. I have mixed their often brilliant themes of religious change and added some of my own interpretations to produce, I hope, a novel way of looking at revivals and revivalists.

According to Wallace and one of his most influential disciples, William G. McLoughlin, a religious revitalization movement—or in other words a revival—occurs "when a society finds its day-to-day behavior has deviated so far from the accepted (traditional) norms that neither individuals nor large groups can honestly (consistently) sustain the common set of religious understandings by which they believe (have been taught) they should act." A period of "individual stress"—or loss of identity—is followed by one of "cultural disorientation" during which the "ordinary stress reduction techniques fail to help those who react to them." Then there arises a charismatic leader or leaders, people who have undergone the traumatic religious experience "that epitomizes the crisis of the culture." Such leaders, in the fourth state of the revitalization movement, "begin to attract the more flexible (usually the younger) members of the society, who are willing to experiment with new mazeways or life-styles." There is often a collective pulling back or retreat to an explicit conservative-negative position and then a sudden leap forward to a new and seemingly radically different "world view." Finally, the revivalists succeed in influencing the more passive individuals—and as the collective "mazeways are cleared. . . . Familiar patterns change, sex roles alter," and a new and revitalized culture clicks into fragile place. It is a religious culture shaped both by the past and the present, and the process repeats itself, in somewhat different form, as groups in each generation attempt to revitalize their way of life.[3]

At the core of the Wallace thesis is an emphasis on what the sociologist Seymour M. Lipset has identified as the need for people under stress to find "a dynamic equilibrium" between what has been referred to as "autonomous action and changing experiences."[4] And, consequently, for Wallace and his disciples, "A religious revival or a great awakening begins when accumulated pressures for change produce such acute personal and social stress that the whole culture must break the crust of custom, crash through blocks in the maze-ways, and find new socially structured avenues along which the members of the society may pursue their course in mutual harmony with one another."[5] And for Wallace the charismatic "prophet" leads the way toward the "dynamic equilibrium." He or she

> reveals (as God's chosen messenger) this new way to his fellow men. Gradually he develops a band of disciples or followers, whom he appoints (or anoints) and they fan out through the social system to proselytize for the new religious order. Among the precepts they inculcate are not only theological statements regarding the nature and will of God and how he is to be worshipped but also (more or less explicitly) a new set of social norms for individual and group behavior. Those who come in contact with the prophet or his charismatic disciples are "touched" by the same divine experience, and this validates both the prophet's vision and the new mazeways he inculcates as God's will for his people.[6]

The charisma of the prophet or prophetess and his or her disciples is not necessarily only an extraordinarily powerful "attribute of individual personality or a mystical quality." There is an important "social relationship" involved in "charisma" as well.[7] As far as the influential sociologist Peter Worsley is concerned, charisma, in fact, provides much "more than an abstract ideological rationale." It is, he argues, stretching Wallace yet a little further, "a legitimization grounded in a relationship of loyalty and identification in which the leader is followed simply because he embodies values in which the followers have an 'interest.' . . . The followers . . . in a dialectical way, create, by selecting them out, the leaders who in turn *command* on the basis on this newly-accorded legitimacy. . . . He articulates and consolidates their aspirations."[8]

The Wallace paradigm seems especially valuable when applied to Henry Alline and Nova Scotia's First Great Awakening. The Wallace revitalization thesis should not be used simplistically, however, to explain all aspects of the widespread social movement that engulfed what is now Nova Scotia and New Brunswick during the American Revolution. Rather, I found that the insights that Wallace provided, largely from his study *The Death and Rebirth of the Seneca* (1970), but also in his seminal article "Revitalization Movements,"[9] could be carefully used to throw light on Henry Alline, his message, and the remarkable impact he had on Nova Scotia and northern New England. Thus for me Wallace's revitalization thesis is more or less a descriptive device rather than an explanatory one. And, moreover, it provides me with the opportunity to locate my reassessment of Alline within the context of Wallace's influential thesis.

My *Ravished by the Spirit: Religious Revivals, Baptists and Henry Alline* was an attempt to associate my work closely with that of Wallace and McLoughlin, the author of *Revivals, Awakenings and Reform* (1978), a historian very much influenced by Wallace. This was not—I hope—an example of guilt by association but rather an example of possible historical relevance and scholarly importance by association. I was eager to locate my work on what I considered the leading edge of American religious scholarship. Since most Canadians remained largely uninterested in what I was doing, I looked longingly southward for inspiration and recognition. Perhaps this was a mistake, perhaps it was not.

I further strengthened my growing dependence on American ideological constructs by using the work of Victor Turner in much the same way I used Anthony Wallace's revitalization thesis. Wallace, for me, threw considerable light on Alline and his disciples and the role they played in triggering scores of revivals in the Maritimes during and after the American Revolution. But as I moved into the post-Alline period, Wallace seemed to become increasingly irrelevant as I was confronted more and more by the question, Why were so many ordinary Nova Scotians and New Brunswickers in the first three or four decades of the nineteenth century—the time of the so-called Second Awakening—so greatly affected by evangelical religion as it was manifested in a series of intense religious revivals that swept the region? I was tempted to appropriate the "social control" model that Paul Johnson used so effectively in *A Shopkeeper's Millennium: Society and Revivals in Rochester, New York, 1815–1837* (1978). Yet when I tried to apply the "social control" model to Yarmouth, Nova Scotia, in the first decade of the nineteenth century, or to Liverpool, Nova Scotia, at the same time, or to other Maritime communities in the 1820s and 1830s as they were convulsed by religious revivals, I saw that "social control" made no sense whatsoever. There was no evidence that members of a middle or upper class in these communities were using religious revivals either to protect increasingly threatened interests or to ensure the existence of a committed labor pool. In fact, the evidence suggested quite the opposite—that the revivals were viewed by the Maritime elite as being almost revolutionary threats to the status quo. They tended to equate revivalism with American and later French republicanism, and they did everything in their power to eradicate what they disparagingly referred to as "New Light Fanaticism."[10] Bishop Charles Inglis of Nova Scotia cogently expressed what he knew to be the Maritime elite establishment view in April 1799: "Fanatics are impatient under civil restraint and run into the democratic system. They are for leveling everything both sacred and civil; and this is peculiarly the case of our New Lights [the disciples of Henry Alline as well as Maritime Methodists] who are, as far as I can learn, Democrats to a man."[11] The Inglis view, it is clear, would prevail in the Maritimes for much of the pre-Confederation or pre-1867 period.

If the Johnson "social control" model was obsolete,[12] then it seemed reasonable for me to accept passively, as a given, the biting, anticipated critique of my neo-Marxist scholar friends and to look seriously at Victor Turner instead. This I did during a 1982–83 sabbatical at Harvard University. I tried to read all that I could find written by Turner and I religiously attended one of his public lectures at Harvard.

I began to realize that Turner, especially in *The Ritual Process: Structure and Anti-Structure* (1979), had provided me with a possible explanatory and descriptive framework in which I could locate the popular evangelical response to revivals and revivalists in the Maritimes in the early nineteenth century. What I had found lacking in Wallace and McLoughlin I discovered often in opaque literary form in Turner.

Through the prism provided by *The Ritual Process*, I began to see late eighteenth- and early nineteenth-century revivals in particular as special "rituals" whereby, as Turner had brilliantly suggested, "well-bonded" human beings had created "by structural means, spaces and times in the calendar," what he has called the "classificatory nets of their routinized spheres of action." And by "verbal and non-verbal means," religious revivals became the technique whereby huge numbers of Maritimers and Canadians were able to break away from their "innumerable constraints and boundaries" and capture what Turner has called the "floating world" of self-discovery, inner freedom, and actualization. Everyone, according to Turner, alternates between "fixed" and "floating" worlds. They oscillate, in other words, between a search for novelty and freedom. Thus, for thousands of Canadians, revivals were occasions to experience first-hand and with intensity what has been called an "anti-structural liminality." The religious revival thus became the social means whereby all sorts of complex and hitherto internalized and sublimated desires, dreams, hopes, and aspirations became legitimized. Often traditional behavior and values were openly challenged; and the "antistructural liminality" of the revival ritual helped to give shape and form, however transitory, to a profoundly satisfying "tender, silent, cognizant mutuality." Often seemingly aberrant behavior, such as women and children exhorting publicly that their husbands and fathers needed to be converted, became "rituals of status reversal." "Cognitively," as Turner points out, "nothing underlines regularity as well as absurdity or paradox" and "emotionally nothing satisfies as much as extravagant or temporarily permitted illicit behavior." Grown men could openly weep during a revival; this was widely perceived as a sign of grace and not a sign of weakness. Married women could publicly chastise their husbands during the revival—the abandoning of deference was simply seen as the acceptable work of the Holy Spirit, as was the often intense criticism by children of their unchristian and worldly parents.

According to Turner, there is in the ritual process an intensely satisfying and intensely pleasurable feeling of fellowship—as the "ecstasy of spontaneous communitas" virtually overwhelms everyone involved directly and indirectly in the ritual process in general and in what I perceived in the revival in particular. What Turner calls the "spontaneous communitas" produced by rituals like revivals had something almost "'magical' about it." People, almost despite themselves, shared a "feeling for endless power" for what seemed eternity but was really a fragile moment. And this feeling was both exhilarating and frightening. When applied specifically to revivals, this bonding—this "mystery of intimacy"—drew people, men, women, and children, toward one another. Christian love, triggered by revival, challenged what seemed to be a selfish, circumscribed, almost worldly fidelity. They saw Christ in their friends and their neighbors, and they wanted ever so desperately to love their friends as they loved their Christ. Some apparently did—or so they wrote—and their joy must have been intense as they looked at the world from the mountain peak of religious ecstasy. Then they realized, often to their bitter sorrow, that "spontaneous communitas" was only a "phase, a moment, not a permanent condition," as the reality of "distancing and of tradition" regained firm control of the community. But it was always a return to the status quo with a difference, for people had behaved differently during the revival and some people had been permanently changed. Some would never replicate their mountain peak religious experience. Others would, as religious revivals became the means whereby their Christian faith was often renewed and revitalized.[13]

The "ecstasy of spontaneous communitas" and the "mystery of intimacy" were two crucially important common themes I perceived in a series of late eighteenth- and early nineteenth-century revivals that I examined in some detail in the early 1980s. Turner's *Ritual Process* gave me the academic courage to pursue my work on Maritime revivals from the bottom up rather than from the top down and from inside rather than from outside. Or at least I wished to move in that direction, despite the fact that I often lacked what one reviewer of *Ravished by the Spirit* referred to as the necessary demographic and statistical data to support my generalizations. But the data, unfortunately, for so-called thick history[14] were not readily available, particularly for the late eighteenth and early nineteenth centuries. But as one moved into the nineteenth century one found more and more material that one could use to reconstruct revivals from the bottom up and from the inside out.[15]

It is noteworthy that no reviewer of *Ravished by the Spirit* pointed out that the book was an attempt to explain why revivalism had become less and less important in Maritime religious culture in the late nineteenth century and the early part of the twentieth century. In addition, no review argued that my book was, in a real sense, a jeremiad in which I attempted to address the remarkable declension of the Maritime Baptists in the twentieth century. Furthermore, the point could also have been made that in *Ravished by the Spirit* I was preoccupied with trying to find out why revivals actually occurred. What were the situational pressures that apparently triggered these "spiritual earthquakes"—as Richard Bushman has called them?[16] Had I been accurate in my earlier work in placing heavy emphasis on sociopsychological factors? For example, as late as 1976 I wrote the following about Henry Alline and Nova Scotia's First Great Awakening:

> Henry Alline was one Nova Scotian who was able to perceive a special purpose for his fellow colonists in the midst of the confused Revolutionary situation. He was the charismatic leader of the intense religious revival which swept the colony during the war period. The revival was not merely a "retreat from the grim realities of the world to the safety and

pleasantly exciting warmth of the revival meeting," and "to profits and rewards of another character." Nor was it basically a revolt of the outsettlment against Halifax or an irrational outburst against all forms of traditionalism and authority. The Great Awakening of Nova Scotia may be viewed as an attempt by many Yankee inhabitants to appropriate a new sense of identity and a renewed sense of purpose. Religious enthusiasm in this context, a social movement of profound consequence in the Nova Scotian situation, was symptomatic of a kind of collective identity crisis as well as a searching for an acceptable and meaningful ideology. Resolution of the crisis came not only when the individuals were absorbed into what they felt was a dynamic fellowship of true believers but also when they accepted Alline's analysis of contemporary events and his conviction that their colony was the center of a crucial cosmic struggle. . . .

The implication of the conjunction of events of civil war in New England and an outpouring of the Holy Spirit in Nova Scotia was obvious to Alline and the thousands who flocked to hear him. God was passing New England's historical mantle of Christian leadership to Nova Scotia. . . . In the world view of those New Englanders fighting for the Revolutionary cause, Old England was corrupt and the Americans were engaged in a righteous and noble cause. There was therefore some meaning for hostilities. But to Alline the totally "inhuman War" had no such meaning. Rather, along with all the other signs of the times, it could only indicate one thing, that the entire Christian world, apart from Nova Scotia, was abandoning the way of God.[17]

By the early 1980s, however, I had come increasingly to realize that there probably was something more in the First Great Awakening than the mere resolving of the collective identity crisis of Nova Scotians. This did not, of course, mean that I enthusiastically abandoned one of the key theses of *A People Highly Favoured of God.* Nothing could have been further from the truth, for my scholarly attachment to the "Stewart-Rawlyk" thesis remained strong. In my view many Nova Scotians were certainly disoriented by the often conflicting forces unleashed by the American Revolution, and the powerful "sense of mission" theme articulated by Alline helped them deal with their collective "confusion, trouble and anguish."[18] Yet there was also a spiritual and religious dimension to their reaction as well—

a dimension with which Goldwin French in his perceptive review of
*A People Highly Favoured of God* felt Gordon Stewart and I had
not adequately dealt.[19] And what seemed to help me to respond
positively to the French critique almost a decade after it was made
were the insights I had gained from my reading of Wallace and Turner,
in particular. These two social anthropologists gave me a certain
degree of academic respectability and encouragement at a time when
I had serious reservations about being too sympathetic or showing
too much empathy for the Canadian evangelical tradition.

I felt a deep inner need in 1982 and 1983 to reexamine the Nova
Scotia revivalist tradition in general and Henry Alline in particular.
But I did not want to jettison whatever academic reputation I had
by being too closely associated with revivals and revivalists—even
in the distant Canadian past. I understood only too well from my
vantage-point at Queen's University the compelling power of the
secular bias of much Canadian historical writing, and I did not want
to be pushed even further to the outer margins of my profession.
My work on the Maritimes had already done this to a certain degree,
I was sure, since for so many Canadian historians Maritime historians
are of peripheral importance, cut off as they are from the Central
Canada and the Western cutting edge of the discipline. Further under-
scoring, for many, the marginality of my work was the fact that so
much of it dealt with the seventeenth and eighteenth centuries—the
so-called Dark Ages of Canadian history. Canadian events prior to
1867, the year of Confederation, according to the standard version
of Canadian history, were and are of little lasting consequence or
importance. Thus my regional emphasis and my research period had
already pushed me out of the mainstream of Canadian historiography.
Writing about revivals and revivalists would, I was certain, push me
even further to the outskirts.

But it became clear to me as early as October 1981, when I was
asked by Acadia Divinity College to give the 1983 Hayward Lectures,
that I had less and less to lose in so doing. And there was perhaps
something to gain. I could at least be involved in a vigorous North
American debate about the evangelical tradition. I had realized by
the mid–1970s that even though many Canadian scholars were not
very interested in my work about New England-Nova Scotia relations
in the seventeenth and eighteenth centuries, some American scholars
definitely were. And, furthermore, I knew from reviews, letters, and
invitations, that a number of American religious scholars were, in
fact, taking some of my work on Maritime religion very seriously
indeed. I saw this first in Stephen Marini's dissertation, "New England Folk Religions, 1770–1815: The Sectarian Impulse in Revolu-

tionary Society," later published by Harvard University Press under the title *Radical Sects of Revolutionary New England* (1982). Then I saw it in the work of Nathan Hatch, a historian at Notre Dame, and Mark Noll of Wheaton College, Illinois—among others. And I was naturally drawn to their intellectual milieu and their attempt to reassess the impact of the evangelical tradition on American religious, social, political, and economic development. I found myself invited to annual seminars at Cape Cod, organized by Hatch and Noll, at which aspects of the North American evangelical tradition were examined from a variety of different perspectives. At the seminars I met George Marsden, the author of *Fundamentalism and American Culture: The Shaping of Twentieth-Century Evangelicalism, 1870–1925* (1980). Widely regarded as a "remarkable accomplishment,"[20] Marsden's volume has been described by Martin Marty of the University of Chicago—with good reason—as one of the most important books about American religion published in the twentieth century.

What Marsden had done, as far as I was concerned even before I met him, was to make academically respectable the serious and sympathetic study of American Fundamentalism. If Marsden could do this for American fundamentalism, why could I not at least attempt to throw some scholarly light on Canadian revivals and revivalists in the eighteenth and nineteenth centuries—happenings and people with whom I was not necessarily unsympathetic? It was also important to me that in his *Fundamentalism* Marsden was not afraid to grapple with his own religiosity; he had met frontally the question of how his own evangelical commitment impinged upon his scholarly inquiry. This was a problem that I too had to face since, although I may not have been as committed as was Marsden to a North American evangelical scholarly perspective, I was, nevertheless, an active Baptist layperson and a former deacon of the First Baptist Church, Kingston. I was determined that my new work would be both sympathetic and critical of the evangelical tradition.

There is a remarkable "Afterword" in Marsden's *Fundamentalism*—an "Afterword" permeated by the author's rigorous integrity and scholarly honesty. It is an "Afterword" that has been permanently etched into my consciousness. Leonard Sweet's article, "Wise as Serpents, Innocent as Doves," superbly analyzes the crucial role that Marsden has played in the "New Evangelical Historiography."[21] According to Marsden:

> It is basic Christian doctrine that there is an awesome distance between God and his creation, and yet that God nevertheless enters human history and acts in actual historical

circumstances. The awareness that God acts in history in ways that we can only know in the context of our culturally determined experience should be central to a Christian understanding of history. Yet the Christian must not lose sight of the premise that, just as in the Incarnation Christ's humanity does not compromise his divinity so the reality of God's work in history, going well beyond what we might explain as natural phenomena, is not comprised by the fact that it is culturally defined.

Then Marsden continues:

The history of Christianity reveals a perplexing mixture of divine and human factors. As Richard Lovelace has said, this history, when viewed without a proper awareness of the spiritual forces involved, "is as confusing as a football game in which half the players are invisible." The present work, an analysis of cultural influences on religious belief, is a study of things visible. As such it must necessarily reflect more than a little sympathy with the modern mode of explanation in terms of natural historical causation. Yet it would be a mistake to assume that such sympathy is incompatible with, or even antagonistic to, a view of history in which God as revealed in Scripture is the dominant force, and in which other unseen spiritual forces are contending. I find that a Christian view of history is clarified if one considers reality as more or less like the world portrayed in the works of J. R. R. Tolkien. We live in the midst of contests between great and mysterious spiritual forces, which we understand only imperfectly and whose true dimensions we only occasionally glimpse. Yet, frail as we are, we do play a role in this history, on the side either of the powers of light or of the powers of darkness. It is crucially important then, that, by God's grace, we keep our wits about us and discern the vast difference between the real forces for good and the powers of darkness disguised as angels of light.

As far as Marsden is concerned, the "Christian historian," though attached to certain theological criteria, may nevertheless "refrain from explicit judgments on what is properly Christian" while at the same time concentrating "on observable cultural forces." "By identifying these forces," he or she "provides material which individuals of various theological persuasions may use to help distinguish God's genuine work from practices that have no greater authority than the customs or ways of thinking of a particular time and place."[22]

Though I have some serious intellectual reservations about the Lovelace-Tolkien-Marsden view of cosmic reality, I see it as a more plausible explanatory device for historical development and change than many widely used and academically popular theories. Though this view may not influence directly my own historical approach, it nevertheless has compelled me to consider more sympathetically the possibility of an empathetic approach to the evangelical tradition. If neo-Marxists can write neo-Marxist history, why should not evangelical Christian historians—like Marsden—write from an evangelical Christian perspective? And, furthermore, why should not a scholar knowledgeable and at least sympathetic to the evangelical tradition today write about the evangelical tradition of yesterday? There is no reason for me to make pious and "explicit judgments on what is properly Christian." It is my hope, as it is Marsden's, that by identifying some of "these observable cultural forces," I will help people whose theological views are quite different from mine to "distinguish God's genuine work from practices that have no greater authority than the customs or ways of thinking of a particular time and place." At one time such an approach would have been anathema to me. Today it is not, largely because of the indirect and direct influence of American Christian scholars like George Marsden.

Since the latter part of the nineteenth century, revivalism has not been a crucially important formative force in Canadian religious life. When sustained religious revivals have occurred in the twentieth century, for example, they have usually taken place in a peripheral region—like the isolated eastern shore of Nova Scotia in the early 1920s or northern Saskatchewan in the 1970s. In a sense, these twentieth-century revivals were nineteenth-century social movements; they affected local communities, often as the result of a powerful symbiotic relationship linking preachers and an "agitated community," swelling and raging like a sea in the storm.[23]

Why was the cutting edge of Canadian revivalism significantly dulled by so-called modernity? According to the distinguished Princeton theologian J. Gresham Machen, writing in September 1912, "We may preach with all the fervor of a reformer and yet succeed in winning a straggler here and there, if we permit the whole collective thought of a nation or of the world to be controlled by ideas which, by the relentless force of logic, prevent Christianity from being regarded as anything more than a harmless delusion."[24] As far as Machen was concerned, these pernicious "ideas" were Christian modernism, and he was convinced that modernism was destroying the essential fundamentals of the true Christian faith. Most Canadian evangelicals in the twentieth century and most Canadian liberals would have endorsed Machen's contention. In fact, this Whig interpretation of the decline of evangelical Canadian Christianity in late Victorian Canada and beyond has now become the standard version of Canadian historiography. In his prize-winning volume, *The Regenerators: Social Criticism in Late Victorian English Canada* (1985), Ramsay Cook implicitly and explicitly argues that the profound doubt triggered by Darwinism and biblical higher criticism led to the secularization of Canadian evangelicalism and the transformation of pietism into an essentially lifeless social religion.

Census data appear to support this contention. During the last fifty years, for example, the fastest growing religious group in Canada has been that which defines itself as having "no religion." In 1981, 7.2 percent of the Canadian population located themselves in this category—1,752,380 Canadians out of a total population of 24,083,495.[25] The number of Canadians with "no religion" was, it should be noted, larger than the combined number of *all* Canadian Baptists and Presbyterians. And in British Columbia in 1981, the largest religious group in the province, some 20.5 percent of the population, was the "no Religion" one.[26] If there is a religious revival occurring in contemporary Canada, it may be argued, it is a revival that is transforming thousands of nominal Canadian Christians into nonbelievers.

There is yet another way to look at the apparent decline of Canadian revivalism and of Canadian evangelism during the past century. It may be argued that the evangelical consensus and revivalistic religion were not necessarily battered into supine nothingness from outside by Darwinism and higher criticism. Rather, the evangelical consensus disintegrated from within as evangelical Christianity lost its collective soul to North American consumerism—the insidious antithesis of essential Christianity. The simple Christian message based upon self-abnegation and sacrifice was replaced by the narcissistic gospel of intense "therapeutic self-realization."[27] By the last two decades of the nineteenth century, it has been recently observed, "the leaders of the W.A.S.P. bourgeoisie felt cramped . . . over-civilized . . . cut off from real life—threatened from without by an ungrateful working-class, and from within by their own sense of physical atrophy and spiritual decay." Moreover,

> The old religious sanctions for the moral life, a life of sacrifice and toil, had begun to disintegrate. . . . A crisis of

purpose, a yearning for a solid, transcendent framework of meaning, was not just Henry Adams' worry, but that of a much wider group. In this time of cultural consternation, the new professional-managerial corps appeared with a timely dual message. On the one hand, they preached a new morality that substantiated the old goal of transcendence to new ideals of self-fulfillment and immediate gratification. The late nineteenth-century link between individual hedonism and bureaucratic organizations—a link that has been strengthened in the twentieth century—marks the point of departure of a modern American consumer culture. The consumer culture is not only the value-system that underlies a society saturated by mass-produced and mass-marketed goods, but also a new set of sanctions for the elite control of that society.[28]

This inner transformation of both North American society and Protestantism is of crucial importance to any sophisticated understanding of late nineteenth-century and twentieth-century Canadian revivalism. Consumerism, in a profound sense, it may be argued, cut the essential heart out of the evangelical consensus and out of revivalism. The marriage between "individual hedonism" and "bureaucratic organization" was especially noticeable in the so-called modern revivalistic tradition. Here the linking of the two produced not only a largely superficial narcissistic therapeutic gospel but also one profoundly affected by misogyny and male clerical control. No longer would revivals be community outpourings of guilt and the resolution of guilt, of broken relationships being rebuilt and renewed, of shared intense "communitas" shaped by women, children, and men. With the professionalization of the evangelical male clergy came control from the top down and a deep suspicion of popular religious movements that they could not manipulate—especially movements involving women. It should never be forgotten that, as Tom Harpur points out, "from one very important point of view, the whole of organized religion is a not-too-subtle form of power-seeking and control."[29] Thus the symbiotic link between community and preacher was snapped, and in the process the revival became a largely empty shell devoid of intense, transforming Christian ecstasy and love. It must be reemphasized that in the long and in the short run North American consumerism had a far greater negative impact on the late nineteenth-century evangelical consensus than did the various manifestations of so-called modern scholarship. At the center of this inner decay, as Douglas Frank contends—persuasively, as far as I am concerned—was the cancer of consumerism, "based on self-indulgence."[30] The testimony of an American woman some eighty years ago upon visiting a department store, the key economic institution of the consumer society, cuts to the heart of the issue:

> I felt myself overcome little by little by a disorder that can only be compared to that of drunkenness, with the dizziness and excitation that are peculiar to it. I saw things as if through a cloud, everything stimulated my desire and assumed, for me, an extraordinary attraction. I felt myself swept along toward them and I grabbed hold of things without any outside and superior consideration intervening to hold me back. Moreover I took things at random, useless and worthless articles as well as useful and expensive articles. It was like a monomania of possession.[31]

Other women made similar comments—"my head was spinning," "I felt completely dizzy," "I am just as if I were drunk." These comments were made by middle-class women who had been arrested for shoplifting. They were, it has been observed, "an odd foreshadowing of Billy Sunday's contention that alcohol was the cause of virtually all crime." The women's addiction, however, was "to consumer gratification." "The pathological frenzy to which some women were driven," it is clear, "had become simply the seamier side of the new consumer society, where the old virtues of thirst and self-control were giving way to a culture of gratification."[32] These women, drunk on goods, were striking symbols of the new consumer society.

It was virtually impossible for most evangelical leaders in the post–1800 period to attack frontally the insidious anti-Christian bias of consumerism. Instead, many would become its ardent disciples, enthusiastic advocates of the fundamental goodness of economic growth and technological development. They were certainly unwilling to see what Karl Marx saw in "modern bourgeois society" in the 1880s and beyond. For Marx such a society "has conjured up such gigantic means of production and of exchange" and has in the process, become "like the sorcerer who is no longer able to control the powers of the subterranean which he has called up by his spells." Marx then went on: "Constant revolutionizing of production, uninterrupted disturbance of all social relations, everlasting uncertainty and agitation, distinguish the bourgeois epoch from all earlier ones. All fixed, fast-frozen relations, with their train of ancient and venerable prejudices and opinion, are swept away, all new-formed ones become antiquated before they can ossify. All that is solid melts into air, all that is holy is profane."[33] Marx laid bare the essential nature of life in modernizing society and he intuitively realized what had happened to North American evangelicalism. The "holy" had, in a profound sense, become "profane" and "all that was solid" had melted into nothingness.

Few, if any, Canadian evangelicals in the late nineteenth century and early twentieth century would have, or more accurately, could have accepted the validity of Marx's penetrating prophetic insight into the essential nature of bourgeois-industrial society. Yet, as the nineteenth century blurred into the twentieth, a number of concerned evangelicals came to realize that something fundamentally destructive was beginning to undermine the theological and ideological underpinnings of their church and their society. But instead of focusing, as Marx had done, on the distinguishing features of the "bourgeois society," or as others had done on the evils of "consumerism," most of these disconcerted evangelicals concentrated their concern on what to them was theological modernism—the way in which Darwinian scientific progress and biblical scholarship was significantly altering the older evangelical consensus. Many of these evangelicals would become known as fundamentalists, and their growing obsession with preserving theological purity would be matched by a remarkable degree of "violence in thought and language."[34] These people would find it far easier to be judgmental than forgiving, destructive than constructive, and confrontational than accommodative. They were so concerned with defending what they felt was the pristine purity of Christianity that they had little time and energy to reach out and evangelize the unchurched. Many of the closed-minded fundamentalists were apparently content to encourage what has been aptly called the "circulation of the Saints"[35] rather than unstructured revivalistic outreach. They needed to control everything—the past, the present, and the future—and their growing preoccupation with premillennial dispensationalism only underscored the fact that having lost control of contemporary North American society they were even more determined to control the future.

Many of those North American revivalists who reached out in the twentieth century to the unconverted did so largely as prophets of religious consumerism. Salvation, for a Billy Sunday, the great early twentieth-century American evangelist who often visited Canada, was a very simple matter and a person "can be converted without any fuss." For Sunday, moreover, as one of his disciples expressed it, "Religion loses whatever traits of femininity it may have possessed, before the Sunday campaign is over." The revival had become a simple, male-dominated consumer response "without any fuss" to be used by the best religious salesman in the community. Cheap grace, emptied of sacrifice, commitment, and a deep suspicion of contemporary values, had become the "thin veneer over an increasingly secularized and consumer-oriented product."[36] And television evangelism, in the post–World War II period, became the most sophisticated purveyor of this "product." Is it surprising that as the twentieth century unfolded, Canadian life, at every level of experience, was increasingly Americanized, and Canadian religious values began to reflect so slavishly those being created at the center of the consumerism's empire?

At one time Canadian revivalists and revivals openly challenged the status quo; they frontally attacked the values of contemporary society, and they encouraged and facilitated the growth of a sense of community. During the revivals, women, men, and children were all one in Christ and were seen as spiritual equals. Of course, revivals, like most intense love relationships, were followed by declension, and many who had had mountain peak experiences found soon after that the embers had cooled in the depths of spiritual despair. Yet for a moment—and for some for an eternity—they had been almost magically drawn together as a people of God. Then, perhaps because they were so human, they could not endure in a "spirit of brokenness, confession and repentance."[37] It was difficult for them to be satisfied with Christ and to resonate with Jacques Ellul that "Beyond Jesus, beyond him there is nothing—nothing but lies."[38] In the twentieth century, however, much of what would be preached by the new prophets of religious consumerism would in fact be "nothing but lies." And the decline in importance of Canadian revivalism in the late nineteenth century and the twentieth century may, in fact, be a significant religious statement. Instead of being attracted to what is seen as the hypocrisy of the Christian gospel, and revolted by its spiritual hubris, tens of thousands of Canadians are satisfied with abandoning Christianity completely. This may be the most important religious movement in Canada in the 1980s and 1990s. And rather than weakening the true evangelical impulse in Canada, this movement may, in an ironic manner, be responsible for revitalizing a tradition—an evangelical tradition that in the twentieth century has been largely denuded of Christ-like love and sacrifice by a myriad of confused and some would say false prophets.

## NOTES

1. See the very critical review by Gordon Stewart in the *Journal of the Canadian Church Historical Society* 28 (1986): 45–46.

2. See my discussion of this in *Wrapped up in God: A Study of Several Canadian Revivals and Revivalists* (Burlington, Ont.: Welch Publishing Co., 1988), ix–xi.

3. See the brief but very cogent summary of the Wallace thesis in William G. McLoughlin, *Revivals, Awakenings and Reform: An Essay on Religion and Social Change in America, 1607–1977* (Chicago: University of Chicago Press, 1978), 12–23.

4. Quoted in McLoughlin, *Revivals*, 15.

5. Ibid., 16.

6. Ibid.

7. Ibid., 17.

8. Quoted in ibid., 17. See Peter Worsley, *The Trumpet Shall Sound* (New York: Schocken Books, 1968).

9. Wallace, "Revitalization Movements," *American Anthropology* 58 (1956): 264–81.

10. See Bishop Charles Inglis to the Reverend Jacob Bailey, 3 April 1799, Public Archives of Nova Scotia, MG1 Vol. 93(a).

11. Ibid.

12. See the important article by Leonard I. Sweet in *The Evangelical Tradition in America*, ed. L. I. Sweet (Macon, Ga.: Mercer University Press, 1984), 37.

13. Turner, *Ritual Process*, 94–140.

14. Stewart, review in *Journal of the Canadian Church Historical Society*, 45–46.

15. One historian has, I think, been unusually successful in writing "thick history" about revivals: Randolph A. Roth, *The Democratic Dilemma: Religion, Reform, and the Social Order in the Connecticut River Valley of Vermont, 1791–1850* (New York: Cambridge University Press, 1987). Roth has brilliantly blended demographic data into his unusually perceptive reading of the Yankee roots of Christian revivalism to produce a groundbreaking study. Though sometimes reductionist in his search for explanations, Roth nevertheless paints a marvelous picture of what he refers to as the "most powerful spiritual work" of revival in the Connecticut River Valley in the 1791 to 1850 period (219).

16. See Bushman, *From Puritan to Yankee: Character and the Social Order in Connecticut, 1690–1765* (Cambridge: Harvard University Press, 1967).

17. See my "summary article," "Nova Scotia and the American Revolution," *New Edinburgh Review* no. 3516 (1976): 107–8.

18. See G. A. Rawlyk and Gordon Stewart, "Nova Scotia's Sense of Mission," *Social History/Histoire Sociale* 2 (1981): 5–17.

19. See the French review article, "Religion and Society in Late Eighteenth Century Nova Scotia," *Acadiensis* 4 (Spring 1975): 107.

20. See, for example, some of the comments about the book on the back cover of the 1982 paperback edition.

21. Leonard I. Sweet, "Wise as Serpents, Innocent as Doves: The New Evangelical Historiography," *Journal of the American Academy of Religion* 56 (Fall 1988): 397–415.

22. Marsden, *Fundamentalism*, 229–30.

23. Quoted in Nathan O. Hatch, *The Democratization of American Christianity* (New Haven: Yale University Press, 1989), 52.

24. Quoted in George M. Marsden, *Reforming Fundamentalism: Fuller Seminary and the New Evangelicalism* (Grand Rapids: William B. Eerdmans, 1987), 31.

25. See Rawlyk, *Wrapped up in God*, 153.

26. Ibid., 154.

27. See R. W. Fox and T. J. Jackson Lears, eds., *The Culture of Consumption* (New York, 1983), xi.

28. Ibid., xi, xi–xii.

29. T. Harpur, *For Christ's Sake* (Toronto: University of Toronto Press, 1986), 53.

30. Douglas W. Frank, *Less than Conquerors: How Evangelicals Entered the Twentieth Century* (Grand Rapids: William B. Eerdmans, 1986), 222.

31. Quoted in Frank, *Less than Conquerors*, 222.

32. Ibid., 223.

33. Karl Marx and Friedrich Engels, *The Communist Manifesto* (New York: Russell and Russell, 1964), 63.

34. N. Furniss, *The Fundamentalist Controversy, 1918–1931* (New Haven: Yale University Press, 1954), 36.

35. Quoted in Frank, *Less than Conquerors*, 264.

36. Ibid., 264, 277.

37. Ibid., 277.

38. Quoted in ibid., 277.

# Contributors

RANDALL BALMER is associate professor of religion at Barnard College. He is the author of *A Perfect Babel of Confusion: Dutch Religion and English Culture in the Middle Colonies* (Oxford, 1989).

DANIEL H. BAYS, professor and chair of the department of history at the University of Kansas at Lawrence, is the director of the History of Christianity in China Project. He is the author of *China Enters the Twentieth Century: Chang Chih-tung and the Issues of a New Age, 1895–1909* (Michigan, 1978).

DAVID BEBBINGTON is a reader in history at the University of Stirling in Scotland and has written numerous articles on the history of British evangelicalism. He is the author of *Evangelicalism in Modern Britain* (Unwin Hyman, 1989).

EDITH L. BLUMHOFER is associate professor of history at Wheaton College and project director at the Institute for the Study of American Evangelicals. She is the author of *Restoring the Faith: The Assemblies of God, Pentecostalism, and American Culture* (Illinois, 1993), as well as several other books and articles on pentecostalism and women in evangelicalism.

JOHN B. BOLES, managing editor of the *Journal of Southern History*, is the Allyn and Gladys Cline Professor of History at Rice University. He has written extensively about Southern religion and is the author of *The Great Revival, 1787–1805: The Origins of the Southern Evangelical Mind* (Kentucky, 1972); *Religion and Antebellum Kentucky* (Kentucky, 1976); and editor of *Masters and Slaves in the House of the Lord: Race and Religion in the American South, 1740–1870* (Kentucky, 1988).

DAVID BUNDY, associate professor of church history and librarian at Christian Theological Seminary in Indianapolis, is the author of numerous articles on early church history and European pentecostalism, including *Keswick: A Bibliographical Introduction to the Higher Life Movements* (1975, repr. 1985).

RICHARD CARWARDINE is lecturer in American History at the University of Sheffield, England. He is the author of *Transatlantic Revivalism: Popular Evangelicalism in Britain and America, 1790–1865* (Greenwood, 1978), and a variety of essays on antebellum politics and popular religion.

FREDERICK HALE is an independent scholar and a prolific author in church history and theology.

DAVID EDWIN HARRELL, JR., Daniel F. Breeden Eminent Scholar in the Humanities at Auburn University in Auburn, Alabama, is the author of a variety of articles, essays, and books on pentecostalism and evangelicalism. His most recent books are *Pat Robertson: A Personal, Religious, and Political Portrait* (Harper & Row, 1987) and *Oral Roberts: An American Life* (Indiana, 1985).

GERALD MORAN is a professor of history at the University of Michigan-Dearborn and is the author of numerous articles on religion in Colonial America and coauthor of *Religion, Family, and the Life Course: Explorations in the Social History of Early America* (1992).

GEORGE RAWLYK is professor of history at the Queen's University in Kingston, Ontario. He is the author of *Ravished by the Spirit: Religious Revivals, Baptists, and Henry Alline* (McGill–Queens, 1984) and is the editor of *Henry Alline: Selected Writings* (Paulist, 1987).

EVERETT A. WILSON, former vice president for academic affairs at Bethany Bible College in Santa Cruz, California, is now co-director of the Centro de Investigaciones Culturales y Estudios Linguisticos in San Jose, Costa Rica. Dr. Wilson is the author of several articles on Latin American pentecostalism.

# Index

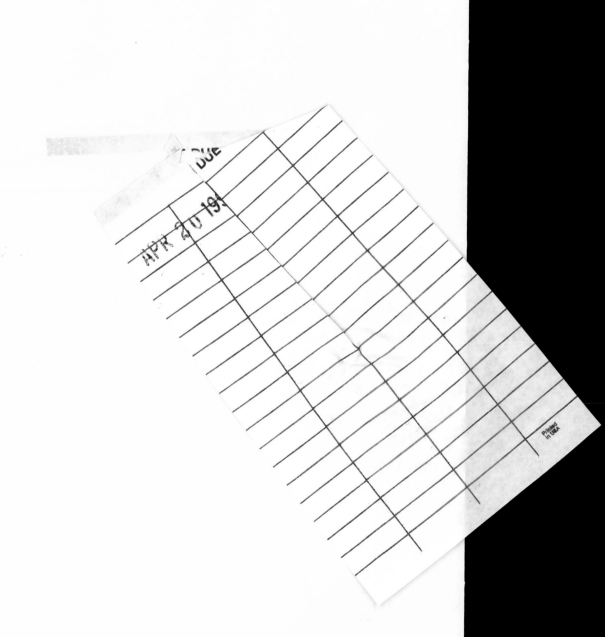